Super Safari 1

Teacher's Book

CB081711

Lucy Frino with Herbert Puchta, Günter Gerngross, & Peter Lewis-Jones

CAMBRIDGE
UNIVERSITY PRESS

CAMBRIDGE
UNIVERSITY PRESS

University Printing House, Cambridge CB2 8BS, United Kingdom

One Liberty Plaza, 20th Floor, New York, NY 10006, USA

477 Williamstown Road, Port Melbourne, VIC 3207, Australia

314–321, 3rd Floor, Plot 3, Splendor Forum, Jasola District Centre,
New Delhi – 110025, India

79 Anson Road, #06–04/06, Singapore 079906

Cambridge University Press is part of the University of Cambridge.

It furthers the University's mission by disseminating knowledge in the pursuit of education, learning, and research at the highest international levels of excellence.

www.cambridge.org
Information on this title: www.cambridge.org/9781107481800

First published 2015

Printed in Great Britain by CPI Group (UK) Ltd, Croydon CR0 4YY

A catalog record for this publication is available from the British Library

ISBN 978-1-107-48180-0 Teacher's Book Level 1
ISBN 978-1-107-48177-0 Student's Book with DVD-ROM Level 1
ISBN 978-1-107-48178-7 Workbook Level 1
ISBN 978-1-107-48186-2 Teacher's DVD Level 1
ISBN 978-1-107-48181-7 Class Audio CDs Level 1
ISBN 978-1-107-47679-0 Flashcards Level 1
ISBN 978-1-107-48184-8 Presentation Plus DVD-ROM Level 1
ISBN 978-1-107-47729-2 Posters Level 1
ISBN 978-1-107-47732-2 Puppet

Additional resources for this publication at www.cambridge.org/supersafari/ame

Contents

Teaching notes

Map of the book

Hello! (pages 4–7)

Vocabulary	Chant: Grammar
Gina, Polly, Leo, Mike	Hello! I'm (Jo).
Total physical response: Stand up, sit down, say "hello"	**Song:** **Hello!**

1 My class (pages 8–15)

Vocabulary	Chant: Grammar	Story and value	CLIL	Thinking skills
bag, pencil, book, chair	Look! It's my (chair).	***The chair*** Saying *sorry*	School behavior	Classifying
Total physical response: Hands up, hands down, clap your hands		**Song:** **In the classroom**		

2 My colors (pages 16–23)

Vocabulary	Chant: Grammar	Story and value	CLIL	Thinking skills
red, blue, green, yellow	It's (yellow).	***The painters*** Cheering someone up	Rainbow colors	Testing predictions
Total physical response: Show me something red, show me something green, show me something yellow		**Song:** **Stand up and paint with me!**		

3 My family (pages 24–31)

Vocabulary	Chant: Grammar	Story and value	CLIL	Thinking skills
dad, mom, brother, sister	Who's this?	***Family and friends*** Caring about family and friends	Understanding age	Ordering
Total physical response: Go to sleep, wake up, give your dad a hug		**Song:** **Rosemary, Rosemary**		

4 My toys (pages 32–39)

Vocabulary	Chant: Grammar	Story and value	CLIL	Thinking skills
ball, car, puzzle, doll	I have a (car).	***The puzzle*** Helping	Big and small	Sorting
Total physical response: Throw your ball, catch your ball, oh, no, clean up		**Song:** **I have a ball**		

5 My numbers (pages 40–47)

Vocabulary	Chant: Grammar	Story and value	CLIL	Thinking skills
one, two, three, four	one book, two books	***Where's Polly?*** Playing together	Quantity	Describing with numbers

Total physical response: Four, three, two, one

Song: **Sing some more**

6 My pets (pages 48–55)

Vocabulary	Chant: Grammar	Story and value	CLIL	Thinking skills
bird, rabbit, fish, cat	What is it?	***The cat*** Working as a team	Species	Making deductions

Total physical response: Jump, walk, fly, swim

Song: **What is this?**

7 My food (pages 56–63)

Vocabulary	Chant: Grammar	Story and value	CLIL	Thinking skills
pasta, salad, rice, cake	I like (rice).	***The cake*** Sharing	Solids and liquids	Focusing on detail

Total physical response: Look! Pasta, eat the pasta, it's yummy, wash your face

Song: **I like yummy lunch!**

8 My clothes (pages 64–71)

Vocabulary	Chant: Grammar	Story and value	CLIL	Thinking skills
T-shirt, pants, dress, shoes	I don't like (the purple dress).	***The party*** Including your friends	Wearing a costume	Categorizing

Total physical response: Put on the shoes, put on a T-shirt, put on a hat, say "hello" to your dad

Song: **Clothes**

9 My park (pages 72–79)

Vocabulary	Chant: Grammar	Story and value	CLIL	Thinking skills
slide, merry-go-round, seesaw, swing	The (swing)'s fun.	***The park*** Taking turns	Circles and triangles	Sequencing

Total physical response: Sit down on the seesaw, down you go, up you go, oh, no

Song: **Let's go to the park**

Phonics (pages 80–89)

Unit 1:	Unit 2:	Unit 3:	Unit 4:	Unit 5:	Unit 6:	Unit 7:	Unit 8:	Unit 9:	Phonics
"p" pencil	"b" bag	"d" dad	"c" car	"t" two	"e" eggs	"s" salad	"n" nose	"i" igloo	review

Review pages 90–94 **Certificate:** 95 **Stickers:** End section

Introduction

About *Super Safari*

What is *Super Safari?*

Super Safari is an English course for pre-school children. The course can be taught in three levels (Levels 1, 2, and 3) or two levels (Levels 2 and 3), as the language introduced in Level 1 is constantly recycled in the higher levels of the course. *Super Safari* helps children get used to learning in a classroom and develop key linguistic and interpersonal skills, all the while having as much fun as possible. The approach ensures that children using *Super Safari* begin their English-learning journey with enthusiasm and confidence.

A flexible approach

All three levels of *Super Safari* have been specifically researched to cater for a variety of teaching situations, including those with a higher than usual number of hours of English per week. The units include lessons with a core syllabus focus and additional lessons that can be used flexibly according to the time available for English. (see pages xviii–xix).

Igniting interest

Super Safari 1 and 2 are appropriate for children who have not encountered English before. This will probably also be their first experience of group learning.

The four lively and colorful animal characters in the course guide the children gently into the new world of learning, through stories and effective oral–aural practice. With the support of chants, physical games, and songs, listening and speaking skills are developed gradually, together with fine motor skills in preparation for writing.

Super Safari 3 is appropriate for children who have already had some exposure to English. There is controlled introduction to word recognition in the Student's Book, giving children a head start for reading and writing at the Elementary level.

Catering for multiple intelligences

Pre-school children need opportunities to use all aspects of their intelligence in a stimulating and varied environment. *Super Safari* caters for multiple intelligences in the following ways:

- The course develops linguistic intelligence – children's sensitivity to language and their ability to use language to express themselves and achieve goals. The games, songs, stories, and projects in *Super Safari* always have a linguistic purpose, whether this is introducing new language, practicing and recycling language, or using language to solve a problem or act out a social situation.
- Activities involving TPR or Total Physical Response (requiring children to move in response to linguistic prompts) are designed to cater for bodily-kinesthetic and spatial intelligence. *Super Safari* features a large number of these games because children have high energy levels and love to use their bodies. Channeling their energy into language learning through mime, dance, or team games helps children to concentrate during the other, quieter parts of the lesson and requires careful listening.
- The chants and songs in *Super Safari* appeal to children's musical intelligence. They encourage a focus on the patterns, tones, and rhythms of English, developing both listening and speaking skills.
- Many of the activities in the Workbook (e.g., coloring puzzles, follow the line puzzles, find the one that doesn't belong, and listen and circle) foster the use of logical-mathematical intelligence. Pre-school children are naturally curious and can apply their growing logic and numeracy skills in the English classroom.
- The story in each unit is designed to awaken interpersonal intelligence – the ability to interact with others and work together successfully, vital for children to get the most out of school in the future. The children are encouraged through discussion and Workbook activities to think about the deeper meaning (or "value") of the stories, such as the importance of fair play, waiting your turn, helping, and taking care of your friends.

Applying English across the curriculum

Wider thinking through the application of knowledge is encouraged by content and language integrated learning (CLIL), with topic-based material clearly linked with subjects across the curriculum.

Super Safari 1 components

The Student's Book contains:

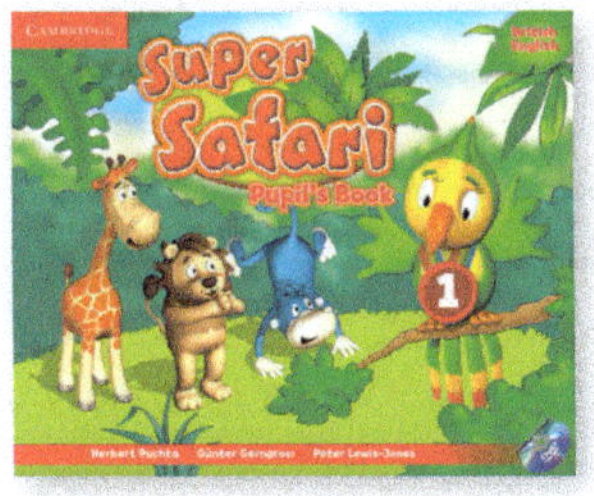

- An introductory *Hello* unit (4 pages) which introduces the animal characters Mike the monkey, Leo the lion, Gina the giraffe, and Polly the parrot, alongside greetings and basic classroom instructions
- 9 core units (8 pages each) with an easy-to-use single-page lesson format
- 10 pages of phonics activities, including basic handwriting skills, one page for each of the 9 core units and one review page
- 5 pages of review material (a listening activity for every two units)
- Stickers to be used in Lesson 6 of each core unit

Each unit offers:

- An opening scene in contemporary and attractive 3D artwork which establishes the topic of the unit story and also provides a vehicle for the presentation of core vocabulary
- A memorable chant to introduce new grammar and review vocabulary
- An engaging song for further language practice
- A story featuring the appealing animal characters, whose interaction illustrates a different value in each unit
- CLIL lessons, broadening the unit topic in the context of other school subjects and offering accessible craft projects

Student's DVD-ROM

This complementary component is included with the Student's Book for children to use at home or in the school computer room. It is also provided with the Presentation Plus DVD-ROM, for teachers to use in the classroom with a computer and a projector. The DVD-ROM offers language reinforcement and consolidation while the children also have fun. It contains:

- 2 interactive vocabulary games per unit
- Animated versions of the Student's Book songs with karaoke

Workbook

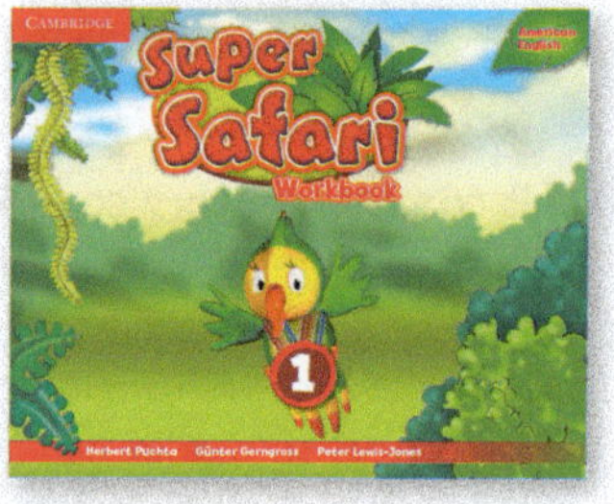

This reinforces language and builds on skills development by offering:

- Visual puzzles, fine motor skills work (circling, joining, matching, and coloring), listening input, and opportunities for oral practice
- A values activity for each unit drawn from the message in the Student's Book story
- Simple craft activities to extend the focus of the CLIL lessons
- An introduction to self-evaluation and an opportunity to review key vocabulary from the unit

- Cutout phonics cards, one set for each phonics lesson
- Cutout Yes/No cards, for use in games (full instructions are supplied in the relevant lessons)
- Cutout masks of the animal characters, for use in the story lessons (full instructions are supplied in the relevant lessons)

Teacher's Book

This Teacher's Book is interleaved with the Student's Book pages. Each page of teaching notes features:

- An Aims box with detailed lesson aims, new and recycled language, any necessary or optional materials, and the language competences that the children will achieve
- Concise and clear instructions for all the Student's Book and Workbook activities
- Additional lesson stages in colored boxes:

  Warm-up: ideas for beginning the lesson, recycling language from the previous lesson, or presenting new language

  Extension activities: optional activities for extending the focus of the lesson, for which any additional materials are listed as optional in the Aims box

  Ending the lesson: simple ideas that are flexible in the time available to bring the lesson to a close, requiring no presentation or extra materials

Posters and Flashcards

The posters and flashcards cover all the core vocabulary. They are ideal for warm-ups, presentations, and games.

Class CDs

The 2 Class CDs contain all the recorded material for the Student's Book and Workbook, including the chants, songs, karaoke versions, and stories.

Puppet

A soft toy puppet version of Polly the parrot for the teacher to use in class. See page xvii for more information about how to use the puppet and related games.

Presentation Plus

This whiteboard software features:

- The Student's Book and Workbook pages
- Teacher's Resources and audio material

It is also packaged together with the material on the Teacher's DVD and Student's DVD-ROM, which provide animated stories, songs, interactive activities, and games for classroom use.

Teacher's DVD

This component features animated stories and songs from the Student's Book with bonus karaoke versions of the songs.

Tour of a unit

Super Safari 1 begins with a *Hello* unit. This is an introductory 4-page unit in both the Student's Book and the Workbook, presenting the animal characters, greetings, and basic classroom instructions. If the children have had any exposure to English, encourage them to use any language they can remember, even if it is not formally presented until later on (e.g., numbers, colors, or additional greetings).

There are then 9 main units, each with 8 lessons. Each page in the Student's Book constitutes a lesson, together with its corresponding Workbook page.

The material is structured in a flexible way to make it suitable for different teaching situations:

- Lessons 1–6 present and practice new core language, as well as including a chant, a song, and a story with follow-up activities.
- Lessons 7 and 8 focus on CLIL, together with creativity (the Workbook project) and review.

Classes with **fewer than 5 hours** of English per week have the option to leave out some or all of Lessons 7 and 8, while still covering the vocabulary and grammar syllabus.

Using all the material in the Student's Book and Workbook provides enough material for classes with **5 hours** per week.

Classes with **more than 5 hours** per week can extend the material by using the phonics material and review lessons at the end of the Student's Book.

Lesson 1

Vocabulary presentation

The core vocabulary of the unit is presented and contextualized in a colorful illustration which also acts as an introduction of the topic of the story later in the unit.

- The children first hear a line or two of dialog.
- The children listen and point to the new vocabulary in the picture and then listen again, this time repeating the words.

- The Workbook offers a variety of practice activities for this lesson, always including oral follow-up.

Lesson 2

Grammar

The key grammar from the unit is presented and practiced in Lesson 2, in a chant based on the unit topic. The vocabulary from Lesson 1 is also reviewed.

- The children first listen to the chant and give a non-linguistic response such as coloring, tracing, or matching.
- They then listen and repeat the chant, sometimes also giving a TPR response (picking up an object, pointing, or doing a mime).
- This is followed by an opportunity to use the language, usually in a game.
- The practice activities in the Workbook often involve drawing and sometimes include listening. There is always oral follow-up.

Lesson 3

Total Physical Response

Further new language is introduced in the form of three or four phrases or instructions, each accompanied by an action.

- The children listen first and either look at the pictures in the Student's Book or watch the teacher demonstrating the action for each phrase.
- The language and actions are repeated until the children feel comfortable joining in (by moving and speaking).
- Each Total Physical Response lesson includes review of the phrases and actions featured in previous units and opportunities for children to respond to new variations of instructions, as they gain confidence with the language.
- The Workbook practice activity requires the children to listen to one or two of the new phrases and choose the correct picture or pictures, by circling.

Lesson 4

Song

The vocabulary and usually the grammar of the unit are combined in a song for children to learn and join in.

- The children first listen to the song, using the pictures to help them follow the meaning.
- They can then join in, according to ability, using the pictures as visual prompts to help them remember the words.
- The next track on the CD after the song is always a karaoke version which you can use once the children are familiar with the song.
- The practice activities in the Workbook are varied. Some require children to listen to some or all of the song and respond by coloring, matching, or tracing. Some do not involve listening.

Lesson 5

While listening to a story

This lesson features the main story for the unit, bringing the unit topic, vocabulary, and structures together. The clear and expressive illustrations invite the children to follow as they listen, and inspire them to act out the story with real emotion in Lesson 6.

- The teaching notes first suggest ways of reviewing the characters and setting the scene of the story (encouraging children to think about where the characters are and what they are doing/are about to do).
- The children then hear the story, which is brought off the page with clear character voices and sound effects to help them follow the action.
- After discussing the story in L1 (the children's own language) where appropriate, the children usually practice some key functional language from the story.
- The Workbook practice is always a listening activity. The children hear one or two lines from the story and color a circle to show which character is speaking from a choice of two.
- The "Ending the lesson" activity in Lesson 5 always practices key language from the story.

Lesson 6

Story follow-up and values

Lesson 6 explores the story in more depth. This lesson uses the unit stickers, which are listed in the Materials section of the Aims box in the teaching notes.

- The children listen to the story again and do the sticker activity. This gives them a chance to review the language and content of the story.
- The teaching notes then guide a brief discussion in L1 of the value illustrated in the story. The children are encouraged to think about what the characters say and do, and to reflect on what is right (or wrong) about the characters' behavior.
- The Workbook presents a similar situation to the value from the story, with a picture illustrating positive behavior. The children complete/draw the smile on a face below the picture, reinforcing the value in the story.
- The optional Extension activity in Lesson 6 is always a suggestion for a group of children to act out the story at the front of the class, using the cutout masks at the back of the Workbook (see pages 93-96) and any other available props. Other groups can then take turns if time allows.

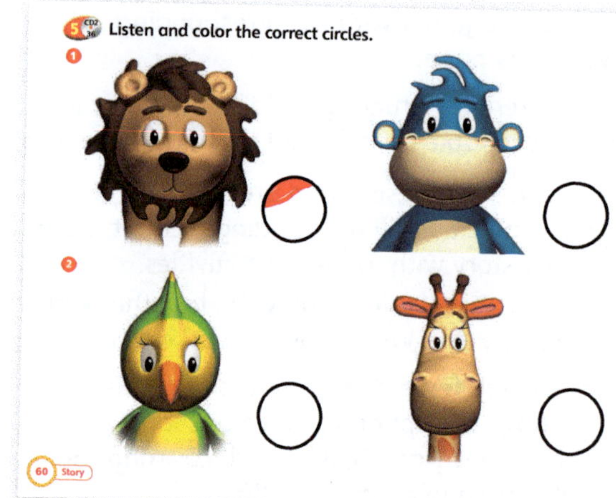

Lessons 7 and 8

CLIL

These two lessons introduce a topic from another area of the curriculum which is related to the overall unit topic. They are designed to encourage the children to explore other subjects through English and then to apply their new knowledge in a craft project.

- The first lesson usually introduces the topic and presents useful words which the children will need to recognize but which are not core vocabulary.
- The Workbook material for Lesson 7 is a creative project, usually carried out individually. The project is illustrated in a series of step-by-step pictures and enables the children to make something which they can take home or display in the classroom. The focus on detail and the skills of cutting, sticking, folding, and drawing involved develop fine motor skills which the children can apply when they begin writing.
- The second CLIL lesson provides opportunities for the children to apply the knowledge from the previous lesson, developing thinking skills such as predicting, making deductions, sequencing, and categorizing. They also review the vocabulary and language from the unit using games and songs.
- The Workbook page for Lesson 8 offers an introduction to self-evaluation. Each item of core vocabulary is illustrated, and children are invited to color the circle next to each word if they can say it. Monitoring while the children are working on this activity allows a simple opportunity for informal assessment.

Optional phonics lessons

Pages 80–88 of the Student's Book contain phonics materials which can be used at the end of each of the 9 core units (Units 1 to 9). There is a set of cutout phonics cards for each of these lessons at the back of the Workbook.

- The teaching notes first provide ideas for focusing on the sound featured in the lesson. The key word on each phonics page is usually a familiar item from the corresponding core unit (e.g., a pencil for Unit 1 (classroom objects)).
- The children then practice forming the corresponding grapheme and saying the sound in a chant. For Units 1 to 3, they practice forming the grapheme in the air with their fingers, in Units 4 to 6 they color in the outline letter on the page and in Units 7 to 9 they trace the letters. The phonics cards in the Workbook are used to reinforce the relationship between the sound and the grapheme.
- The next stage of the lesson is a sound discrimination activity. The children listen to words read by the teacher (they do not need to understand the meaning) and respond when they hear the target sound by showing a phonics card, doing an action or holding up an object.

After the main phonics lessons in the Student's Book, there is a phonics review lesson. This reviews all the sounds focused on so far with a game of bingo, alongside further activities and games.

Review lessons

Pages 90–94 of the Student's Book are Review pages. There is a Review lesson for every two units of the book. In each Review lesson, the children listen to four key pieces of language from the two featured units and choose the correct picture from a selection, by coloring. They then practice the vocabulary and language from the units with a selection of appropriate games.

Teaching with *Super Safari* 1

Teaching very young children

Working with children of pre-school age presents a number of challenges. Young children are only able to concentrate in short bursts (no more than seven to ten minutes at ages three and four). Pre-schoolers' high energy levels make it difficult for them to sit still for long, and they are not used to being in the rather formal setting of the classroom. But young children have an insatiable curiosity, an innate sense of fun, and a lack of self-consciousness, all of which make them excellent language learners. *Super Safari* has been developed with these challenges and advantages in mind, and the range and nature of the activities in the course are perfectly suited to the demands and abilities of this age group.

Keep moving

Super Safari harnesses children's energy with activities involving Total Physical Response, dance, or mime in every lesson. The teaching notes suggest mimes and actions at each stage of the unit – to practice vocabulary in Lesson 1, to accompany the chant in Lesson 2, as an integral part of the Total Physical Response material in Lesson 3, to support and help with comprehension of the song in Lesson 4, and so on. In parallel with activities involving movement at the children's desks, many of the Extension activities are action games, which require the children to jump, run, move like different animals, throw a ball, hit a balloon, pick up objects and put them in a box or basket, or play a traditional game such as *Hide and seek*. Whenever the children are required to move to a larger space for an action game, an alternative is suggested (e.g., pointing instead of moving or using flashcards instead of real objects).

Be creative and have fun

In addition to the project activity in Lesson 7 of each of the 9 core units, there are instructions for a range of hands-on creative activities.

Extension activity

Aim: to encourage the children to join in and focus on their classmates

- If possible, move your class out into the playground, school gym, or an empty classroom.
- Ask the children to stand in a circle. Say the name of one of the children. The class repeat. Throw the soft ball to that child. The child says the name of one of his/her classmates. The children repeat it. Then he/she throws the ball to that child, and so on. Say *Join in!* They can also say *sorry* if they throw the ball too hard.

Extension activity

Aim: to practice responding to *Go to sleep* and *Wake up*

- If possible, move your class out into the playground, school gym, or an empty classroom.
- Play the traditional party game *Sleeping lions* with the children. Put on the CD of relaxing music and say *Go to sleep!* All the children lie down and keep as still and quiet as possible. Walk among the "sleeping lions" and try to make them "wake up" by talking to them / making them laugh. If a child moves or giggles, he/she is "out" – say *Wake up* (name)*!* The child gets up and helps you to try and "wake" the other children. The winner is the child who keeps still and quiet the longest.

Pre-school children are still discovering the world around them, and they learn a great deal by employing all their senses, particularly touch. Making simple models to represent new words (using playdough or cardboard boxes, empty pots, and craft materials) is an excellent aid to learning and memory. The teaching notes also suggest using paint to explore the way colors are formed, sorting objects such as buttons or plastic lids to support work on color, number, and size, and making simple shapes with craft materials.

Super Safari uses young children's boundless imagination and love of play to support learning. There are role play shopping games to practice counting and dressing-up activities to practice clothing and other key vocabulary. Polly the parrot is used to engage the children's curiosity and becomes an imaginary English-speaking friend (see Using the Polly the parrot puppet, on page xvii). Your attitude will also set the tone in the classroom – don't be afraid to have fun with the class when you are playing, dancing, or miming.

Be flexible

Given the short attention span of pre-school children, each lesson needs to have a variety of activities and games, with changes of pace and activity type in order to keep the children interested. There are some set stages in the lesson notes (see The importance of routines on page xiv), but it is important to use the notes according to the way each lesson unfolds. If you find that your class is particularly energetic, you may choose to do an action game before the practice stage of the lesson or gain their attention using the puppet. If your class has a favorite song from the course, sing it as a reward after they have completed an Workbook pencil-to-paper activity. If the weather is very good, choose one of the games the children can play outside. At this age, any language learning is good learning, and after Lesson 4 in each unit, you can alter the order of the lessons and activities to suit your situation and your class. *Super Safari* is designed to be flexible.

Extension activity

Aim: to review vocabulary and practice fine motor skills

- Make a playdough model of an egg. Show the class and ask *What's this?* Tell the children they are going to make a model of something from the lesson – a chicken, a baby, or an egg. Point to the pictures on SB page 30 and elicit the words.
- Hand out playdough to each child. The children make three models each (chicken, chick, and egg). Circulate and help as necessary. Ask *What's this?* Show some of the best models to the class. Confident children can show and say, e.g., *This is my egg*.

Extension activity

Aim: to practice *I like ...*

- Draw a shelf on the board. Stick the food flashcards on the "shelf" and elicit the words.
- Tell the class that you need a volunteer to be a sales clerk.
- Place a grocery bag at the front. Take one of the flashcards from the "shelf" on the board, and show it to the class. Say, e.g., *I like pasta* and put it in your grocery bag. Repeat for the other flashcards.
- Stand next to the sales clerk and pass him/her the items from your bag one by one. Encourage the child to say, e.g., *Pasta, thank you* and pretend to ring up the price on the cash register/calculator. Use play money to "pay." Put the food back in your bag and say *Goodbye!* to the sales clerk. Repeat the whole game with a different volunteer.
- The children can play the game in pairs using imaginary food instead of flashcards.

Getting used to school

Pre-school is often the first time children have socialized regularly with the same group of their peers, and is almost certainly the first time they have been in a classroom. A large part of the role of a pre-school teacher is laying the foundations for learning and behavior which will be vital for the children's entire academic career. Establishing good habits and appropriate behavior patterns, together with a positive attitude and love of learning, at this early stage is therefore extremely important. The colorful, engaging illustrations and attractive materials in *Super Safari* (songs and stories, flashcards, masks, cards, puppet, and accompanying digital activities) are designed to make the learning experience as much fun as possible. The teaching notes also contain advice about introducing routines, praising, and motivating the children.

Familiarizing the children with the classroom

Children are comfortable with familiar things, and the classroom should be a safe, recognizable place where they can explore new things and learn about the world of language. It is a good idea to have designated areas in the classroom, which are always used for the same purpose. Having a "story corner" where the children always sit to listen to stories in Lessons 5 and 6; a "creative corner" where the materials for projects, aprons, etc. are stored; a "nest" for Polly the parrot on one wall, will help the children recognize familiar stages in a lesson. Displaying the children's work throughout the year, with a topic-themed wall display, will give them a sense of achievement and help them remember key language. This is also a useful way to show parents what the children are working on (see Linking school and home, in the next column).

Make sure that classroom furniture is arranged in a way that encourages communication and is not overly formal. The children can sit in small groups or facing each other, rather than always in rows facing the front. The seating arrangements should ideally be flexible, so that chairs and tables can be moved easily for physical activities and games.

Children need to learn which types of behavior are acceptable in the classroom and which are unacceptable. You may wish to introduce a particular way to sit for a story or for listening (e.g., legs crossed, arms folded), a way to attract the teacher's attention (e.g., putting up hands), and a way for the teacher to ask the children to be quiet (such as ringing a bell). Reward good and improved behavior with stickers or by allowing children to help you perform classroom tasks (e.g., cleaning the board, using the whiteboard, sticking flashcards on the board).

Linking school and home

At this age, the most important influences on a child are still his or her parents or carers and the home environment. It is therefore advisable to forge a strong link between school and home and involve parents in their children's learning. The activities provided at the web address at the front of the Student's Book go some way toward doing this. There are also specific points in the Student's Book where a link to home can be made, either by practicing key vocabulary (such as furniture or classroom objects) at home, singing the song at home or in the car (using the DVD-ROM in the Student's Book), or applying values and practicing simple functional language from the story in genuine situations at home (e.g., saying *sorry*). These home–school link points are marked with a "Family fun" icon.

You can keep your children's families involved with the topics covered in the course by encouraging them to look at class displays, inviting them to hear the children performing their favorite chants or songs, and encouraging children to bring items relevant to the topics or CLIL lessons into school.

The importance of routines

Young children respond well to routines. They provide a similar sense of familiarity to a well-organized classroom and are also an opportunity to learn everyday set phrases and practice key language in a natural way. The *Super Safari* teaching notes have the same structure for the beginning and end of each lesson – a Warm-up activity and an Ending the lesson activity. However, there will also be an initial stage of the lesson before the Warm-up, in which you all get ready (e.g., with the children signaling they are ready by sitting in a particular way or getting their books out). You may wish to write the day of the week on the board or display a word card or picture for each day at the beginning of each lesson, talk about the weather, or celebrate a child's birthday by singing a song together. Similarly, after the Ending the lesson activity, you could establish a final signal that the lesson has finished, e.g., by saying a goodbye chant together or singing the "Clean up" song as you clear up (see page T11).

Using books

Children will not be used to working with a textbook, and they need to learn to use two books in one lesson. Establishing effective techniques for having the correct book open at the correct page can save a lot of time.

The right book

The first time you use a book in a lesson, holding up your own Student's Book or Workbook is an obvious cue for the class. You can also save time by asking the children to hold up the book as well. Anyone with the wrong book will quickly see what their classmates are doing and will be able to change books.

The right page

- Say the page number in English and, if possible, in L1. Children of this age may be able to recognize figures 1 to 10, but do not expect them to be able to read figures consistently with success. Show the children the correct page and draw their attention to the pictures, characters, or colors to help them find it quickly.
- Again, asking children to hold up their books, open at the right page, can be a faster way of checking that everyone is ready.

Using pencils and crayons

Many of the activities in *Super Safari* require children to use a pencil or colored pencils/crayons. Hand the materials out at the beginning of the class or make sure the children have them ready to use. Show the number and colors required, naming and counting in English, and ask children to hold up their pencils or crayons to make sure they have the right colors.

The Workbook practice activities which involve drawing lines, circling, and tracing and the Student's Book phonics lessons in later units all help develop the early writing skills of gripping a pencil correctly, controlling the pencil, and working from left to right on the page. Whenever children are working individually on these activities, the teaching notes suggest monitoring and checking they are using the correct grip.

Classroom management

Checking instructions

The key to classroom management is clear instruction, and the larger the class, the more possibility there is that some children will become distracted and are not then sure what to do.

- If children need to move to different desks, a different part of the classroom, or outside for a game, move them first and then explain the activity.
- If they need to take certain materials with them, support your instructions with flashcards or board drawings, e.g., *Take your pencil* (stick the pencil flashcard on the board) *and your book* (stick the book flashcard on the board) *with you*.
- Remember that children are not able to read the written instructions, so focus on the examples in the Workbook and demonstrate them with your finger.
- Even at this young age, there will usually be one or two children able and more than willing to explain the instructions in L1 as a final check if some children still seem unsure.

Involving everyone

In *Super Safari*, presentation and practice activities involving the whole class are balanced with individual practice activities, allowing time for monitoring each child's progress. This combination ensures that all children are actively involved in the lesson.

Children can also be involved in presentation stages of the lesson, by holding flashcards or demonstrating games and activities with you at the front of the class. This takes longer, but there are several benefits:

- It changes the dynamic of the classroom, which helps to keep everyone's attention.
- It provides opportunities for recycling classroom language in a meaningful way as you invite children to stand up, come to the front, pick up a pencil, etc. The whole class can hear this language, and they watch to see how their classmates respond.
- It demonstrates important values: you share your materials with the children, they play with them, take care of them, and give them back safely. *Please* and *Thank you* become common, natural phrases in the classroom.

Confident children will eagerly volunteer to come to the front in every lesson, so you may find it useful to keep a column in your notebook to mark children's names when they have been involved in this way, to ensure that everyone has been asked to take part (for example, F = flashcard, A = acting out).

Using English and L1

With young learners, it is helpful to establish an English-speaking environment as far as is possible, while still fostering an encouraging atmosphere where the children feel at ease and able to contribute. The more you use English, the more natural it will be for children to copy you and to use as much as they can. If you do not speak your children's L1, this will happen as a matter of course, but you will need to monitor your own use of language carefully, use materials such as flashcards and plenty of gesture and mime, to make sure none of the children feel lost or uncomfortable. In a class where everyday classroom business is carried out in English, many children will acquire a little more language passively and may surprise you by using new classroom phrases that they have heard.

The use of L1 can be an effective tool:

- After you have first explained and demonstrated a task in English, use limited L1 to clarify or ask a confident child to explain in L1 for you. However, it is best to avoid doing this all the time. If you always repeat instructions in L1 after first explaining in English, children will learn to expect this and more passive children may "switch off" until they hear the L1 instructions.
- When a child has clear emotional needs, for example if they are unhappy because a craft activity hasn't turned out as they intended, they won't have the necessary English to explain the problem. In these instances, let the child tell you the problem in L1 first (consult a colleague if necessary) but then use English to console them, to praise their work, and to integrate them in the lesson again, e.g., *OK now? Really, your chicken's great! Come and look at* (name)*'s chicken. It's orange like yours*.

Monitoring and assessment

Monitoring in the classroom is essential to ensure that everyone's attention is on the task in hand. It's even more important in the language classroom, particularly at the oral-aural stage. More children will have an opportunity to speak if you encourage this while you are monitoring their work.

As you circulate:

- Use English to praise work and ask questions. The teaching notes provide guidance about when and how to do this, and many of the Workbook activities have a follow-up oral stage which has been specifically designed for authentic communication. Some children may be able to use a few words; most will need questions to prompt them; others may only be ready to listen and agree as you talk about their work.
- Ask children about their classmates' work and encourage them to show interest and to compliment each other.

Using the Workbook self-evaluation feature

Assessment at this early stage of learning is an ongoing process of observation in whole-class work and monitoring at an individual level. Although formal testing is not appropriate in the pre-school classroom, the Workbook self-evaluation feature at the end of each unit can be used for informal assessment. If practical, call children to your desk individually to say the words, while the rest of the class is working on another activity. Check off in the children's books / use a reward sticker to confirm they have said the words.

Using the *Super Safari* songs

Songs are an extremely valuable part of the language-learning process at this stage. Children produce more language in a song than in any other form of practice activity; the rhythmic nature of songs helps develop authentic intonation and pronunciation, and the repetitive nature of song lyrics activates key language many times.

Before playing a song

It may be tempting to explain the song lyrics before children hear them, but it is more motivating to let them simply enjoy the song first. Strong visual support encourages thinking skills and helps children predict what the song is about. The songs in *Super Safari* are clearly illustrated with this in mind, and the teaching notes suggest a quick lead-in to each song based on the picture.

Learning a song

As well as providing a context, the song illustrations act as visual prompts to help support the meaning of the lyrics. Once children are more familiar with the song, they will add in actions (suggested in the teaching notes), for which they will need to stand and sing without looking at their books. It is common for children of this age to "mumble" the less familiar words, but the song structure in many cases will allow time for you to show a flashcard or an object, or do an action to help them join in with the core words.

Performing the songs

The teaching notes suggest different approaches to performing the songs, depending on the type of song and the content – for example, dividing the class into groups taking different roles as they sing. There are karaoke versions of the songs after the main recording. These are best used once the class is confident enough to sing without their books. Where possible, you could use the karaoke versions as a showcase for parents to see what their children have been learning.

Using the *Super Safari* stories

Before playing a story

An effective way to prepare children to listen to a story is to ask them to sit in a part of the classroom or in a circle, making sure they are relaxed but also quiet and ready to listen. Tell children to put their things away to avoid distractions.

While listening to a story

Hold up your book and point to each frame. Encourage children to listen for the sound that signals the end of each frame by cupping your hand to your ear every time it sounds. After working with the first story in the course, they will learn to recognize this.

After listening to a story

The Lesson 5 teaching notes give guidance on how to work with the story. In Lesson 6 there is then the full exploitation of the value illustrated in the story.

Using the masks and Yes/No cards

Masks of the animal characters Mike, Gina, Leo, and Polly are at the back of the Workbook for use in acting out the stories, to practice the characters' names, and for additional activities, detailed in the notes for individual lessons. To make the masks more durable, stick or copy them onto thin cardboard and/or laminate them. If you use them from the pages of the book, use Scotch tape to add strips of paper to fit around the childrens' heads or, if you have to use string, add reinforcers or Scotch tape to strengthen the holes in the masks.

Also at the back of the Workook (pages 91 and 92) is a green card with a check mark on it and a red card with an X on it. These are referred to as "Yes/No cards" in the teaching notes, and can be used at different stages of the lesson to elicit a non-verbal response. The notes explain fully how to introduce and use the cards. It is a good idea to reinforce the cards by copying or sticking them onto thin cardboard or laminating them.

Using the Polly the parrot puppet

Puppets provoke a magical reaction from young children. In their eyes, a puppet has a life of its own, with its own home, character, and language. This makes the puppet an extremely useful tool in the language classroom.

Making your own Polly puppet

If you do not have the Polly puppet, you can make your own using a green sock, thin orange cardboard (for the beak and feet), thin green cardboard (for the wings and tail), and thin black and white cardboard for the eyes.

Bringing Polly to life

To make Polly as magical and appealing as possible, create a home for her in the classroom. This can be a nest (a cardboard box or a basket) or simply your bag. Make sure children do not see you putting Polly on your hand, so that she appears to magically come to life. You can use a special voice for Polly if you wish, but do not distort your pronunciation, as the children need to hear clear examples of language at all times.

Have a set routine for beginning an activity with Polly, e.g., Polly greets the children and they respond *Hello, Polly!* When the activity is finished, get the class to say *Goodbye, Polly!* Make Polly reply and fly back to her home.

Keep in mind that Polly is a parrot, and can do the things that a real parrot does – fly, walk, talk, and sing. Polly can use her skills to help with classroom management, e.g., fly to an individual child if you need to choose a volunteer, help the children learn a song (by singing along), or bring some fun to the class if the children are feeling tired. To gain the most linguistic value from the puppet, make sure that she speaks only English. This will lead the children to communicate with Polly in a very authentic, natural way.

Games with Polly the parrot

Disappearing flashcards

Put on the puppet and greet the class. Make Polly say *Close your eyes*. Mime closing your eyes. Make Polly say *Open your eyes*. Practice these instructions, with Polly "talking" to the class and the children following her instructions. Stick the flashcards on the board. Elicit the words.

Make sure all the children have their eyes closed, and remove one flashcard from the board. Say *Open your eyes*. Polly "points" to the remaining flashcards in turn. The class says the words. She "points" to the space where the missing flashcard was. The class says the missing word. Show them the card and make Polly say *Yes! Good job!* Repeat the game, changing the order of the flashcards.

Follow the leader

Choose a volunteer to be the leader. The rest of the class stands behind the leader in a line. The leader walks around with everyone following. Put on the puppet and greet the class. Make Polly whisper an instruction to the leader. He/She does the action, moving around the space at the same time. The rest of the class follows and say the word (e.g., if the instruction is *Jump!* the child jumps around, and all the other children do the same thing, saying *Jump!*). Make Polly say *Good job! Stop! Change the leader!* The leader then goes to the back of the line and the child at the front is the new leader.

No, Polly!

Put on the puppet and greet the class. Make Polly point at one of the items or flashcards, e.g., a bag, and say the wrong word (e.g., *Pencil*). Frown at Polly and say *Pencil? No, Polly!* Try to make your class laugh. The children say *Bag* to the puppet. Make Polly say *Oh! Bag! Thank you*. Repeat for the other items. Polly says the wrong word each time. Encourage the children to join in when you say *No, Polly!* Repeat with Polly getting the words right. Encourage the class to clap whenever she gets it right (she takes a bow).

Polly says ...

Put on the puppet and greet the class. Make Polly whisper in your ear. Mime listening. Then say, e.g., *Polly says "Stand up."* Encourage the children to follow the instruction. Repeat with different instructions, making Polly "whisper' into your ear each time.

Say *Let's play!* Explain in L1 that the children need to listen carefully and follow your instructions, but only when you say "Polly says." Make Polly whisper in your ear and give instructions as before. The children follow the instructions when they hear "Polly says." Leave out "Polly says" sometimes. The children who follow the instruction that time are "out." Repeat until only a few children remain. They are the winners. Make Polly fly to each of the winners, "land" on their heads or hands and say *Good job!*

Singing Polly

Put on the puppet. Explain in L1 that Polly is going to sing. Say that she is very good at singing, but her memory is not so good.

Give out the No cards. Explain that when the children hear Polly make a mistake, they should hold up the card.

Play the karaoke version of the song. Make Polly sing along, but with the wrong words. Pause when the children hold up their No cards and ask/help a volunteer to say or sing the right words. Make Polly say *Oh, thank you!* and then continue singing.

Teaching without the puppet

There are ideas in the teaching notes for adapting puppet activities if you do not wish to use the puppet. For all the games described above, you can take the role of Polly (for "Polly says," which is a version of "Simon says," any soft toy could be used to replace Polly).

How can I adapt Super Safari to fit my schedule?

Super Safari is designed for schools that dedicate a significant part of the week to English. No two schools are the same, and different pressures on the schedule mean that you, the teacher, may need to adapt the course to fit your schedule.

If you have more time

Repetition, repetition, repetition. Young children learn very quickly but forget just as quickly, which is why it is so important to recycle little and often. If you have more time available, don't be afraid to sing the same song a couple of times in any one lesson and several times during the week. Consider incorporating your class's favorite songs and chants into the welcome routines for every lesson. Similarly, the story in the book can be used several times in many different ways.

Remember, as well as the Workbook, the puppet, flashcards, and posters offer excellent opportunities to further consolidate new language.

If you have less time

If you are short of time, it can be tempting to skip lessons or shorten certain stages. However, when working with pre-school children it is important to maximize input and ensure each lesson has lots of variety and movement. Consider the following ideas as ways to shorten the course, and focus on the activities that make a difference and that children will enjoy.

Do

- Ensure every lesson includes predictable routines for Warm-up, Presentation, Practice, and Ending the lesson.
- Ensure that each lesson has a balance of active and quiet periods.
- Focus on the Presentation and Practice stages of the lesson; this is the main input and fundamental to successful acquisition.
- Focus on the activities in which children hear and use new language.
- Consider leaving the drawing and coloring tasks until the end of the lesson or for homework. Do not ignore these activities altogether: they offer children an excellent opportunity to process the lesson's input.

All the lessons in a unit provide important learning opportunities, but the following chart can help you decide how much time to allocate to each lesson.

Suggested time allocation per unit

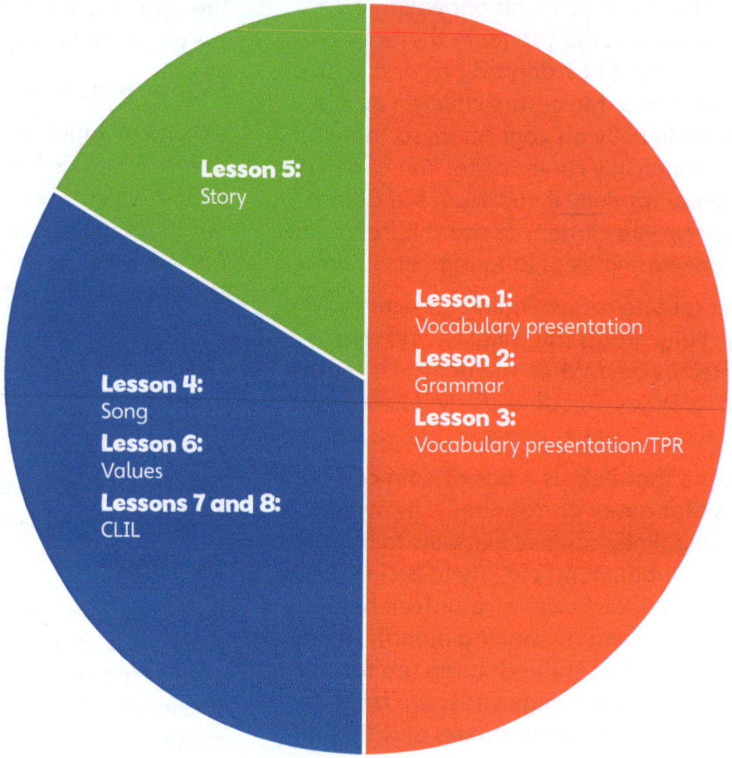

We hope this helps you plan your lessons, but please get in touch at ELTmail@cambridge.org if you have any questions or comments about the course.

Use the table below to help you decide which activity types you can integrate into your lessons depending on the time you have available.

Component	Activity type	If you have more time	If you have less time
Teacher's Book	Warm-up activities Extension activities Ending the lesson activities Lesson 6 (practice)	✓ ✓ ✓ ✓	✗ ✗ ✗ ✗
Student's Book	*Think!* (activity 7) Phonics Review	✓ ✓ ✓	✗ ✗ ✗
Workbook	Value (activity 6) Project (activity 7) Review (activity 8)	✓ ✓ ✓	✗ ✗ ✗
Teacher's DVD	Animated stories Animated songs Animated songs with karaoke	✓ ✓ ✓	✗ ✗ ✗
Student's DVD-ROM	Vocabulary practice game 1 Vocabulary practice game 2 Animated songs* Animated songs with karaoke* ** Also seen on the Teacher's DVD*	✓ ✓ ✓ ✓	✗ ✗ ✗ ✗ *(can be used at home)*

Hello!

1 CD1 02 **Listen and point. Say the names.**

Aims:

- to present and practice character names; to practice saying *Hello*

New language: *Hello*, Gina, Polly, Leo, Mike, *Goodbye*

Materials: CD 1, flashcards (characters), the puppet (Polly), pencils

Language competences: The children will be able to recognize and name the characters in *Super Safari*.

Warm-up

Aim: to present and practice *Hello*

- Smile and wave at the class. The children wave back. Say *Hello* and wave at the same time. The children wave back and say *Hello*. Do this several times until all the children are joining in with *Hello*.
- Turn to one of the children and say *Hello*, (name). He/She replies *Hello*. Encourage the child to say *Hello*, (name) to his/her neighbor. Continue this chain around the class. If you have space in the classroom, the children can sit in a circle for this activity. With a large class, start another chain at the back of the room/the other side of the circle so that the children who are waiting do not become bored.

Presentation

1 CD1 02 SB p4 **Listen and point. Say the names.**

Aim: to present characters

- Help the children find SB page 4. Point to the picture. Wave at the characters and say *Hello!*
- Say *Listen*. Play the audio. The children listen without looking at their books.
- Say *Listen and point*. Play the audio again. Show the children how to point at the characters. Say *Listen and point* again. Play the audio. The children listen and point.
- Play the audio again. The children point and say the names.

Audio script page T95

Practice

- Show the character flashcards in the same order as the picture in the Student's Book. Say each name. The children repeat.
- Stick the character flashcards on the board in the same order. Point to each flashcard one at a time. The children say the name. Point to the flashcards in different orders. The children say the correct name.
- Teach a mime for each of the animal characters:
  Gina = Standing up tall and munching leaves from a tree.
  Polly = Flapping wings and squawking.
  Leo = Growling and leaping.
  Mike = Swinging arms and making a monkey noise.
- Do one of the mimes. The children say the correct name. Repeat with a different mime. Make the mimes as funny as you can.
- The children stand up. Say a name. They do the correct mime. Repeat several times.
- Ask the class to sit down and open their Workbooks.

1 WB p4 **Look and trace. Say the names.**

Aim: to practice character names and recognizing shapes

- Help the children find WB page 4. Point to each character's head one at a time and say the name. The children copy you. Repeat. Ask volunteers to point to the heads and say all the names.
- Say *Look and trace*. Show the children how to trace the lines. They trace the lines using pencils. Monitor and make sure they are tracing and using the correct grip. Ask individual children to point at the pictures and say the names.

Extension activity

Aim: to practice character names

- Talk briefly in L1 about which of the animals has long legs, long hair, strong arms, wings, etc.
- Draw part of one of the characters on the board, e.g., Mike's tail. The children say the name of the character. Repeat with different body parts, e.g., Polly's beak, Gina's long neck, Leo's tail, Polly's feet, Gina's horns, Mike's hand, Leo's nose and mouth.

Ending the lesson

Aim: to review *Hello*

- Put on the Polly puppet and make her say *Hello* to the class. Make her voice friendly and funny. The children reply *Hello, Polly!*
- Make Polly fly to a child and sit on his/her head. The child stands up. Make Polly say *Hello*, (name). The child replies *Hello, Polly!* Repeat several times, moving around the class so that children are watching carefully to see where Polly will "land" next.
- End the lesson by making Polly wave and say *Goodbye!* The children wave and can say *Goodbye* if they wish.

Aims:

- to present *Hello!*, *I'm* ... and practice introducing yourself; to say a chant

New language: Hello! I'm ...

Recycled language: character names, *Hello*, *Goodbye*

Materials: CD 1, flashcards (characters), the puppet (Polly), CD of lively music, pencils, colored pencils or crayons

Language competences: The children will be able to introduce themselves. The children will be able to join in with a chant.

Warm-up

Aim: to review *Hello* and character names

- Show the character flashcards one at a time. Say the names. The children repeat.
- Show the flashcards again. The children say the names.
- Cover each flashcard with a piece of paper. Slowly reveal the picture. The children say the name when they recognize the character.
- Stick the flashcards on the board. Point to each one, wave and say, e.g., *Hello, Mike!* The children repeat. Point to the flashcards in a different order. The children wave and say *Hello*, (name).

Presentation

2 CD1 03 SB p5 **Listen and chant.**

Aim: to present *Hello! I'm ...* and say a chant

- Help the children to find SB page 5. Talk about the picture briefly in L1 (ask where the children are and what they are saying, and what's in the classroom). Use the picture to elicit *Hello!* Point at the girl and say *Jo*. The children repeat. Point at the boy and say *Mo*. The children repeat.
- Play the chant. Point to the girl for verse 1 and the boy for verse 2. The children copy.
- Say *Listen and chant*. Play the chant again line by line. The children listen and repeat. Play the chant again for the children to join in. They point to the children in the picture as they chant.

Audio script page T95

Practice

- Put on the Polly puppet. Make her say *Hello* to the class. The children reply. Make Polly look at you and say *Hello! I'm Polly*. Reply to the puppet *Hello! I'm* (your name). Repeat.
- Make Polly fly to a child and say *Hello! I'm Polly!* Encourage the child to reply *Hello! I'm* (his/her name). Repeat with different children. Ask them to raise their hands if they'd like to speak to Polly.
- The children stand up. Play some music. The children walk around. When the music stops, the children turn to their nearest classmate. They say *Hello! I'm* (name) to each other and wave. Start the music again. Continue until the children are confident with introducing themselves.

2 WB p5 **Draw yourself. Say the sentence.**

Aim: to practice *Hello! I'm ...*

- Draw a simple outline of a head and shoulders on the board (similar to the one on WB page 5). Point and say *I'm* (your name). Draw your eyes, hair, nose, and a smiley mouth. Wave at the picture and say *Hello! I'm* (your name).
- Help the children find WB page 5. Point to the example drawing and the frame. Show some crayons and say *Draw yourself*. The children draw eyes, hair, mouth, etc. according to ability.
- Circulate and ask individuals to say *Hello! I'm* ... Invite volunteers to show their picture to the class and say *Hello! I'm* ....

Extension activity

Aim: to practice the long vowel sound "oh" and listening skills

- If possible, move your class out into the playground, school gym, or an empty classroom.
- Divide the class into two teams. Name one team Mo and the other team Jo. The teams stand at one end of the space (e.g., against one wall or behind a line). Explain in L1 that each team needs to run to the wall or line in front and touch it, then run back. The Mo team runs when you say *Go Mo!* and the Jo team runs when you say *Go Jo!*
- Play the game several times, encouraging the children to listen carefully for the name of their team. Ask a confident volunteer to lead the game by saying *Go Mo!* or *Go Jo!*

Ending the lesson

Aim: to practice the chant

- Divide the class into two groups. Name one group Mo and the other group Jo. They stand up and face each other. Play the chant. For the first verse, Mo group says the *Hello* lines, while Jo group says the *I'm Jo* lines. They change lines for the second verse. Encourage them to wave at each other while saying *Hello*.
- End the lesson by waving and saying *Goodbye!* The children wave. Encourage them to say *Goodbye*.

2 CD1 03 **Listen and chant.**

3 CD1 04 Listen and act.

Aims:

- to present and practice responding to *Stand up, Sit down, Say "hello"*

New language: Stand up, Sit down, Say ...

Recycled language: *Hello! I'm ...*, character names, *Goodbye*

Materials: CD 1, flashcards (characters) or character masks (WB pages 93 to 96), the puppet (Polly), pencils

Language competences: The children will be able to follow classroom instructions.

Warm-up

Aim: to review character names and *Hello! I'm ...*

- Review the character names with the flashcards.
- Hold the flashcard of Gina in front of your face or put on the Gina mask and say *Hello! I'm Gina*. Use a "Gina" voice. Repeat for the other characters.
- Invite four volunteers to the front. Hand out the character flashcards or the four character masks to these children. They take turns to hold their flashcard up or put on their masks and say *Hello! I'm* (the character on the card). Encourage them to use a different voice for the characters. Repeat with different volunteers.

Presentation

3 CD1 04 SB p6 **Listen and act.**

Aim: to present classroom instructions and practice listening and responding physically

- Books closed. Ask the children to sit in a circle. Sit in the center. Play the first line of the audio and do the action (*Stand up*). Encourage the children to copy you. Ask the children to sit down again. Play the first line again. Do the action along with the children. Play the next line and do the action (*Sit down*). The children copy you. Repeat for the rest of the recording.
- Play the audio again without pausing, doing the actions and saying *Hello* along with the children. Repeat this several times, until the children are following the instructions with ease. Play the audio for the children to follow the instructions without your help.

Audio script page T95

Practice

Aim: to practice new instructions and listening

- Put on the Polly puppet. Make the puppet greet the class. Then make her say *Stand up*. The children stand. Repeat with the other new instructions. *Say "hello"* and *Sit down*. The children follow.
- Make Polly give the instructions in different orders and more quickly, as the children become confident.

3 CD1 05 WB p6 **Listen and circle.**

Aim: to practice new instructions, listening, and pencil control

- Help the children find WB page 6. Point to the first picture and say/elicit *Look! Stand up*. Point to the second picture. Say/Elicit *Say "hello."*
- Say *Listen and circle*. Trace a large circle in the air with your finger. Say *Draw a circle*. Encourage the children to copy you, practicing the circle shape with their fingers in the air.
- Say *What can you hear?* Play the audio. *Hello?* (gesture "yes"). Confirm the instructions in L1. Play the audio. Ask the children to point at the correct answer. They finish drawing the circle around the second picture. Circulate and elicit *Say "hello"* from individual children.

Audio script page T95

Extension activity

Aim: to practice responding to instructions

- Pretend to be a robot. Say *Hello!* in a robot voice, sit down with arms and legs making jerky movements like a robot, and stand up in the same way. Repeat, encouraging the children to copy you.
- Explain to the class in L1 that they are all robots and you are going to give them instructions. The children stand up. Give instructions (e.g., *Sit down, Stand up, Say "hello," Say "goodbye," Sit down*). The children follow using robot movements and robot voices. Make this into a fun game by speeding up.

Ending the lesson

Aim: to practice following instructions

- Divide the class into four groups. Name the groups Gina, Polly, Leo, and Mike. Give instructions from the lesson, but naming a group each time, e.g., *Mike, stand up* (only the children in the Mike group stand up). Repeat with different instructions and character names. If your class has made the character masks, they can wear them for this game (e.g., all the children in the Gina group wear their Gina mask).
- End the lesson by asking each group to say *Goodbye*.

Aims:

- to sing a song; to review character names and encourage children to reflect on their learning

New language: *Clap your hands, Let's go*

Recycled language: *Stand up, Sit down, Say "hello,"* character names

Materials: CD 1, flashcards (characters), colored pencils or crayons

Optional: the puppet (Polly)

Language competences: The children will be able to join in with a song. The children will be able to reflect on their learning.

Warm-up

Aim: to present *Clap your hands* and review classroom instructions

- Clap your hands. Encourage the children to copy. Say *Clap your hands* as the children clap. Choose individual children and say, e.g., *Elena, clap your hands.*
- Put on the Polly puppet. Make her give instructions to the class (*Stand up, Sit down, Say "hello," Say "goodbye,"* and the new instruction *Clap your hands*). The children respond. Speed up as they become more confident.

Presentation

4 CD1 06 07 SB p7 **Listen and sing.**

Aim: to sing a song

- Help the children find SB page 7. Point to the children on SB page 7 and ask what they are doing in L1. Elicit *Hello.*
- Play the song. The children listen and point to the pictures.
- Play the song again. The children follow the instructions (they begin the song sitting down and stand up for the first line of verse 2).
- Play the song again, pausing to teach each line.
- Using L1, you may want to use the artwork as an opportunity to highlight how children can be different but still an important part of our community. Emphasize how everybody wants to feel included and take part in all the same fun and games.

Audio script page T95

Review

4 WB p7 **Say the names. Color the circles.**

Aim: to review character names and create a record of learning

- Review the character names using the flashcards.
- Help the children find WB page 7. The children color the circles if they can say the names on their own.
- Circulate and ask individual children to say the names.

Extension activity

Aim: to practice giving instructions

- Put on the puppet. Make her greet the class and then "sit" on your desk or a chair. Give Polly instructions and make the puppet "follow" by doing the actions, e.g., *Stand up, Polly! Say "hello," Polly! Clap your hands!* (Polly "claps" her wings together), etc.
- Choose volunteers to give Polly instructions in the same way. Make the game funny by having Polly get tired/fed up as the children speed up their instructions.

Ending the lesson

Aim: to practice the song

- Play the song. The children sing along and follow the instructions.
- Wave and say *Goodbye* to end the lesson. The children copy you.

4 CD1 06 07 **Listen and sing.**

Family fun!

1 My class

1 CD1 08 **Listen and point. Say the words.**

Aims

- to present and practice classroom objects

New language: *bag, pencil, chair, book*

Recycled language: *Hello, Goodbye*, character names (*Leo, Polly, Mike, Gina*)

Materials: CD 1, flashcards (characters, classroom objects), classroom objects, the puppet (Polly), character masks, pencils

Optional: a strong light source, e.g., an adjustable lamp or projector, five or six familiar objects or toys which cast clear shadows (e.g., a pencil, a ball, a book, a teddy bear, a doll)

Language competences: The children will be able to name classroom objects.

Warm-up

Aim: to review greetings and character names

- Say *Hello* in a whisper. The children whisper *Hello* back. Repeat with different tones of voice and volumes.
- Show the character flashcards and say the names. Repeat. Stick the flashcards on the board. Point to the characters one at a time and say their names. The children repeat.
- Teach the chant below. Practice it line by line, then say it as a class. Point to the character flashcards on the board as prompts.

  Le, Le, Le, O, O, O, Leo! Leo! Leo!
  Gi, Gi, Gi, Na, Na, Na, Gina! Gina! Gina!
  Pol, Pol, Pol, Ly, Ly, Ly, Polly! Polly! Polly!
  Mike! Mike! Mike!
- Remove the flashcards and stick the character flashcards (turned around to the blank side) on the board. Point to one of the masks. Ask *Who's this?* Repeat the question in L1. Elicit the name. Repeat for all the characters several times.

Presentation

1 CD1 08 SB p8 **Listen and point. Say the words.**

Aim: to present classroom objects

- Help the children find page 8 of the SB. Point to the picture on SB page 8 and ask *Where's Polly?* The children point to Polly. Repeat with the other characters.
- Point to the classroom objects in the picture and ask *What's this?* The children reply in L1. Say *Listen.* Play the audio. The children just listen the first time. Say *Listen and point.* Play the audio. The children point. Play the audio again. The children point and say the words.

  Audio script page T95

Practice

- Put your bag, a book, and a pencil on your desk. Place your chair so the children can see it. Point to one of the items (e.g., the chair) and ask *What's this?* The children give the answer in chorus. Repeat for the other objects.
- The children stand up. Ask them in L1 to put their Student's Books in their bags and put their bags, Workbooks, and just a pencil on their table. Say one of the four classroom objects. The children point to the correct item. Repeat several times, getting faster and faster.
- Ask the class to sit down and open their Workbooks.

1 WB p8 **Look and match. Say the words.**

Aim: to practice classroom objects and recognizing shapes

- Help the children find WB page 8. Point to each object one at a time and say the words. The children copy you. Repeat. Ask volunteers to point to the pictures on the right and say the words.
- Say *Look and match.* Show the children how to draw lines from left to right to match the objects. They draw using pencils. Monitor and make sure they are tracing from left to right and using the correct grip. Circulate and ask individual children to point at the pictures and say the words.

Extension activity

Aim: to raise awareness of how shadows are created

- Put Polly near your light source (a lamp or projector) so that the children can see her shadow on the wall. Say the word *Shadow* and elicit the translation in L1.
- Place other items, toys, or the character masks near the light source to make different shadows. Say *What's this?* or *Who's this?* Elicit the words in L1 or English.

Ending the lesson

Aim: to review classroom objects

- Stick the classroom object flashcards on the board. Put on the Polly puppet. Make Polly "point" to each flashcard on the board and ask *What's this?* The children say the word. Do this several times.
- Play *Disappearing flashcards* using the classroom objects flashcards (see Introduction, page xvii).

Aims

- to present *Look! It's my ...* and practice classroom objects; to say a chant

New language: *Look! It's my (chair)*

Recycled language: classroom objects

Materials: CD 1, flashcards (classroom objects), classroom objects, the puppet (Polly), pencils

Optional: Yes/No cards (WB pages 91 and 92)

Language competences: The children will be able to refer to their possessions. The children will be able to join in with a chant.

Warm-up

Aim: to review classroom objects

- Show the classroom object flashcards one at a time. Say the words. The children repeat. Show the flashcards again. The children say the words without you.
- Play *No, Polly* (see Introduction, page xvii), using real classroom objects.

Presentation

2 CD1 09 SB p9 **Listen and trace. Chant.**

Aim: to present *Look! It's my ...* and say a chant

- Help the children to find SB page 9. Point to each object at the bottom of page 9 and ask *What's this?* The children say the words. Show how to follow the lines from the children to the objects with your finger. The children copy.
- Say *Listen and trace.* Play the first verse of the chant and show how to trace the first line from the boy to the chair with a pencil. Do the same for the next three verses. Circulate and check they are tracing from left to right and using the correct grip. Play the whole chant for the children to listen and check.
- Say *Listen and chant.* Play the chant again line by line. The children listen and repeat. Play the chant again for the children to join in. They point to or hold up their own possessions as they say each verse (chair, pencil, bag, etc.).

Audio script page T95

Practice

- Place a book, a bag, and a pencil on your table at the front of the class. Point to each item and say *Look! It's my (book).*
- Put on the Polly puppet. Say to Polly *It's my bag.* Polly "flies" to your bag and lands on it. Say *Good job, Polly!* The children clap. Repeat with the other objects. Call a volunteer to the front. Say, e.g., *It's my book.* The child points to the correct object. Repeat with different volunteers.
- Move around the class. Point at an item which belongs to an individual child (book, bag, pencil, or chair). Encourage the child to say *It's my (book).* Repeat with different children.

2 CD1 10 WB p9 **Listen and connect the dots. Say the sentence.**

Aim: to practice listening, pencil control, and classroom objects

- Help the children find WB page 9. Point to the first picture and show children how to connect the dots with a pencil. Say *Listen and connect the dots.*
- Play the audio. The children listen and find the first picture. Pause until everyone has finished. They connect the dots as they find each picture.
- Play the audio again. The children point at their pictures and repeat the words and the sentence.

Audio script page T95

Extension activity

Aim: to practice *It's my ...* and classroom objects

- Give each child their Yes/No cards. Show the Yes card, smile and nod, and say *Yes!* The children copy. Show the No card, frown, and say *No!* The children copy. Repeat until they are doing this with ease. Say *Yes* or *No* in different orders. Children pick up the correct card.
- Show the children one of your classroom objects and say a false sentence, e.g., show a pencil and say *It's my bag.* The children say *No!* and hold up the No card. Repeat with different objects, mixing up true and false sentences.

Ending the lesson

Aim: to practice the chant

- Divide the children into four groups. Name them Chair, Pencil, Bag, and Book. Play the chant. The children in each group stand up and join in with the correct verse.

2 CD1 09 Listen and trace. Chant.

Family fun! Look! It's my (chair).

3 CD1 11 Listen and act.

Aims

- to present and practice *Hands up*, *Hands down*; to practice following instructions

New language: *Hands up*, *Hands down*

Recycled language: classroom objects, *Look! It's my (chair)*, *Clap your hands*, *Stand up*, *Sit down*

Materials: CD 1, flashcards (classroom objects), classroom objects, the puppet (Polly), pencils

Language competences: The children will be able to follow classroom instructions.

Warm-up

Aim: to review referring to possessions

- Review the classroom objects with the flashcards or real items.
- Do one of the mimes below. The children say the correct object, e.g., *Bag*. Say *Yes! It's my (bag)*.

  Bag = Picking up a backpack and putting it on your back.

  Pencil = Sharpening a pencil and then writing with it.

  Chair = Lifting a chair, putting it down, and then sitting on it.

  Book = Taking a book off a shelf, opening it, and looking through the pages.
- Invite volunteers to do one of the mimes for the class. When their classmates guess, encourage them to say *Yes! It's my ...* .
- Show items of your own and say, e.g., *Look! It's my pencil*. The children do it in pairs.

Presentation

3 CD1 11 SB p10 **Listen and act.**

Aim: to review classroom instructions and present *Hands up*, *Hands down*

to practice listening and responding physically

- Books closed. Ask the children to sit in a circle. Sit in the center. Clap your hands and say the phrase at the same time. The children copy. Repeat with *Stand up* and *Sit down*. Do this until the children are joining in with ease. Then give instructions without doing the actions yourself.
- Play the first line of the recording and do the new action (*Hands up*). Encourage the children to copy you. Play the next line and do the new action (*Hands down*). The children copy you. Repeat for the rest of the recording.
- Play the audio again without pausing, doing the actions along with the children. Repeat this several times, until the children are following the instructions with ease. Then play the audio for the children to do the actions without your help.
- Give the children instructions in a different order, adding *Stand up* and *Sit down*, e.g., *Stand up, Hands up, Clap your hands, Hands down, Sit down*. They follow your instructions. Speed up when they are confident.

Audio script page T95

Practice

3 CD1 12 WB p10 **Listen and circle.**

Aim: to practice new instructions, listening, and pencil control

- Help the children find WB page 10. Point to the first picture and say/elicit *Look! Hands up*. Point to the second picture. Say/Elicit *Hands down*.
- Say *Listen and circle*. Trace a large circle in the air with your finger. Say *Draw a circle*. Encourage the children to copy you, practicing the circle shape with their fingers in the air.
- Say *Listen. Hands down* or *hands up?* Play the audio. Ask the children to point at the correct answer. They draw the circle around the second picture and say *Hands down*.

Audio script page T95

Extension activity

Aim: to practice classroom instructions

- Clap your hands once, and then do one action. Say the action at the same time, e.g., *Hands up*. The children copy you. Repeat with different actions. Once the children are saying the actions confidently, do just the actions, and ask the children to say the words.

Ending the lesson

Aim: to practice following instructions

- The children stand behind their desks, with their chairs nearby. Ask them to put a pencil and a book on their desks. Put on the Polly puppet. Polly gives instructions (e.g., *Stand up, Hands up, Hands down, Clap your hands, Sit down*). The children follow. Once the children are following with ease, introduce new instructions with the items on their desks (e.g., *Pencils up, Pencils down, Books up, Books down*). Repeat all the instructions in different orders and speed up.

Aims

- to present and practice *Clean up (your) (bag)*; to review classroom instructions; to sing a song

New language: *Clean up (your ...)*

Recycled language: classroom objects, *Stand up, Sit down, Clap your hands, Hands up, Hands down*

Materials: CD 1, the puppet (Polly), pencils

Optional: small bag, a pencil, a book, and a cardboard box/basket for each team of three to six children (the cardboard box/basket must be large enough to hold the bag, pencil, and book)

Language competences: The children will be able to join in with a song.

Warm-up

Aim: to review classroom instructions

- Give instructions (*Stand up, Hands up, Hands down, Sit down, Clap your hands*). The children follow.
- Ask the children to put their bag, pencil, and book on their desks.
- Play *Polly says ...* (see Introduction, page xvii). Review known instructions and include *Bags up/down. Pencils up/down* and *Books up/down.*

Presentation

4 CD1 13 14 SB p11 **Listen and sing.**

Aim: to present *Clean up your (chair)* and sing a song

- Ask about known classroom objects on SB page 11. Say, e.g., *Point to a chair.* The children point. Ask in L1 what the children in the picture are doing. Elicit that they are cleaning up and say *Clean up* in English. The children repeat.
- Play the song. The children just listen.
- Play the song again. The children look at the picture and point to the book, chairs, pencils, or bag at the appropriate point in the song.
- Play the song again, pausing to teach each line. When they are confident, they can stand up and mime cleaning up each of the items mentioned as they sing.

Audio script page T95

Practice

4 WB p11 **Follow the path.**

Aim: to practice *Clean up* and pencil control

- Point to the book and ask *What's this?* Elicit *Book*. Say *Clean up your book.* The children repeat. Mime drawing a line from the girl, through the maze to the shelf. The children use a pencil to solve the maze. Circulate and check they are drawing a line from left to right and using the correct grip. Encourage the children to chant *Clean up your book* as they draw.

Extension activity

Aim: to practice following instructions and take part in a team game

- If possible, move your class into the playground, school gym or an empty classroom.
- Divide the class into teams of three to six. The teams stand in lines, with one child at the front. In front of each team, place a bag, then a pencil and a book and, furthest away, a cardboard box/basket. Make sure there is plenty of space between each object.
- Show the children how to play. Say *Clean up your bag*. The first child in each team runs to pick up the bag in their line of objects, puts it in the box/basket, and runs to the back of their team. Say *Clean up your pencil.* The children now at the front run, pick up their team's pencil, and put it in their box/basket. They run to the back of their team. Do the same for the book.
- Practice the game slowly at first. You will need to take the objects out of the boxes/baskets once you have given all three instructions, and place them in line again. Mix up the order of the instructions to keep children listening carefully.
- Make the game competitive – the fastest child wins a point each time.

Ending the lesson

Aim: to practice the song

- Say *Listen and clean up!* Play the song. The children sing and clean up their own books, chairs, and pencils, and close their bags.

Note: You can play this song and clean up at the end of every lesson.

4 CD1 13 14 **Listen and sing.**

5 CD1 15 Sticker The chair

Values

1 2 3 4

Aims

- to present a picture story; to review language from the unit

New language: *please, stop it, sorry*

Recycled language: classroom objects, *Hello, Sit down, It's my chair*

Materials: CD 1, flashcards (characters, classroom objects), the puppet (Polly), character masks

Language competences: The children will be able to listen and follow a picture story. The children will be able to use *please*.

Warm-up

Aim: to review characters and classroom instructions

- Show each of the character flashcards and ask *Who's this?* Children say the names. Repeat. Stick the flashcards on the board.
- Put on the Polly puppet. Play *No, Polly!* (see Introduction, page xvii) with Polly pointing at the character flashcards and saying the wrong names.
- Make Polly give instructions to review *Stand up, Sit down, Clap your hands, Hands up,* and *Hands down.* The children listen and follow.

Presentation

5 CD1 15 SB pp12–13 **Story: The chair**

Aim: to listen and follow a picture story

- Point to Polly in the first picture on SB page 12 and ask *Who's this?* The children say *Polly.* Repeat for Gina. Ask where Polly and Gina are in L1 (in the classroom / at school). Point to the characters in picture 2 and ask their names. Point to the new character in picture 3 and ask *Who's this?* The children tell you in L1 that it's the animals' teacher, a zebra. Point to the chair and ask *What's this?*
- Play the CD. The children point at the pictures as they listen.
- Play the story again, stopping after each picture. The children explain what's happening in L1. Elicit translations for *please, stop it,* and *sorry.*
- Divide the class into four groups. Name each group after one of the characters in the story. They put on the appropriate character mask. Ask the children to put a bag, a pencil, and a pen on their desks and stand up. Give instructions using *please*, e.g., *Leo! Sit down, please* (only the children in the Leo group sit down). Repeat with different instructions and character names. Include new instructions *Pencils up, please, Bags down, please,* etc.

Audio script page T95

Practice

5 CD1 16 WB p12 **Listen and color the correct circle.**

Aim: to listen and identify the correct picture

- Point to the first picture on WB page 12. Ask *Who's this?* The children say the name. Repeat for the second picture. Say *Listen. Mike or Gina?* Play the audio. Elicit the answer *Mike.*
- Show the children how to color the correct circle. Play the audio again. Check their work as they color.
- Play the recording again. The children repeat Mike's line.

Audio script page T95

Extension activity

Aim: to practice careful listening and classroom instructions

- Put on the puppet. Make Polly say *Stand up* to the children in an impolite way. Gesture to the children to remain sitting down. Say *Polly! Say "please!"* Make Polly say *Stand up, please!* The children stand up.
- Explain in L1 that the children must only do what Polly says if they hear the word *please.* Make Polly give different instructions, some with *please*, some without. The children only carry out the polite ones!

Ending the lesson

Aim: to practice *please*

- Elicit a translation for *please.* Show the classroom object flashcards. The children say the words. Repeat with the characters. Stick all the flashcards on the board at a height your class can reach.
- Invite a volunteer to the board and say, e.g., *Pencil, please.* The child takes the flashcard from the board and passes it to you. Say *Thank you.* Repeat with different volunteers.
- Ask the children to put a pencil, a book, and a bag on their desks. Children practice asking for items in pairs by saying, e.g., *Book, please.*

Aims

- to talk about the meaning of a story; to review language from the unit

Recycled language: classroom instructions, classroom objects, language from the story

Materials: CD 1, flashcards (characters), Unit 1 stickers, colored pencils or crayons, the puppet (Polly)

Optional: character masks, three chairs

Language competences: The children will be able to appreciate the values shown in the story. The children will practice saying *sorry*.

Warm-up

Aim: to review classroom instructions and *please*

- Show the character flashcards. The children say the names.
- Mix the flashcards up and hand them out randomly to four children. Give instructions using *please*, e.g., *Leo! Stand up, please.* The child with the Leo flashcard stands up. Repeat with different instructions for the four children. Then take back the flashcards by asking, e.g., *Leo, please*. Say *Thank you* when the child gives you the card. Repeat with four different children.

Practice

5 CD1 15 SB pp12–13 **Story: The chair Listen to the story. Stick.**

Aim: to review the story

- Ask the children to tell you what they remember about the story in L1.
- Play the story again, pausing after each picture to ask about the names of the characters, the classroom objects in the picture, and what is happening.
- Hand out the stickers for Unit 1. Say, e.g., *Bag*. The children point to the correct sticker on the sheet. Repeat for the other items.
- Point to the picture on SB page 13. Say *Where's the bag?* The children point to the sticker outline. Mime peeling the sticker of the bag off the sheet. The children peel off the sticker and hold it up. Check that they all have the correct sticker. Then say *Stick it, please*. Mime sticking it in the right place. The children stick the sticker in their books. Repeat for the other stickers.

Audio script page T95

Story values SB pp12–13

Aim: to think about the meaning of the story: being kind and saying *sorry*

- Play the story again. The children listen and point. Pause after picture 4 and talk in L1 about the way the characters are feeling. Ask in L1 *Why are Leo and Mike fighting?* (Because they both want the chair.) *How does the teacher feel?* (Annoyed/Angry.) *Why?* (Because this isn't the way we behave in class/it isn't kind.) Play the rest of the story and ask in L1 *What do Leo and Mike say at the end of the story?* Elicit *Sorry* in English and in L1. Ask the children when they would say *sorry*. Talk about how important it is to say *sorry* to a friend if you have upset him/her.
- Say *Sorry!* The children repeat. Say the word at different volumes. The children repeat it at the same volume each time.

6 WB p13 **Complete the face. Color the picture.**

Aim: to apply values from the story to new situations

- Tell the children in L1 *We're going to look at some children now. Look at the picture and think. Is he kind?* Help the children find WB page 13. Point to the happy face and explain in L1 that if they think the boy is doing the right thing and saying *sorry*, they trace a happy smile. Show them how to trace the line with a pencil. Circulate and check as they trace. Then the children can color the picture.

Extension activity

Aim: to reinforce understanding of the story

- Invite five volunteers to the front. Assign them the roles of Gina, Polly, Leo, Mike, and the teacher. The children playing the main characters put on the masks. Arrange three chairs near the children. Play the story. The children act out the story along with the CD. Encourage the children to join in with the CD and the child who is playing the teacher to act like a teacher.
- Invite another group of five children to come to the front and act.

Ending the lesson

Aim: to practice saying *sorry*

- Put on the Polly puppet. Make Polly pick up a pencil from your desk and throw it on the floor. Point to the pencil, look angry, and say *Polly! Look! It's my pencil!* Make Polly look down/sad and have her say *Sorry!* Repeat with Polly throwing or knocking items belonging to individual children on the floor (books, bags, pencils). Encourage the children to say *Polly! Look! It's my ...* Have Polly say *sorry* each time.
- Invite volunteers to wear Polly and practice saying *sorry* in the same way.

5

School behavior

6 CD1 17 **Listen and point. Say the words.**

Aims

- to integrate other areas of the curriculum through English: Social studies

New language: *Listen, Join in*

Recycled language: *Look*, classroom instructions, *Hello! I'm ...*

Materials: CD 1, the puppet (Polly), a piece of paper or thin cardboard for each child with a simple outline of a person, colored pencils or crayons, an outline drawing of you (colored in with the correct hair color, clothes, etc. (as on WB page 14)

Optional: a soft ball

Language competences: The children will be able to recognize social skills required in the classroom.

Warm-up

Aim: to review classroom instructions and encourage children to work together

- Put on the puppet. Give the class instructions using Polly, e.g., *Stand up, please. Hands up. Hands down. Sit down. Clap your hands. Pencils up.*
- Invite four to six volunteers to the front. They stand in a row. Say *Listen and say.* Explain to the first child in L1 that he/she needs to listen to your instruction and then tell it (in English) to the next child. He/She shouldn't actually do the action. Explain that you want the instruction to get to the last person in the row, then he/she does the action and says it. Tell the children at the front to listen very carefully to their friends. Whisper an instruction into the first child's ear. He/She whispers it to the next person and so on down the line. The last child does the action and says the instruction, then goes to the beginning of the line. Repeat with a different instruction.
- Talk briefly in L1 about how important it is to listen in class. Explain that in today's lesson you are going to think about other things which are important when we are in a group at school.

Presentation

6 CD1 17 SB p14 **Listen and point. Say the words.**

Aim: to present social skills

- Ask the children to look at SB page 14. Elicit *Look* and *Listen* for the first two pictures.
- Play the recording. The children listen and point to each picture one at a time.
- Translate *join in* into L1. Talk about the way we need to join in with activities and games in class. Remind children to use *please* and *sorry* and be kind.

Audio script page T95

Practice

7 WB p14 **Make a model of yourself.**

Aim: to take part in a craft activity and encourage recognition of self
to review *Hello! I'm ...*

- Show the pictures on WB page 14. Explain in L1 that you are all going to make models of yourselves. Hold up a simple outline you have completed of yourself (with the correct hair color, clothes, etc.). Make the outline say *Hello! I'm* (your name).
- Hand an outline of a person on paper or thin cardboard to each child. Say *Color you!* Circulate and help the children draw the face and use the correct colors for their hair, tops, pants, etc.
- Ask volunteers to show their finished models to the class and say *Hello! I'm* (name).

Note: If you wish, the children can stick their models onto a piece of poster paper with the title *Our class*. Display the finished poster and say *Look, our class!* Explain in L1 that we all need to work together in class.

Extension activity

Aim: to encourage the children to join in and focus on their classmates

- If possible, move your class out into the playground, school gym, or an empty classroom.
- Ask the children to stand in a circle. Say the name of one of the children. The class repeats. Throw the soft ball to that child. The child says the name of one of his/her classmates. The children repeat it. Then he/she throws the ball to that child, and so on. Say *Join in!* They can also say *sorry* if they throw the ball too hard.

Ending the lesson

Aim: to review social skills from the lesson

- Teach the following mimes for the three skills from the lesson:

  Look = Hold both hands up to your eyes, as if looking through binoculars.

  Listen = Cup one hand around one ear.

  Join = Join your hands together in front of you as if shaking hands with yourself.
- Say each word. The children mime. When they are confident with the mimes, they say and mime at the same time.
- Say the words in a rhythmic phrase while you mime: *Look, Listen, Please, Join in.* The children copy.

Aims

- to review language and values from the unit; to encourage children to reflect on their learning

Recycled language: *Look, Listen, Join in,* classroom objects

Materials: flashcards (classroom objects), the puppet (Polly)

Optional: playdough or modeling clay (one piece for each child)

Language competences: The children will be able to use language from the unit. They will be able to reflect on their learning.

Warm-up

Aim: to review social skills

- Repeat the mime and chant from the previous lesson (see page T14, Ending the lesson). Talk briefly in L1 about the importance of looking, listening, and joining in.

Review

7 Think! SB p15 **Look and complete the faces.**

Thinking skills: classifying behavior

- Draw two faces with eyes but no mouths on the board (like the ones on SB page 15). Draw a smile on one face, a sad mouth on the other. Ask in L1 which is *Yes* and which is *No*. Ask the children to practice drawing a happy face and a sad face on a piece of paper or with their fingers in the air.
- Point to the children in the first picture on SB page 15. Say *Yes. Look!* Show the children how to trace the sad mouth on the face. Explain in L1 that the children need to look at the other picture and trace the happy mouth on the face if they think the behavior is good. Circulate and help as necessary.
- Check answers. Elicit in L1 that the children are listening and joining in in the second picture. Point at the pictures and say *Look, Listen, Join in.* The children repeat.

8 WB p15 **Say the words. Color the circles.**

Aim: to create a record of learning

- Point to the pictures on WB page 15. The children say the words together.
- The children color the circles if they can say the words on their own.
- Circulate and help as necessary. Ask individual children to say the words.

Extension activity

Aim: to review classroom object vocabulary

- Make a playdough model of a chair. Show the class and ask *What's this?* Tell the children they are going to make models of the classroom items from the unit. Stick the classroom object flashcards on the board and elicit the words.
- Hand out playdough to each child. The children make a model for each of the words (or they work in pairs and make two models each). Circulate and help as necessary. Ask *What's this?* Show some of the best models to the class.

Ending the lesson

Aim: to review language from the unit

- Play the children's favorite game from the unit or sing the unit song.

Phonics

- See page T80 for Unit 1 Phonics.

Review

- See page T90 for *Hello!* unit & Unit 1 Review.

7 Think! Look and complete the faces.

1

2

Phonics → page 80 Review → page 90

2 My colors

1 CD1 20 **Listen and point. Say the colors.**

Aims

- to present and practice colors

New language: *red, blue, green, yellow*

Recycled language: classroom objects, *Hello, Look, Polly, Gina*

Materials: CD 1, flashcards (colors), the puppet (Polly), red, blue, green, and yellow flags or scarves in a bag, colored pencils or crayons, items to sort into color groups (e.g., red, blue, green, and yellow feathers, crayons, beads, ribbons, etc.)

Optional: classroom objects that are red, blue, green, and yellow

Language competences: The children will be able to name colors.

Warm-up

Aim: to introduce colors

- Put on Polly the puppet and make her say *Hello* in a friendly way as before. The children say *Hello, Polly*.
- Polly says *Look! A bag!* and flies to get the bag with the scarves or flags in the four colors (red, blue, green, yellow). Take a scarf/flag from the bag very slowly and make Polly look at it and say, e.g., *Look! Red!* The children repeat the color if they wish. Repeat with all the scarves/flags.
- Put the scarves/flags back in the bag.
- Make Polly take the bag in her beak and fly away.

Presentation

1 CD1 20 SB p16 **Listen and point. Say the colors.**

Aim: to present color words

- Point to the picture on SB page 16. Point to Polly and say *Who's this?* Elicit *Polly*. Repeat for Gina. Say *Listen*. Play the audio. The children just listen.
- Say *Listen and point*. Play the audio. Show the children how to point at the colors on Gina's palette. Say *Listen and point* again. Play the audio again. The children point.
- Say *Say the colors*. Play the audio again. The children point and say the words.

Audio script page T96

Practice

- Put a selection of colored items onto different tables (e.g., feathers on one table, beads on another, crayons on another). Tell the children to sort them into red, blue, green, and yellow piles. The children say the colors as they do the activity.
- Put on Polly the puppet and make her fly around, checking the activity and asking individual students to say the colors.

1 WB p16 **Look and color. Say the colors.**

Aim: to practice colors

- Point to the classroom objects in the picture. Ask *What's this?* The children say the words.
- Point to the dots on the bag and say/elicit *Red*. Show a red crayon or pencil and mime coloring red all the spaces marked with a red dot. Repeat for the other colors. Say *Look and color*. Circulate and check that the children are coloring using the correct colors. Ask individuals to say what color they are using.
- When the children have finished coloring say *Say the colors*. Point to the picture of the book. Ask *What's this?* Elicit *Book* and *Yellow*. Repeat for the other items.

Extension activity

Aim: to practice color recognition and pronunciation

- Before the lesson, hide some red, blue, green, and yellow pencils/crayons/books around the classroom (there should be one for each child). In L1 explain that there are objects hidden around the room and that each child must find one of them. When they have found one (pencil) they take it back to their table and sit down.
- Give the children two minutes to find one (pencil) each.
- Hold up a (blue) (pencil) at the front of the class and say *Blue*. The children say the color. Ask individual children to hold up the object they found, say the color and name the object.

Ending the lesson

Aim: to review colors

- Put on the puppet. Play *Disappearing flashcards* using the color flashcards (see Introduction, page xvii).

Aims

- to practice describing classroom objects using colors; to say a chant

New language: *It's (yellow)*

Recycled language: *red, blue, green, yellow,* classroom objects, *Look! It's my ...*

Materials: CD 1, the puppet (Polly), flashcards (classroom objects and colors), colored pencils or crayons, Yes/No cards

Optional: pieces of plain white paper for drawing, a drawing you have made and colored e.g., a green bag

Language competences: The children will be able to talk about the colors of classroom objects. The children will be able to join in with a chant.

Warm-up

Aim: to practice color words and listening skills

- Review the colors with the flashcards.
- Make sure the children each have red, blue, green, and yellow pencils/crayons.
- Put on the puppet. In L1 tell the children that Polly is going to check that she has the correct colored pencils/crayons today.
- Say *Blue*. Polly finds and holds up a blue pencil/crayon. Repeat for the other colors. Make Polly nod/clap excitedly after she finds each color.
- Tell the children that Polly wants to know whether they have the correct colors, too. Polly says, e.g., *Red*. The children hold up their red pencils/crayons. Repeat for the other colors and circulate with Polly to check and praise.

Presentation

2 CD1 21 SB p17 **Listen and color. Chant.**

Aim: to present *It's (yellow)* and say a chant

- Point to each of the items on SB page 17 asking *What's this?* The children say the word.
- Make sure the children have the right colored pencils/crayons. Say *Listen and color.* Play the first verse of the chant and show how to choose the correct object and color it. Play the chant. Pause to give the children time to color.
- Say *Listen and chant.* Play the chant again verse by verse. The children listen and repeat. Play the whole chant for the children to join in. They point to the pictures they colored in as they chant.

Audio script page T96

Practice

- Have the Yes/No cards ready. Put on the puppet. Say *Look, Polly!* Pick up, e.g., a blue book. Say *Look! It's my book. It's red.* Make Polly shake her head and hold up the No card. Make her say *It's blue!* Repeat with another object, but say the correct color. Polly nods her head and holds up a Yes card.
- Give out the Yes/No cards. Hold up a red pencil and say *Look! It's my pencil. It's yellow.* Make Polly hold up a No card. The children copy and join in with Polly as she says *It's red!* Repeat for other objects and colors, mixing correct and incorrect sentences. The children hold up their Yes/No cards, following Polly's lead.
- Once the children are following with ease, play the game without Polly helping.

2 WB p17 **Look and color. Say the sentences.**

Aim: to practice *It's (yellow)*

- Elicit the colors at the top. Say *Look and color.*
- Show the children how to follow the line from the red paint to the car. Point to the blue paint. The children follow with their fingers in the same way. They color the car blue. Repeat for the last car.
- Point to the red car and say *It's red.* The children point at the car and repeat *It's red.* Point to the other pictures. The children say the sentences all together. Call on volunteers to point to a picture in their book and say *It's ...* and the color.

Extension activity

Aim: to practice talking about a picture

- Stick the classroom object flashcards on the board. Tell the children to choose one of the objects to draw.
- Tell the children to color their object red, green, blue, or yellow.
- Hold up the drawing you did. Say *Look! It's my bag. It's green.*
- Choose volunteers to come to the front and talk about their pictures in the same way.

Ending the lesson

Aim: to practice the chant and thinking skills

- Stick the classroom object flashcards on the board. Say a verse from the chant, adapting it for the color of the object on the flashcard, e.g., *Look! It's my chair. It's red, it's red. Look! It's my chair. It's red, it's red.*
- Repeat with different flashcards. Encourage the children to join in and check pronunciation.

2 CD1 21 Listen and color. Chant.

3 CD1 22 23 Listen and act. Listen and color.

1

2

3

Aims

- to present and practice *Show me something …* ; to practice following instructions

New language: *Show me something …*

Recycled language: colors, classroom objects, *Look! It's my … , It's (yellow)*, instructions (*Stand up, Sit down, Clap your hands, Hands up, Hands down*)

Materials: CD 1, flashcards (colors and classroom objects), classroom objects, the puppet (Polly), a variety of yellow, green, blue, and red classroom objects for yourself and each child, e.g., pencils, books, bags, chairs

Optional: bean bags or colored scarves in red, yellow, blue, and green (one set for each team of children)

Language competences: The children will be able to follow instructions.

Warm-up

Aim: to review colors and *It's (yellow)*

- Review the colors with the color flashcards and the classroom object flashcards.
- Hold up a book and say *Look! It's my (book). It's …* . Elicit the correct color. Repeat with other classroom objects. The children say *It's red/blue/green/yellow*, as appropriate.

Presentation

3 CD1 22 SB p18 **Listen and act.**

Aim: to review colors and present *Show me something …*
to practice listening and responding physically

- Play the first line of the audio and pick up your red object. Encourage the children to copy. Play the next line and pick up your green object. The children pick up their green objects in the same way. Repeat for the rest of the audio. Do this until the children are joining in with ease.
- Play the audio again, pausing for the children to pick up the items, but without your help this time.
- Say, e.g., *Show me something green*. The children pick up a green object. Repeat for other colors.

Audio script page T96

3 CD1 23 SB p18 **Listen and color.**

Aim: to practice new instructions and listening

- Say *Listen and color*. Remind the children in L1 to color the circle below the pictures the correct color. Play the first line of the audio and point to the first circle. Then play the rest of the audio, pausing for children to color the circle each time.

Audio script page T96

Practice

3 CD1 24 WB p18 **Listen and circle.**

Aim: to practice new instructions, listening, and pencil control

- Point to the first picture and say *Show me something yellow*. Point to the second girl and say *Show me something …* and elicit *Blue*.
- Say *Listen and circle*. Trace a large circle in the air with your finger. Encourage the children to copy you.
- Say *Listen. Show me something blue* or *Show me something yellow*. Play the audio. Ask the children to point to the correct answer. They draw the circle around the first picture.

Audio script page T96

Extension activity

Aim: to practice following instructions and take part in a team game

- If possible, move your class into the playground, school gym, or an empty classroom.
- Divide the class into teams. The teams stand in lines, with one child at the front. In front of each team, place the four colored things in a group. The things should be pretty far from the teams.
- Say *Show me something green!* The first child in each team runs to pick up their team's green object and bring it to you. Then they go to the back. Say *Show me something blue!* The children now at the front run, pick up the blue item, and bring it to you. They run to the back. Repeat for *yellow* and *red*.
- Speed up as the children become more confident.

Note: If you cannot move your class, put the items or the classroom object flashcards on a desk at the front. A child from each team comes to the front. Give an instruction, e.g., *Show me something blue*. The first child to find the correct item wins a point.

Ending the lesson

Aim: to practice following instructions

- Put on the puppet. Polly says *Show me something* (color). The children pick up an object in the correct color and say the color. Repeat with different instructions. Speed up so that the children have to listen and respond quickly.

Aims

- to present and practice *Paint*; to sing a song with the class; to practice following instructions

New language: *Paint with me, Paint your (bag) (blue)*

Recycled language: colors, classroom objects, *Show me something (yellow), Stand up*

Materials: CD 1, red, blue, green, and yellow objects (enough for two or three items for each pair of children), classroom objects, flashcards (colors and classroom objects), the puppet (Polly), paintbrushes (one for you and one for each child)

Optional: a piece of paper for each child with four colored blobs on it – red, green, yellow, and blue (like a simple artist's palette)

Language competences: The children will be able to join in with a song.

Warm-up

Aim: to review *Show me something (yellow)*

- Before the lesson, hide a variety of red, green, yellow, and blue objects. Make sure each pair of children will have two or three items.
- Put on the puppet. Make Polly ask *Show me something blue.* In L1, tell the children to stand up and find something of the correct color in pairs. When they have found something, they hold it up. Polly flies around checking and clapping, saying *Good job! It's blue.*
- Repeat with Polly asking for the different colors.

Presentation

4 CD1 25 26 SB p19 **Listen and sing.**

Aim: to present *Paint (with me / your bag (blue))* and sing a song

- Stick the classroom object flashcards on the board and elicit the words. Give out the paintbrushes if you have some.
- Point to the picture on SB page 19. Mime painting on the picture of the chair using a real paintbrush and say *Paint the chair.* Hand out a paintbrush to each child. Mime painting the bag in the picture and say *Paint your bag.* The children copy you, using a paintbrush or their fingers.
- Play the audio, pausing the song after the first verse. The children listen and mime painting the pencil in their books.
- Say *Stand up.* Play the chorus *Stand up and paint with me* and mime painting together with your brushes in the air. Pause the song and say *Sit down, please.*
- Repeat this with each verse.
- Play the song again all the way through without pausing. The children mime painting the different objects in their books and standing up when the chorus plays, without your help.

Audio script page T96

Practice

4 CD1 27 WB p19 **Listen again and color.**

Aim: to practice listening, identifying colors, and following instructions

- Point to the can of yellow paint in the picture. Ask *Red, yellow, green, or blue?* Elicit *Yellow.*
- Point at the pencil on the left and say *Listen. Red, green, yellow, or blue?* Play the first verse of the song. Elicit the answer *Blue.* Show the children how to color the pencil blue. Play the song verse by verse, pausing for the children to color in the book, bag, and chair. Circulate and check they are using the correct colors. Ask individuals while pointing at the picture in their book *Red?* Elicit *Red* from the child. Say *Yes, red bag.*

Audio script page T96

Extension activity

Aim: to practice listening skills and review *Paint your (chair) (yellow)*

- Hand out a piece of paper with red, green, yellow, and blue splotches on it to each child (to act as an artist's palette). Hand out the paintbrushes.
- Give instructions for the children to act out with their palettes and paintbrushes, e.g., *Paint your chair yellow.* Repeat with different objects and colors.
- Once they are confident, the children can play this game in pairs, with one child giving the instructions and the other miming. Then they swap roles.

Ending the lesson

Aim: to practice the song

- Draw a chair, bag, book, and pencil on the board. Invite a volunteer to stick the color flashcards on the board, matching them to the items you have drawn as they appear in the song. Ask every time before they stick the card, *What's this? What's the color?* Help them with the answer until they say it alone.
- Play the song again for the children to sing along, using the flashcards on the board as prompts.

4 CD1 25 26 **Listen and sing.**

5 CD1 28 Sticker The painters

Values

1

2

3

4

Aims

- to present a picture story; to review language from the unit

New language: *Wow, Thank you, Poor (Gina)*

Recycled language: colors, *please*, *Hello*, *Look*, character names

Materials: CD 1, flashcards (characters, colors), the puppet (Polly), colored pencils or crayons

Optional: a photocopied picture of a very simple flower shape for coloring in (one for each child)

Language competences: The children will be able to listen to and follow a picture story. The children will be able to use *Thank you*.

Warm-up

Aim: to review characters and greetings

- Stick the character flashcards on the board. Point at the flashcard for Gina and say *Hello, Gina*. The children repeat. Point at the other characters to elicit *Hello* (character name).
- Play *Disappearing flashcards* using the character flashcards (see Introduction, page xvii).

Presentation

5 CD1 28 SB pp20-21 **Story: The painters**

Aim: to listen and follow a picture story

- Point to Gina in the first picture and ask *Who's this?* The children say *Gina*. Point to the other characters in the picture and ask their names. Point to picture 2 and ask where they all are in L1 (Gina's house). Ask why Gina is on the couch/ what Gina is pointing to. The children tell you she has a problem with her leg. Point to the paints in picture 4 and ask what the characters are doing. The children answer in L1.
- Play the CD. The children point to the pictures as they listen.
- Play the story again, stopping after each picture. The children explain what's happening in L1. Elicit translations for *Poor (Gina)*, *Wow* and *Thank you*.
- Put on the puppet. Hold her with her head down to make her appear sad. Make her whisper in your ear. In L1, explain that Polly has lost her voice. Look at Polly and say *Poor Polly*. Encourage the children to repeat. Repeat *Poor Polly* and pet her. Ask volunteers to come to the front, say *Poor Polly* and pet the puppet. Polly says *Thank you* each time they pet her, with her voice getting stronger and better until she is talking normally and happy again. If it is possible and you have a small class, give each child a turn.

Audio script page T96

Practice

5 CD1 29 WB p20 **Listen and color the correct circle.**

Aim: to listen and identify the correct picture

- Point to the first picture on WB page 20. Ask *Who's this?* The children say the name. Repeat for the second picture. Say *Listen. Leo or Gina?* Play the audio. Elicit the answer *Gina*.
- Show the children how to color the correct circle. Play the audio again. Check their work as they color.
- Play the audio again. The children repeat Gina's line.

Audio script page T96

Extension activity

Aim: to practice colors, *Poor* ... and *Thank you*

- Stick the color flashcards on the board. The children say the words. In L1, tell the children that they are going to color in pictures to make Polly feel better. Give out the flower pictures and make sure the children have red, blue, green, and yellow pencils/crayons on their tables. The children color in the pictures. Circulate and ask individuals *What color is this?*
- Put on the puppet. Make her look sad/sick. Elicit *Poor Polly*. Ask volunteers to come up to Polly and give her a picture. When the child gives Polly the picture, Polly says *Thank you*. Give back all the pictures.
- The children work in pairs. One child pretends to feel sick, the other says *Poor* (child's name) and gives them their picture. The child responds *Thank you*.

Ending the lesson

Aim: to practice *please* and *Thank you*

- Stick the color flashcards on the board at a height your children can reach.
- Call a volunteer to the front. Say, e.g., *Green, please!* The child finds the correct flashcard and gives it to you. Say *Thank you*. Repeat with different volunteers.
- The children can repeat the activity in pairs, using red, green, blue, and yellow crayons or colored pencils.

Aims

- to talk about the meaning of a story; to review language from the unit

Recycled language: colors, *Show me something (yellow), Paint … , Thank you, Poor …*

Materials: CD 1, flashcards (colors), Unit 2 stickers, colored pencils or crayons, the puppet (Polly), a selection of red, yellow, green, and blue toys/objects, pencils

Optional: character masks

Language competences: The children will be able to appreciate the values shown in the story. The children will practice saying *Poor …* and *Thank you*.

Warm-up

Aim: to review colors and *Thank you*

- Put objects of different colors at the front of the class (red, blue, green, and yellow). Ask a volunteer to come to the front. Put on the puppet and make her say *Show me something red*. The child picks up something red and gives it to Polly. Polly says *Thank you*.
- The children work in pairs. Give a selection of the colored objects to each pair. They repeat the activity one at a time, saying *Show me something …* and *Thank you*.

Practice

5 CD1 28 SB pp20–21 **Story: The painters**
Listen to the story. Stick.

Aim: to review the story

- Ask the children to tell you what they remember about the story in L1.
- Play the story again, pausing after each picture to ask about what is happening and the names of the colors at the end.
- Hand out the stickers for Unit 2. Say, e.g., *Red*. The children point to the correct sticker on the sheet. Repeat for the other sticker.
- Point to the picture on SB page 21. Say *Where's red?* The children point to the red can of paint. Mime peeling the sticker off the sheet. The children peel off the sticker and hold it up. Check that they all have the correct sticker. Then say *Stick!* The children stick the sticker in their books. Repeat for the other sticker.

Audio script page T96

Story values SB pp20–21

Aim: to think about the meaning of the story: cheering someone up and saying *Thank you*

- Play the story again. The children listen and point. Pause after picture 2 and ask in L1 *How does Gina feel?* (Sad.) Play the rest of the story and ask in L1 *How do the other characters feel?* (They feel sad for Gina.) *What do they do to make Gina feel better?* (They paint the cast on her leg.) *How does Gina feel in the end?* (She feels happy and thankful.) Ask in L1 *What does Gina say at the end?* Elicit *Thank you*. Ask the children when they say thank you. Talk about how important it is to help your friends feel better when they are sad.
- Ask a volunteer to come to the front and pretend he/she has hurt one leg. Say *Poor* (child's name). Give him/her a chair to sit on. Explain/Elicit that you have done something kind. Ask the children what the child should say and elicit *Thank you*. Repeat the activity with other children. The children then act the situation out with a partner.

6 WB p21 **Complete the face. Color the picture.**

Aim: to apply values from the story to new situations

- Tell the children in L1 *We're going to look at some children now. Look at the picture and think. How does the boy on the floor feel?* (Sad.) *What is the other boy saying? Poor …* (child's name). *Who is helping?* (The girl, the teacher, and the boy.)
- Point to the happy face and explain that if they think the children and the teacher are doing the right thing, they should trace the happy smile. Show them how to trace the line with a pencil. Circulate and check. Then, the children can color the picture.

Extension activity

Aim: to reinforce understanding of the story

- Invite four volunteers to the front. Assign them the roles of Gina, Polly, Leo, and Mike. Put two chairs together to make a couch for Gina to lie on. The children playing the main characters put on the masks. Play the story. The children act out the story along with the CD. Encourage the rest of the children to act being sad or happy as appropriate.
- Invite another group of four children to come to the front and act.

Ending the lesson

Aim: to practice saying *Poor …* and *Thank you*

- Put on the puppet. Make her look sad again. Elicit *Poor Polly!* Elicit some ideas from the class for cheering up Polly. Ask a volunteer to come and try to cheer Polly up. Polly looks up and says *Thank you*.

Family fun!

Rainbow colors

6 CD1 30 **Listen and point. Say the colors.**

Aims

- to integrate other areas of the curriculum through English: Physics

New language: *rainbow, orange*

Recycled language: colors

Materials: CD 1, flashcards (colors), the puppet (Polly), materials for the project (a paper plate and a piece of paper for each child, paints in red, orange, yellow, green, and blue (one set per table), a paper plate painting you have prepared (similar to the one on WB page 22), a large bowl, and a spoon

Optional: colored scarves/large strips of paper (red, yellow, orange, blue, green), a camera, Scotch tape

Language competences: The children will be able to name some of the colors of the rainbow in English. They will think about where and when rainbows appear.

Warm-up

Aim: to review colors and introduce the topic of rainbows

- Draw a rainbow on the board or show a picture of a rainbow. Say *Wow! Look! A rainbow!* Move your hand in a rainbow shape as you say *Rainbow*. The children copy.
- In L1, ask the children where we see rainbows, if they have ever seen a real one, and what colors did they see. Ask when rainbows appear.

Presentation

6 CD1 30 SB p22 **Listen and point. Say the colors.**

Aim: to focus on the different colors in a rainbow

- Point to the picture on SB page 22. Say *Rainbow* as you move your finger over the rainbow. Point to one of the colors and ask *What color is this?* The children answer, e.g., *It's red*. Repeat for yellow, green, and blue. Ask whether the children can see any other colors in the rainbow. Elicit and translate *orange* into L1.
- Say *Listen and point*. Play the audio, pausing after the first set of colors. The children listen and point to the colors in the rainbow. Repeat for the next two sets of colors.
- Say *Say the colors*. Play the whole recording again for the children to listen and repeat. Ask which set of colors was in the right order of the rainbow (the first set).

Audio script page T96

Practice

7 WB p22 **Make a mixed-color painting.**

Aim: to take part in an art project and experiment with mixing colors

- Show the pictures on WB page 22. Show the children a painting you have already made. Explain what you did, using the pictures on page 22. Talk about how the colors mix together when the plate is turned around on the paper.
- Hand out the materials. Circulate and help the children. Ask individuals to name the colors as they paint.
- Help the children turn their plates around on the paper (it may help to stick the paper to the table).
- Ask volunteers to show their finished paintings and talk about the colors they can see.

Where the colors have mixed together, talk about the results. Say, e.g., *Yellow and blue … green! Red and yellow … orange!*

Extension activity

Aim: to consolidate knowledge about rainbows

- If possible, move your class into the playground, school gym, or an empty classroom.
- Work together to create a giant rainbow using the scarves/strips of paper. Chant the colors with the children. Take a photograph of the finished rainbow.

Note: If you do not have a large space, the children could work individually to make their own picture of a rainbow using strips of paper and glue.

Ending the lesson

Aim: to review the colors of the rainbow and mixed colors

- Put on the puppet. In L1, say *Polly is going to show us some magic with colors! She is going to mix colors together to make new colors*. Take out the bowl and spoon and color flashcards.
- Put the green flashcard into the bowl secretly. Make Polly put the yellow and blue flashcards into the bowl. Elicit the colors. Polly mixes the colors around with the spoon. Polly pulls out the green flashcard! Say *Wow! Good job, Polly! It's green*. The children say the color. Repeat with *red* and *yellow* making *orange*. Use an orange piece of thin cardboard to illustrate orange.

Aims

- to review language and values from the unit; to encourage children to reflect on their learning

Recycled language: colors, classroom objects, *Paint your ...* , *Thank you*

Materials: flashcards (colors), food coloring in red, yellow, and blue, four half-full plastic bottles of water

Optional: a photocopy of a page with classroom objects for coloring – a chair, a book, a pencil, a bag (one copy for each child), red, yellow, green, and blue paint, paintbrushes

Language competences: The children will be able to use language from the unit. They will be able to reflect on their learning.

Warm-up

Aim: to review knowledge of mixing colors

- Show the children the plastic bottles with water. Tell them they are going to help make some colored water. Put a drop or two of red food coloring into one of the bottles. Ask *What color is it?* The children answer *Red*. Put one or two drops of yellow food coloring into another bottle of water and ask *What color is it?* The children answer *Yellow*. Then pour some water from the red bottle into the yellow, put the lid on, and shake it around. Ask the children to predict what the color will be in L1. Hold up the bottle and ask *What color is it?* The children reply *Orange*. Repeat using blue and yellow to make green water. Ask some of the children to help. Say *Thank you* when they put the drops in the water.

Review

7 Think! SB p23 **Look and say the colors. Color.**

Thinking skills: testing predictions

- Point to the cans of paint in the first picture on SB page 23. Say *Look and say the colors.* The children look at the paints and say *Yellow* and *Blue*. In L1, tell the children to think about what happens when those colors are mixed together. They can look at the picture of the rainbow on page 22 to help. Point to the empty can of paint and say *Color.* The children color in the can of paint with the correct color (green). Tell the children to hold up their books and say the color.
- Repeat for the second set of paint pots (orange). Circulate and help, listening to the color words.

8 WB p23 **Say the colors. Color the circles.**

Aim: to create a record of learning

- Point to the paint splotches on WB page 23. The children say the colors together.
- The children color the circles if they can say the words on their own.
- Circulate and help as necessary. Ask individual children to say the colors.

Extension activity

Aim: to review *Paint your ...*

- Give out the photocopies with pictures of classroom objects.
- Tell the children they are going to use their colors to paint the objects as you say them. Say, e.g., *Paint your bag red. Paint your book blue.* The children listen and paint using the correct colors.
- Circulate and help as necessary.
- Show some of the best pictures to the class.

Note: If you do not have pictures, act out the painting as on page T19.

Ending the lesson

Aim: to review language from the unit

- Play the children's favorite game from the unit or sing the unit song.

Phonics

- See page T81 for Unit 2 Phonics.

7 Think! Look and say the colors. Color.

1

2

Phonics → page 81 Review → page 91

3 My family

1 CD1 32 **Listen and point. Say the words.**

dad, mom, brother, sister

Aims

- to present and practice family words

New language: *mom, dad, brother, sister, Who's this?*

Recycled language: *It's my ...* , classroom objects, colors

Materials: CD 1, a pencil, book, and bag of known colors (red, blue, green, yellow, orange), flashcards (family), the puppet (Polly), pencils

Optional: Leo character mask, Yes/No cards

Language competences: The children will be able to name family members.

Warm-up

Aim: to review *It's my ...* , classroom objects and colors

- Show a book of a known color and say *It's my ...* . The children say *Book*. Say *Yes! It's my book*. The children repeat. Say/Elicit the color, e.g., *It's yellow*, by asking *What color is it?* Repeat with a pencil and a bag.
- Circulate and point to individual children's bags, pencils, books, and chairs which are red, blue, green, orange, or yellow. Ask *What's this?* Children say *It's my (chair). It's (blue)* or simply *Chair. Blue* according to ability.

Presentation

1 CD1 32 SB p24 **Listen and point. Say the words.**

Aim: to present family words

- Point to the picture of Mike and ask *Who's this?* The children say *Mike*. Repeat for Leo.
- Point to the picture Leo is holding and ask *Who's this?* Elicit *Leo's family* in L1.
- Say *Listen*. Play the audio. The children just listen the first time.
- Say *Listen and point*. Play the audio. The children listen and point to the animals.
- Play the audio again. The children point and say.

Audio script page T96

Practice

- Show the family flashcards. Say each word. The children repeat.
- Show the flashcards in different orders. The children say the correct word.
- Ask the children to sit in a circle. Place the family flashcards in the center, face up. Choose a confident child and say, e.g., *Teresa, dad!* The child comes to the center of the circle to collect the correct flashcard and sits back down. Point to the flashcard and ask *Who's this?* He/She holds up the card and says, e.g., *(It's) dad*.
- Repeat with different children for the other flashcards. Replace the flashcards when all four are taken, and call on different children. Once the children are confident, call two children to take different flashcards, *e.g., Carlos, mom! Isabel, brother!* The two children come to the center together and see who can choose the correct card the quickest. The game can also be played calling three children, or even four children, to take the cards.
- If you have less space, stick the flashcards on the board and call children to come to the front and choose.

3

1 WB p24 **Look and circle the different picture. Say the words.**

Aim: to practice family words

- Point to the pictures in the first row and say *mom, mom, sister, mom*. The children copy you. Point to the picture of the sister and say *Look! Sister is different*. Confirm in L1. Show the children how to complete the circle around this picture.
- The children find the different picture in the other rows and circle with a pencil. Circulate and help as necessary. Ask individual children to point at the rows and say the words.

Extension activity

Aim: to practice family words and *It's my ...*

- Give each child their Yes/No card. Show the Yes card. The children say *Yes!* Show the No card. The children say *No!* Repeat until they are doing this with ease. Say *Yes* or *No* in different orders. Children pick up the correct card.
- Put on the Leo character mask. Wave at the children and say *Hello, I'm Leo* (in a Leo voice). The children say *Hello, Leo!* Show the children one of the family flashcards and say a false sentence, e.g., show the brother flashcard and say *It's dad*. The children say *No* and hold up the No card. Repeat with different family flashcards, mixing up true and false sentences.

Ending the lesson

Aim: to review family words

- Put on the puppet. Play *Disappearing flashcards* with the family words (see introduction, page xvii).
- Make Polly wave and say *Goodbye!* The children wave and say *Goodbye, Polly!*

Aims

- to present *Who's this?* and practice *It's my ...* and family words; to say a chant

New language: *Who's this?*

Recycled language: *mom, dad, brother, sister, It's my ...* , classroom instructions *(Stand up, Clap your hands*, etc.)

Materials: CD 1, flashcards (family and characters), colored pencils or crayons, a piece of card or thick paper (to cover the flashcards), pencils

Optional: a soft scarf to use as a blindfold

Language competences: The children will be able to answer the question *Who's this?* and name family members. The children will be able to join in with a chant.

Warm-up

Aim: to review family words

- Show the family flashcards one at a time. Say the names. The children repeat.
- Show the flashcards again. The children say the names.
- Divide the class into four groups. Name them Mom, Dad, Brother, and Sister. Give instructions for each group to follow, e.g., *Mom, stand up* (only the children in the Mom group stand up). Repeat with different instructions and family words, calling on the groups in different orders. Include *Hands up, Hands down*, and *Clap your hands*.

Presentation

2 CD1 33 SB p25 **Listen and trace. Chant.**

Aim: to present *Who's this?*, review family members and say a chant

- Use the pictures on SB page 25 to elicit the family words.
- Point to the question mark hiding picture 1 and ask *Who's this?* Play the first verse of the chant. Show the children how to trace the line from the question mark to the picture of the mom. Repeat the audio. The children trace the line with a pencil. Make sure they are tracing from left to right.
- Repeat for the rest of the chant, pausing after each verse for the children to trace.
- Say *Listen and chant*. Play the chant again line by line. The children listen and repeat.

Audio script page T96

Practice

- Choose a confident child. Point to one of the pictures on SB page 25 and ask *Who's this?* The child replies, e.g., *Sister.* Say *Yes, it's the sister.* Repeat with the other pictures.
- Children do the same activity in pairs. Child A points to one of the pictures on SB page 25 and asks *Who's this?* Child B replies *Mom. / It's the mom.* Circulate and encourage the children to pronounce the consonant sounds "s" and "th" in *Who's this?*

2 WB p25 **Draw a family member. Say the sentence.**

Aim: to practice *Who's this? It's my ...* and family words

- Draw a simple outline of a figure (similar to the one on WB page 25). Draw eyes, hair, a smiley mouth, and simple clothes (e.g., a skirt and top) on the figure. Point and say *Look! It's my mom!*
- Point to the example drawing, then to the frame on WB page 25. Show some crayons and say *Draw your mom, dad, brother, or sister.* Make sure the children understand that they need to draw someone from their own family. The children complete the outline with details according to ability.
- Circulate and ask individuals *Who's this?* They reply *It's my ...* . Invite volunteers to stand up and show their picture. The whole class points and asks *Who's this?* The child replies, e.g., *It's my brother.*

Extension activity

Aim: to practice asking and responding to *Who's this?*

- Choose a volunteer and blindfold him/her with a soft scarf. Make sure he/she can't see anything. Bring another child to the front. Turn the blindfolded child around several times, then move him/her toward the other child. Ask *Who's this?* The rest of the class repeats the question with you. The child with the blindfold has to feel the other child's face, hair, and clothes and then guess the name, e.g., *(It's) Anna!* When the blindfolded child has guessed the name, repeat the game with different children.

Ending the lesson

Aim: to practice responding to *Who's this?*

- Hold up a character flashcard covered with a piece of thin cardboard or thick paper. Slowly reveal the picture, looking at it and asking *Who's this?* The children say, e.g., *(It's) Gina.* Repeat with the other characters.
- Say *Goodbye!* as usual to end the class.

2 CD1 33 Listen and trace. Chant.

3 CD1 34 35 Listen and act. Listen and color.

1

2

3

Aims

- to present and practice responding to *Go to sleep, Wake up, Give your dad a hug*

New language: *Go to sleep, Wake up, Give your dad a hug,* family

Recycled language: family words, instructions (*Stand up, Sit down, Hands up, Hands down,* etc.)

Materials: CD 1, flashcards (family), the puppet (Polly), CD of lively music

Optional: CD of relaxing music

Language competences: The children will be able to follow new and familiar instructions.

Warm-up

Aim: to review family words, *Who's this?* and *It's ...*

- Review the family words with the flashcards.
- Put on the puppet. Play *No, Polly!* with the family flashcards.

Presentation

3 CD1 34 SB p26 **Listen and act.**

Aim: to present new instructions and practice listening and responding physically

- Books closed. Ask the children to sit in a circle. Sit in the center. Play the first line of the audio and do the action (*Go to sleep*). Encourage the children to copy you (e.g., by resting their heads on their hands / lying down). Say *Go to sleep!* Do the action again, along with the children. Play the next line and do the action. The children copy. Repeat for the rest of the recording (mime hugging for *Give your dad a hug*).
- Play the audio again without pausing, doing the actions with the children. Repeat several times, until the children are confident. Play the audio for the children to follow the instructions without your help.

Audio script page T96

Practice

3 CD1 35 SB p26 **Listen and color.**

Aim: to practice new instructions and listening

- Say *Listen and color*. Remind the children in L1 to color the circles below the pictures the correct color. Play the first line of the audio and point to the first circle. Then play the rest of the audio, pausing for children to color the circle each time.

Audio script page T96

3 CD1 36 WB p26 **Listen and circle.**

Aim: to practice new instructions, listening, and pencil control

- Point to the pictures on WB page 26 and elicit *Go to sleep* and *Wake up*.
- Say *Listen and circle*. The children practice the circle shape in the air.
- Say *Listen. Go to sleep or wake up?* Play the audio. The children point to the correct picture. They draw a circle around the first picture. Circulate and elicit *Go to sleep* from individuals.

Audio script page T97

Extension activity

Aim: to practice responding to *Go to sleep* and *Wake up*

- If possible, move your class out into the playground, school gym, or an empty classroom.
- Play the traditional party game *Sleeping lions* with the children. Put on the CD of relaxing music and say *Go to sleep!* All the children lie down and keep as still and quiet as possible. Walk among the "sleeping lions" and try to make them "wake up" by talking to them / making them laugh. If a child moves or giggles, he/she is "out" – say *Wake up* (name)*!* The child gets up and helps you to try and "wake" the other children. The winner is the child who keeps still and quiet the longest.

Ending the lesson

Aim: to practice following instructions

- Put on the puppet. Make her fly and "land" on an individual and give one instruction to that child, e.g., *Go to sleep, Stand up, Clap your hands, Give Polly a hug*. Polly can fly back to individuals and say, e.g., *Wake up, Sit down* so that everyone is awake and sitting down at the end of the activity.
- End the lesson by asking the children to say *Goodbye!* to Polly.

Aims

- to sing a song with the class; to review family words, *Who's this?* and *It's my ...*

New language: *Please show me (your family)*

Recycled language: *Go to sleep, Wake up, Give ... a hug, Look! It's my ...* , family words, *Who's this?*

Materials: CD 1, the puppet (Polly), flashcards (family), pencils

Optional: character masks, bags, books

Language competences: The children will be able to join in with a song.

Warm-up

Aim: to review *Go to sleep, Wake up,* and *Give ... a hug*

- Put on the puppet. Play *Polly says ...* (see Introduction, page xvii). Review known instructions and include *Go to sleep, Wake up* and *Give (your friend) a hug.*

Presentation

4 CD1 37 38 SB p27 **Listen and sing.**

Aim: to review family words, to present *family*, and sing a song

- Review family words with the flashcards.
- Point to the little girl in the foreground on SB page 27 and say *Look! It's Rosemary. Hello, Rosemary.* The children say *Hello, Rosemary*, and repeat the name after you several times.
- Point to Rosemary's family (sitting on the wall) on SB page 27. Say *Look! It's a family. It's Rosemary's family.* Say, e.g., *Point to the mom.* The children point. Repeat several times.
- Play the song. The children listen and point to the appropriate person for each verse.
- Play the song again, pausing to teach each line. The children point to the people in Rosemary's family as they sing.

Audio script page T96

Practice

4 CD1 39 WB p27 **Listen and match.**

Aim: to practice *Who's this? It's my ...* and pencil control

- Point to head and shoulders pictures one at a time and ask *Who's this?* Elicit *Sister* and *Mom.* Point to the first silhouette and say *Listen and match.* Play the audio. Elicit the answer and show the children how to draw a line to match the head and shoulders picture of Rosemary's mom to the silhouette. Play the audio again. The children listen and draw a line. Repeat for the second picture. Circulate and check the children are drawing a line from left to right and using the correct grip. Ask individuals *Who's this?* They say *It's (the) mom.*

Audio script page T96

Extension activity

Aim: to practice *Show me your (bag)*, classroom objects, and character names

- Make sure each child has a pencil, bag, and book at hand. Give out the character masks (four masks per child).
- Say *Show me your book* and hold up a book. The children copy. Repeat with different objects and characters (for the masks, say, e.g., *Show me Leo* – children hold up the Leo mask or put it on).
- Once the children are following with ease, give instructions without showing the items yourself. You can make the game competitive – the fastest child to show you the item or character wins a point each time. To make sure everyone joins in, you can call on individual children to show you an item/ character (e.g., *Antonio, show me Gina*).

Ending the lesson

Aim: to practice the song

- Divide the class into two groups. One group is the snail, the other group is Rosemary. Play the song. The groups join in with the questions or answers, as appropriate. Swap roles and repeat.

4 CD1 37 38 **Listen and sing.**

5 CD1 40 Sticker Family and friends

Values

Aims

- to present a picture story; to review language from the unit

New language: *Wow, This is my friend*

Recycled language: *family, Who's this? It's my …*

Materials: CD 1, flashcards (family and Mike), character masks, five "frames" made from paper or cardboard to fit around the outside of the family and Mike flashcards (to make them look like portraits), colored pencils or crayons

Optional: photographs of members of your own family (mom, dad, brother, sister) – large enough to display on the board, Yes/No cards

Language competences: The children will be able to listen and follow a picture story.

Warm-up

Aim: to review family words and *This is my …*

- Play the song (CD 1, Track 37). The children join in. Encourage them to clap along to the rhythm of the lines in the chorus: *Rosemary, Rosemary, please show me your family.*

Presentation

5 CD1 40 SB pp28–29 **Story: Family and friends**

Aim: to listen and follow a picture story

- Point to Leo in the first picture on SB page 28 and ask *Who's this?* The children say *(It's) Leo.* Repeat for Mike. Ask what Leo and Mike are doing in L1 (looking at pictures in a gallery).
- Play the CD. The children point at the pictures as they listen.
- Play the story again, stopping after each picture. The children explain what's happening in L1. Elicit a translation for *This is my friend.*
- Stick the family flashcards on the board. Put on the Leo character mask. Hand a Mike character mask to each student. The children put on the Mike mask. Play the story. The children join in with Mike's question and his reactions each time, pointing at the flashcards on the board. You join in with Leo's answers and gesture toward the flashcards as if introducing your family.

Audio script page T96

Practice

5 CD1 41 WB p28 **Listen and color the correct circle.**

Aim: to listen and identify the correct picture

- Point to the dad in the first picture on WB page 28. Ask *Who's this?* The children say *Dad.* Repeat for the second picture. Say *Listen. Dad or sister?* Play the audio. Elicit the answer *Sister.*
- Remind the children that they have to color the correct circle. Play the audio again. Check their work as they color.
- Play the recording again. The children repeat the question and answer exchange.

Audio script page T97

Extension activity

Aim: to practice *This is my …* and family members

- Stick photographs of your family on the board. For each picture, encourage the class to ask you *Who's this?* Reply *This is my (dad)*, etc. Repeat two or three times.
- Give each child their Yes/No cards. Say *Yes* or *No* in different orders. Children pick up the correct card.
- Point to one of the photographs of your family and say a false sentence, e.g., point to the photograph of your sister and say *This is my mom.* The children say *No* and hold up the No card. Repeat with different photographs, mixing up true and false sentences.

Ending the lesson

Aim: to practice *This is my …* , family members and careful listening

- Stick the flashcards of the family and of Mike in different places in the classroom, with a thin cardboard or paper "frame" around each one if possible, to make them look like the portraits on SB page 28.
- The children stand up. Put on the Leo character and say (in a Leo voice) *This is my dad.* The children run to the correct flashcard. Repeat with the different family members and Mike (for Mike say *This is my friend*).
- If you do not have space in your classroom, the children can stand at their desks and point to the correct picture.
- Once the children are playing with ease, a confident volunteer can put on the Leo mask and lead the game.

Aims

- to talk about the meaning of a story; to review language from the unit

Recycled language: family members, language from the story

Materials: CD 1, photographs of your own family (mom, dad, brother, sister), flashcards (family), Unit 3 stickers, colored pencils or crayons, CD of lively music, pencils

Optional: Leo and Mike character masks, family and Mike flashcards with paper/thin cardboard frames (to make them look like portraits)

Language competences: The children will be able to appreciate the values shown in the story. The children will be able to introduce a friend with *This is my friend*.

Warm-up

Aim: to review family members

- Show the photographs of your family and say *This is my mom*, etc. The children can join in.
- Hand the photographs to different children. Say a sentence, e.g., *This is my sister.* The child with the correct photograph stands up and brings you the photograph. Repeat for the other photographs. Do the activity again with different children.

Practice

5 CD1 40 SB pp28–29 **Story: Family and friends Listen to the story. Stick.**

Aim: to review the story

- Ask the children to tell you what they remember about the story on SB pages 28 and 29 in L1.
- Play the story again, pausing after each picture to ask about the people in the pictures and elicit what Leo and Mike are saying.
- Hand out the stickers for Unit 3. Say, e.g., *Dad.* The children point to the correct sticker on the sheet. Repeat for *mom.*
- Point to the picture on SB page 29. Say *Where's Leo's mom?* The children point to the sticker outline. Mime peeling the sticker of mom off the sheet. The children peel off the sticker and hold it up. Check that they all have the correct sticker. Then say *Stick.* The children stick the sticker in their books. Repeat for the other sticker.

Audio script page T96

Story values SB pp28–29

Aim: to think about the meaning of the story: caring about family and friends

- Play the story again. The children listen and point. Pause after picture 4 and ask in L1 *Is Leo happy to show Mike his family?* (Yes, he is.) Play the rest of the story and ask in L1 *Who is Leo's friend?* (Mike.) *Is Mike happy to be in the picture?* (Yes, he is.) Talk about how important it is to care for both our family and our friends.

6 WB p29 **Complete the face. Color the picture.**

Aim: to apply values from the story to new situations

- Tell the children in L1 *We're going to look at some children now. Look at the picture and think. Is she caring for her friend?* Talk in L1 about how sharing things with someone shows that you care. Point to the happy face and explain in L1 that if they think the girl is doing the right thing, they trace the happy smile. Show them how to trace the line with a pencil. Circulate and check as they trace. When they finish tracing, the children color the picture.

Extension activity

Aim: to reinforce understanding of the story

- Stick the flashcards of the family and Mike to the board with frames around them to make them look like portraits. Invite two volunteers to the front. Assign them the roles of Leo and Mike. The children put on the Mike and Leo masks. Play the story. The children act out the story along with the CD, gesturing toward the pictures on the board. Encourage the children to join in with the CD and laugh at the end.
- Invite another pair of children to come to the front and act or repeat, with the class working in pairs at the same time, miming pointing to pictures.

Ending the lesson

Aim: to practice introducing someone with *This is my friend,* (name)

- Ask two volunteers to come and stand at the front. One says, pointing at the other, *This is my friend,* (name). The children repeat. The volunteers then swap roles. They then go back to their seats. Repeat with different children.
- The children stand up. Play some music. The children walk around. When the music stops, they make groups of three or four. They take turns introducing each other, saying *This is my friend,* (name). Start the music again. The children move around once more. Continue until the children are confident with introducing their friends.

Family fun!

Value: Caring about family and friends

Animal families

6 CD1 42 **Listen and point. Trace and say the words.**

Aims

- to integrate other areas of the curriculum through English: Biology

New language: *egg, baby, chicken*

Recycled language: *mom, dad, brother, sister, This is my …*

Materials: CD 1, flashcards (family), the puppet (Polly), a toy or hard-boiled egg, a picture of a baby, materials for the project (a paper plate, yellow crayon or pencil, two stick-on eyes, a tail, beak, and wings made of colored paper, scissors, and glue for each child), a "rocking chicken" you have prepared (similar to the one on WB page 30)

Optional: playdough or modeling clay (one piece for each child)

Language competences: The children will be able to understand that a baby chick is younger than an adult chicken.

Warm-up

Aim: to present *egg* and review *This is my …* and family words

- Put on the puppet. Play *Disappearing flashcards* using the family flashcards (see Introduction, page xvii).
- Make Polly take the toy egg/hard-boiled egg out of your bag. She says *Look! This is my egg.* Make her sit on the egg. Say *Egg.* The children repeat. Polly passes the egg to volunteers, saying *This is my egg.* The child says *Egg.* To get it back, make Polly say *My egg, please!*

Presentation

6 CD1 42 SB p30 **Listen and point. Trace and say the words.**

Aim: to present *baby* and identify the members of an animal family

- Ask the children to look at SB page 30. Point to the egg and ask *What's this?* Elicit *Egg.* Say *Point to the mom.* Help the children to point to the correct picture. Repeat for *Dad.* Point to the chick and say *This is the baby.* Show the picture of a baby and say the word. Students repeat.
- Play the first section of the recording. The children listen and point to each picture one at a time. Join in yourself. Repeat for the second section. Play the third section for the children to point without your help.
- Point to the line around the first picture and trace it with your finger. At the same time, say *Dad.* The children copy. Do the same for the other three pictures. The children trace around the pictures and say the words.
- Talk in L1 about which is younger, the baby or the mom. Then ask which is younger, the egg or the chick, to get the children thinking about age.

Audio script page T97

Practice

7 WB p30 **Make a rocking chicken.**

Aim: to take part in a craft activity and encourage recognition of parts of a bird

- Show the pictures on WB page 30. Explain in L1 that you are all going to make a chicken which rocks. Hold up the chicken you have made and say *This is my chicken.* The children repeat *Chicken.* Explain how you made the chicken in L1, using the pictures on WB page 30.
- Hand out the materials. Circulate and help the children color the plate yellow, fold it and stick on the wings, tail, beak, and eyes. Cut out the parts of the chicken for the children (beak, wings, tail) in advance. Ask individual children *What's this?* Elicit *Chicken* and the parts of the bird in L1.
- The children practice making their chickens "rock" once the glue is dry.

Extension activity

Aim: to review vocabulary and practice fine motor skills

- Make a playdough model of an egg. Show the class and ask *What's this?* Tell the children they are going to make a model of something from the lesson – a chicken, a baby, or an egg. Point to the pictures on SB page 30 and elicit the words.
- Hand out playdough to each child. The children make three models each (chicken, chick, and egg). Circulate and help as necessary. Ask *What's this?* Show some of the best models to the class. Confident children can show and say, e.g., *This is my egg.*

Ending the lesson

Aim: to review new words *egg, baby, chicken*

- Teach the following mimes for the new words in the lesson:

  Egg = Curl up with hands over head to make an egg shape.

  Baby = Move your arms as if rocking a baby.

  Chicken = Fold your arms with elbows out and "flap" them while moving your head like a chicken.
- Say each word. The children mime with you. When they are confident with the mimes, they say and mime at the same time.
- The children work in pairs. Child A says one of the words, Child B mimes. Then they swap. Circulate and check.

Aims

- to review language and values from the unit; to encourage children to reflect on their learning

Recycled language: *chicken, baby, egg, mom, dad, brother, sister*

Materials: flashcards (family)

Optional: simple outline cutouts of men, women, boys, girls, and babies (enough for each child to choose two adults and two or three children/babies), glue, a piece of paper or thin cardboard for each child

Language competences: The children will be able to recognize the order of a simple life cycle (egg – chick – adult bird). The children will be able to use language from the unit.

Warm-up

Aim: to review vocabulary from the previous lesson

- Repeat the mimes from the previous lesson (see page T30, Ending the lesson) to elicit and practice *egg, baby,* and *chicken*. Talk briefly in L1 about which is younger/smaller.

Practice

7 Think! SB p31 **Follow the path.**

Thinking skills: ordering

- Point to the photographs on SB page 31. Elicit the words. Say, e.g., *Point to the chicken*. The children point. Repeat with *Egg* and *Baby*. The children will point to the two photographs for baby. Ask in L1 *Which is the youngest? / Which is the smallest?* The children point to the photograph on the bottom left.
- Explain in L1 that the children have to draw a path from each photograph – from the youngest/smallest to the oldest. Point to the egg and say in L1 *The egg is first*. Ask *What's next?* The children point to the photograph of the chicken on the eggs. Repeat with the other two photographs.
- Point at the photographs in age order. The children copy you.

8 WB p31 **Say the words. Color the circles.**

Aim: to create a record of learning

- Point to the pictures on WB page 31. The children say the words together.
- The children color the circles if they can say the words on their own.
- Circulate and help as necessary. Ask individual children to say the words.

Extension activity

Aim: to make a family picture and think about age

- Take a piece of paper or thin cardboard and choose some of the cutout figures (e.g., one man, one woman, a boy). Stick the figures on your piece of paper. Show the children and say *This is my family. This is my dad. This is my mom. This is my brother.*
- Hand out a piece of paper or thin cardboard to each child and spread out the cutout figures on desks around the class. The children choose figures to make up their family and stick them on the paper. Circulate and help as necessary. Ask individuals about their pictures and encourage them to make sentences in English (e.g., *This is my dad. This is my sister.*). Ask in L1 who is the youngest/oldest in the picture.
- Invite volunteers to show their pictures to the class.

Ending the lesson

Aim: to review language from the unit

- Play the children's favorite game from the unit or sing the unit song.

Phonics

- See page T82 for Unit 3 Phonics.

Review

- See page T91 for Unit 2 & Unit 3 Review.

7 Think! **Follow the path.**

Phonics → page 82 Review → page 91

4 My toys

1 CD1 45 **Listen and point. Say the toys.**

4

Aims

- to present and practice toys

New language: *ball, car, puzzle, doll, It's a (blue) (ball)*

Recycled language: *my, Hello, Look*, colors, characters

Materials: CD 1, flashcards (toys), real toys (a ball, a toy car, a jigsaw puzzle, and a doll), the puppet (Polly), colored crayons or pencils (red, blue, green, orange, and yellow) for each child, Yes/No cards

Optional: small classroom objects (a book, a pencil), a tray, and piece of cloth (to cover the tray)

Language competences: The children will be able to name toys.

Warm-up

Aim: to introduce the topic

- Show one of the real toys and say, e.g., *Look! My car.* Repeat with *ball, puzzle,* and *doll*. Point to all of the toys and say *My toys!* Give each of the toys to children in different parts of the classroom. They pass the toys around for everyone to look at. Collect the toys and put them at the front.

Presentation

1 CD1 45 SB p32 **Listen and point. Say the toys.**

Aim: to present toys

- Point to the characters and ask *Who's this?* The children say the names.
- Say *Listen*. Play the audio. The children just listen.
- Say *Listen and point*. Play the audio. The children listen and point to the toys.
- Play the audio again. The children point and say.

Audio script page T97

Practice

- Show the toy flashcards. Say each word. The children repeat. Say the words at different volumes. The children repeat in the same way.
- Teach the following mimes:
  Ball = Bouncing a ball.
  Car = Holding a steering wheel.
  Puzzle = Hands in front of you, palms toward you, interlinking your fingers.
  Doll = Rocking a baby in your arms.
- Say each word. The children mime with you. When they are confident, they say and mime at the same time.
- Say one of the words. The children do the mime without your help. Choose a volunteer. He/She says a word. You do the mime.

1 CD1 46 WB p32 **Listen and color. Say the toys.**

Aim: to practice toys, review colors, and practice listening skills

- Make sure each child has crayons or pencils (red, blue, orange, green, and yellow). Hold up a yellow pencil and say *Look! It's yellow! It's a yellow pencil. Show me yellow.* The children pick up the correct color. Do the same for the other colors. Repeat, but without showing the color yourself. The children pick up the correct color.
- Say *Listen and point*. Then say, e.g., *It's a doll.* The children point to the correct picture. Repeat for the rest of the toys.
- Say *Listen and color.* Play the first line of the audio. Point to the picture of the ball and ask *What color?* The children reply *Blue*. Show the children how to color the picture. Play the rest of the audio. Pause after each item for the children to color.
- Point to the finished pictures and ask *What's this? What color is it?* Rephrase the responses, e.g., *Yes! It's a ball. It's blue. It's a blue ball.*

Audio script page T97

Extension activity

Aim: to practice toys

- Put the real toys, the pencil, the book, and Polly onto a tray. Pick up each item and ask *What's this?* and (if it's red, green, yellow, orange, or blue) *What color is it?* Place all the items back on the tray and say *Look! Remember!* Let them look for one minute at the objects on the tray, then cover it with a large cloth. Turn away and secretly remove one of the items (you can ask the children to close their eyes). Show the tray again and ask *What's missing?* Elicit guesses from different volunteers. You can also ask *What color is it?* Hold up the missing item and elicit the name and the color.
- Repeat the game several times, removing a different item each time.

Ending the lesson

Aim: to review toy words

- Put on the puppet. Play *No, Polly!* with the toy flashcards/real toys. Polly makes right or wrong sentences about the color of the toys, e.g., *It's a red car.* Give out the Yes/No cards. Say *Show me No*. The children hold up the correct card. Repeat for Yes. Do as many sentences as time allows.
- Make Polly wave and say *Goodbye!* The children wave and say *Goodbye, Polly!*

Aims

- to present *I have a (car)* and practice toys; to say a chant

New language: *I have a (car)*

Recycled language: *ball, car, puzzle, doll,* classroom objects

Materials: CD 1, flashcards (toys, classroom objects), real toys (ball, car, puzzle, doll) and real classroom objects (bag, pencil, book), CD of lively music, colored pencils or crayons, Yes/No cards

Optional: character flashcards, character masks

Language competences: The children will be able to talk about possession with *I have a …* . The children will be able to join in with a chant.

Warm-up

Aim: to review toys

- Show the toy flashcards one at a time. Say/Elicit the names. The children repeat.
- Show the flashcards again. The children say the names.
- Repeat the mime activity from page T32 Practice.

Presentation

2 CD1 47 SB p33 **Listen and match. Chant.**

Aim: to present *I have a …* , review toys and say a chant

- Show the car flashcard or toy car and elicit the word. Say *Look! I have a car.* Repeat for the other toys.
- Point to the first picture on SB page 33. Say *Listen and match* and play the first line of the chant. Trace the line from the boy to the car with your finger. The children copy. Repeat for the other toys.
- Play the chant again. The children draw the lines with a pencil.
- Say *Listen and chant.* Play the chant again line by line. The children listen and repeat. Play the chant again for the children to join in. They trace the lines they drew as they chant.

Audio script page T97

Practice

- Hold up a toy and say, *I have a … .* The children name the toy. Say the whole sentence (e.g., *Yes! I have a puzzle.*). Repeat with different toys and classroom objects.
- Give out the Yes/No cards. Say *Show me No.* The children hold up the correct card. Repeat for Yes.
- Hold up a doll and say *I have a ball.* The children hold up the No card. Repeat for the other toys and classroom objects, mixing correct and incorrect sentences.

Note: Alternatively, move your children to a larger space and stick a Yes card to one wall and a No card to another wall. Hold up an object and make a true or false sentence. The children run to the correct wall.

2 WB p33 **Draw a toy. Say the sentence.**

Aim: to practice *I have a …* and toys

- Point to the example drawing on WB page 33 then the frame. Show some crayons and say *Draw a toy.* Make sure the children understand that they can draw a car, ball, doll, or puzzle.
- Circulate and say *I have a …* to individual children. They reply according to what they're drawing, e.g., *Car.* Encourage them to say the sentence *I have a car.* Invite volunteers to show their picture and say, e.g., *I have a doll.*
- Invite volunteers to stand up and show their picture.

Extension activity

Aim: to practice *I have a …*

- Stick the character flashcards on the board and elicit their names.
- Divide the class into four groups. Give out the character masks, one type to each group.
- Stick a toy flashcard next to each character flashcard. Point to the Gina group and to the doll flashcard and say *I have a …* The children in that group say *Doll.* Encourage them to say the whole sentence *I have a doll.* Repeat for the other groups. Change the order of the toy flashcards and elicit the new sentences. Speed up as the children get the idea.

Ending the lesson

Aim: to practice *I have a …*

- The children sit in a large circle. Hand out toys and classroom objects (doll, car, puzzle, ball, pencil, book, bag) to six children (not next to each other). Alternatively, use flashcards. Elicit a sentence from each of the children with an object/card, e.g., *I have a book.* Play the music. The children pass the objects to their left. When the music stops, elicit sentences from the children who are now holding the objects. Repeat until everyone has had at least one turn to speak.

2 CD1 47 Listen and match. Chant.

1
2
3

3 CD1 48 49 Listen and act. Listen and color.

1

2

3

4

Aims

- to present and practice responding to *throw* and *catch;* to review toys

New language: *Throw your ... , Catch your ... , Oh, no!*

Recycled language: toys, *I have a ... , Clean up the ...* , instructions (*Hands up, Hands down, Go to sleep, Wake up, Show me something (green)*, etc.), colors

Materials: CD 1, flashcards (toys, classroom objects, characters), a large soft ball, the puppet (Polly)

Optional: toy car, doll, puzzle, soft ball, and cardboard box/basket for each team of three to six children (the cardboard box/basket must be large enough to hold all the toys)

Language competences: The children will be able to follow new and familiar instructions.

Warm-up

Aim: to review toys, classroom objects, and *I have a ... .*

- Review the toys with the flashcards. Show each flashcard and elicit the word. Confirm by saying a sentence with *I have* (e.g., *I have a puzzle*). Practice the classroom object words and *I have* using the flashcards in the same way.
- Put the toy and classroom object flashcards together, mix them up and take one, holding it so the children can't see what it is. Say *I have a ...* Volunteers guess by saying one of the words. When a child guesses correctly, say the whole sentence, e.g., *Yes! I have a chair!* Repeat with different flashcards. Then make the activity competitive by dividing the class into teams.

Presentation

3 CD1 48 SB p34 **Listen and act.**

Aim: to present new instructions and practice listening and responding physically

- Books closed. Ask the children to sit in a circle. Sit in the center. Throw a soft ball into the air and say *Throw*. Catch it and say *Catch*. Repeat several times. Encourage the children to mime as you throw and catch, then join in with the words. Let volunteers try throwing and catching the ball.
- Set the ball aside. Play the first line of the audio and mime throwing. The children copy. Say *Throw your ball.* Do the action again, along with the children. Play the next line and do the action. The children copy. Repeat for the rest of the recording.
- Play the audio again without pausing, doing the actions with the children. Repeat several times. Play the audio for the children to follow the instructions without your help.
- Give more instructions, adding language from earlier units, e.g., *Stand up. Throw your ball.* The children follow. Speed up when they are confident.

Audio script page T97

Practice

3 CD1 49 SB p34 **Listen and color.**

Aim: to practice new instructions and listening

- Say *Listen and color.* Explain in L1 that the children have to choose the correct color to color the circles below the pictures. Play the first line of the audio and point to the example circle next to picture 1. Then play the rest of the audio, pausing for children to color the circle each time.

Audio script page T97

3 CD1 50 WB p34 **Listen and circle.**

Aim: to practice new instructions, listening, and pencil control

- Point to the pictures on WB page 34 and elicit *Clean up* and *Throw your ball.*
- Say *Listen and circle. Clean up or throw your ball?* Play the audio. The children point to the correct picture. They draw the circle around the second picture. Circulate and elicit *Throw your ball* from individuals.

Audio script page T97

Extension activity

Aim: to practice following instructions and take part in a team game

- If possible, move your class out into the playground, school gym, or an empty classroom.
- Divide the class into teams of three to six. In front of each team place a doll, a car, a ball, a puzzle and, furthest away, a box or basket.
- Say *Clean up the doll!* The first child in each team runs to pick up the doll in their line of objects, puts it in the box/basket, and runs to the back of their team. Say *Clean up the car!*
- Practice the game slowly at first. You need to take the objects out of the boxes once you have given all the instructions, and place them in line again. Mix up the order of the instructions.
- Make the game competitive.

Ending the lesson

Aim: to practice following instructions

- Put on the puppet. Play *Polly says ...* using known instructions, *throw*, and *catch* (see Introduction, page xvii).

Aims

- to sing a song with the class; to present and practice *big* and *small*

New language: *big, small,* adjectives: *a (big) (red) (ball)*

Recycled language: toys, colors, classroom objects, *Show me (something) (blue), throw, catch, mom, dad, brother, I have a ...*

Materials: CD 1, a soft ball, toys, classroom objects, pencils and crayons in known colors, a big ball, a small ball, large circles of red and blue thin cardboard, small circles of red and blue thin cardboard (enough for a quarter of the class to have big red circles, a quarter big blue circles, etc.), pencils

Optional: big and small toys and classroom objects, one for each child

Language competences: The children will be able to join in with a song.The children will be able to describe the color and size of an object.

Warm-up

Aim: to review *throw*, *catch*, toys, classroom objects, and colors

- The children stand in a circle. Place toys and classroom objects in the centre. Elicit the words and colors. Say, e.g., *Angela, please show me the doll.* The child picks up the doll and brings it to you. She puts it back. Repeat with different children and different objects. When the children are confident, add in colors, e.g., *Philippe, please show me the red pencil / something red.*
- Say, e.g., *Victor, catch the ball,* and throw the soft ball. Say *Victor, throw the ball.* The child throws the ball back to you. Encourage him to say (Your name), *catch the ball.* Repeat with different children. When the children are confident, let them choose who to throw to. They say (Name), *catch the ball* each time.

Presentation

4 CD1 51 52 SB p35 **Listen and sing.**

Aim: to present *big* and *small* and sing a song

- Show the children a big ball and say *A big ball.* Hold up a small ball and say *A small ball.* Repeat several times. Encourage the children to join in. Then hold up the big ball and say *I have a big ball.* Repeat with *I have a small ball.*
- Point to the little girl on SB page 35 and say *Look! It's Rosemary. Children, say hello to Rosemary.* The children say *Hello, Rosemary.* Point to Rosemary's family and ask *Who's this?* The children say *Brother/Mom/Dad.* They say hello to each of them.
- Say, e.g., *Point to a big ball.* The children point. Repeat several times, mixing up big and small. Then say, e.g., *Point to a small, red ball.* The children point to the first ball. Repeat for *big, red ball/small, blue ball/big, blue ball.*
- Play the song. The children listen and point to the appropriate ball.
- Play the song again, pausing to teach each line.

Audio script page T97

Practice

4 CD1 53 WB p35 **Listen again. Trace and color.**

Aim: to practice listening and identifying size and color

- Point to the picture on the left and say *Listen. Big or small? What color?* Play the first verse of the song. Elicit the answer A *big, red ball.* Show the children how to trace around the ball and color it red. Play the song verse by verse, pausing for the children to trace and color. Circulate and check they are using the correct colors.
- Say, e.g., *I have a small, blue ball.* The children say the correct person from WB page 35, e.g., *Dad.*

Audio script page T98

Extension activity

Aim: to practice *I have a (big/small) (blue) ... ,* toys and classroom objects

- Hand each child a big or small toy/classroom object. Elicit sentences from volunteers about their object, according to ability, e.g., *I have a ball. / I have a small book. / I have a small, blue pencil.*
- Ask all the children to say a sentence to their neighbor. They take turns speaking. Circulate and check/help. Then say *Pass it on.* Show the children how to pass their object to the person on their right. Repeat the pairwork activity, with the children making a sentence about their new object. The game continues until the children have made five or six sentences.

Ending the lesson

Aim: to practice the song

- Divide the class into four groups (Brother, Mom, Dad, and Rosemary). Hand out the colored circles to match the balls in the song. Play the song. The groups join in with the correct verse and hold up their circles as they sing. Everyone sings the chorus.

4 CD1 51 52 **Listen and sing.**

Family fun!

The puzzle

5 CD1 54 Sticker

Values

Aims

- to present a picture story; to review language from the unit

New language: *Where is it? Is it there? It's there*

Recycled language: toys, classroom objects, colors, *big/small, I have … , Thank you, egg*

Materials: CD 1, a large soft bag, eight to ten big and small toys, including a puzzle, and classroom objects (most of these should be red, yellow, green, or blue), Leo mask, a cushion, the puppet (Polly), a toy egg/hard-boiled egg

Language competences: The children will be able to listen and follow a picture story. The children will be able to respond to the questions *Where is it?* and *Is it there?*

Warm-up

Aim: to review *I have a big/small (red) (ball)*

- Show the children each of the big/small objects you have brought to class. Say, e.g., *I have a small, red car.* Then put it in the bag.
- Invite a volunteer to come to the front. With eyes closed, he/she takes an object out of the bag. Encourage the child to make a sentence with *I have … ,* according to ability. The child takes the object back to his/her place. Repeat with different volunteers. Collect the objects by saying, e.g., *Where's my small, red car?* The child with the correct object puts it back in the bag. Say *Thank you,* (name). *Good. I have my small, red car.*

Presentation

5 CD1 54 SB pp36–37 **Story: The puzzle**

Aim: to listen and follow a picture story

- Point to the characters on SB page 36 and ask *Who's this?* The children say, e.g., *(It's) Gina.* Review toys by asking, e.g., *Where's the car?* The children point. Ask what Leo is doing in L1 (a puzzle) and why he is sad (the last piece is missing).
- Play the CD. The children point to the pictures as they listen.
- Play the story again, stopping after each picture. The children explain what's happening in L1. Elicit translations for *Where is it? Is it there?* and *It's there!*
- Put on the Leo character mask. Play the story. Pretend to be Leo and join in with his reactions/ questions. Point to a shelf in the classroom/open a cabinet and lift the cushion as in the story. The children join in with the other animals' lines. At the end, turn around and pretend you are Leo, looking at your tail. Encourage the children to point and join in with *Look! It's there!*

Audio script page T97

Practice

5 CD1 55 WB p36 **Listen and color the correct circle.**

Aim: to listen and identify the correct picture

- Point to the characters in the pictures on WB page 36. Ask *Who's this?* Say *Listen and color the circle.* Point to the circles. Play the audio. Elicit the answer (the second picture).
- Play the audio again. Check the children's work as they color.
- Play the recording again. The children repeat the question and answer exchange.

Audio script page T97

4

Extension activity

Aim: to practice *big/small,* colors, *Where is it?, Is it there?,* and *There it is!*

- Place three or four of the items from the beginning of the lesson in different places around the classroom (if possible, when the children are not looking). Make sure the children can see the items. Say, e.g., *My book! My big, green book. Where is it?* Go around the classroom looking. As you look, ask the class and individuals *Is it there?* They respond *No!* When the children point to the object and say *Look!/It's there!* "find" the object and say *Thank you! I have my big, green book.* Repeat with the rest of the objects.

Ending the lesson

Aim: to practice *Where's my … ?, Is it there?* and *There it is!*

- Put on the puppet. Make her pick up an egg. Point and ask her *What's this?* Polly says *My egg. I have an egg.* Say *Polly, let's play a game!* Make Polly cover her eyes with her wings and hide the egg somewhere in the classroom. The children can suggest places in L1. Say *OK, Polly!* Make Polly uncover her eyes and say *My egg! Where is it?* She flies around the room looking for the egg on shelves, in cabinets, under the cushion, etc. Make Polly ask *Is it there?* each time. The children respond *No!* Make Polly point to the egg and say *It's there! Look! I have my egg.*
- Make Polly wave and say *Goodbye!* The children wave and say *Goodbye, Polly!*

Aims

- to talk about the meaning of a story; to review language from the unit

Recycled language: toys, classroom objects, language from the story

Materials: CD 1, Unit 4 stickers, colored pencils or crayons, pencils

Optional: character masks, a large jigsaw piece, Scotch tape

Language competences: The children will be able to appreciate the values shown in the story. The children will be able to use and respond to language from the story.

Warm-up

Aim: to review language from the story

- Before the class, hide things that you need around the room (e.g., your bag, your book, a pencil, your chair). Pretend that you have lost the items and say, e.g., *My bag! Where's my bag?* Move around the classroom looking, and asking *Is it there?* The children help by saying *No* and pointing or saying *It's there!* "Find" each thing and say *Thank you!*

Practice

5 CD1 54 SB pp36–37 **Story: The puzzle**
Listen to the story. Stick.

Aim: to review the story

- Guide the children to tell you what they remember about the story on SB pages 36 and 37. Ask while miming *Why is Leo sad? What has he lost? Where does he look? Who helps him?*
- Play the story again, pausing after each picture to ask what is happening, and elicit what the characters are saying.
- Hand out the stickers for Unit 4. Say *Where's the car?* The children point to the correct sticker on the sheet. Repeat for *ball.*
- Point to the picture on SB page 37. Say *Where's the ball?* The children point to the sticker outline. Mime peeling the sticker of the ball off the sheet. The children peel off the sticker and hold it up. Check that they all have the correct sticker. Then say *Stick.* The children stick the sticker in their books. Repeat for the other sticker.

Audio script page T97

Story values SB pp36–37

Aim: to think about the meaning of the story: helping

- Play the story again. The children listen and point. Pause after picture 2 and ask in L1 *What's Gina doing?* (She's helping look for the puzzle piece.) Play the rest of the story and ask about what Polly and Mike are doing. Talk about how important it is to help people. Ask the children how they help people at school and at home.

6 WB p37 **Complete the face. Color the picture.**

Aim: to apply values from the story to new situations

- Tell the children in L1 *We're going to look at a boy and a woman now. Look at the picture and think.* Talk in L1 about how we can help someone who is not as strong as us. Ask in L1 *What is the boy doing?* (Helping.) *What is the woman saying?* (Thank you.) Point to the happy face and remind the children in L1 that if they think the boy is doing the right thing, they trace the happy smile. Show them how to trace the line with a pencil. Circulate and check as they trace. Then the children can color the picture.

Extension activity

Aim: to reinforce understanding of the story

- Invite four volunteers to the front. Assign them the roles of Gina, Polly, Leo, and Mike. The children playing the main characters put on the character masks. Stick a large jigsaw piece to the back of the child playing Leo using Scotch tape. Play the story. The children act out the story along with the CD. Encourage them to join in with the CD and look around as the characters do ("Gina" looking on a shelf, "Polly" opening a cabinet and "Mike" looking under a chair). The child playing Leo "finds" the jigsaw piece after the others point to it on his back.
- Invite another group of four children to come to the front and act.

Ending the lesson

Aim: to practice helping and thanking someone for their help

- Ask the children to put three objects in front of them (e.g., a book, a red pencil, and a yellow pencil). Demonstrate with a volunteer. Put three items on your desk and ask the child, e.g., *Where's my book?* Encourage the child to point to it and say *Look! It's there!* Say *Thank you* and pick it up. The children practice the same dialog in pairs with the items in front of them. Circulate and help as necessary.

Family fun!

Big and small

6 CD1 56 **Listen and point. Trace and say the words.**

1

2

3

4

5

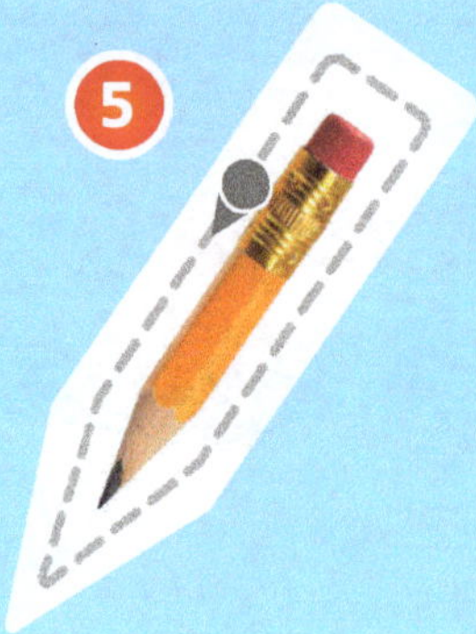

6

Aims

- to integrate other areas of the curriculum through English: geometry

Recycled language: *big*, *small*, toys, classroom objects, colors

Materials: CD 1, flashcards (toys), big and small toys/bags/books (some in known colors), the puppet (Polly), air-drying modeling clay (one piece for each child), paints and paintbrushes, pencils

Optional: eight to ten pictures or photographs of big and small things (e.g., a truck, a large building, a tree, an airplane, an elephant, a tennis ball, a mouse, a piece of candy, a daisy, an ant)

Language competences: The children will be able to differentiate between big and small objects.

Warm-up

Aim: to review toys and *big/small*

- Put some big and small objects at the front of the classroom (e.g., a big book and a small book, a big toy car and a small toy car, a big ball and a small ball, a big bag and a small bag). Hold up an object and ask *Is it big or small?* The children respond. Repeat with different objects.
- Put on the puppet. Make Polly say, e.g., *Oscar, please show me a small bag*. The child comes to the front and holds up the correct object. Polly says *Thank you!* Repeat with different volunteers.

Presentation

6 CD1 56 SB p38 **Listen and point. Trace and say the words.**

Aim: to differentiate between big and small objects

- Ask the children to look at SB page 38. Point to the first picture and ask *What's this?* Elicit *Car*. Ask *Big or small?* Elicit *A big car*. Repeat for the other pictures.
- Play the first section of the recording. The children listen and point to each picture one at a time. Join in yourself. Play the second section for the children to point without your help.
- Point to the line around the first picture and trace it with your finger. At the same time, say *A big car*. The children copy. Do the same for the other pictures. The children trace around the pictures and say the phrases.

Audio script page T97

Practice

7 WB p38 **Make a big toy and a small toy.**

Aim: to take part in a craft activity and encourage recognition of size and shape

- Show the pictures on WB page 38. Explain in L1 that you are all going to make a big toy and a small toy, like the boy in the picture. Point to the toys he has made one at a time and ask *What is it? Is it big or small?*
- Hand out the materials. Circulate and help the children make their toys. Ask individual children *What's this? Is it big or small?*
- The children paint their toys then leave them to dry. Ask volunteers to show their toys to the class and say, e.g., *A small doll* or *I have a small doll*.

Extension activity

Aim: to extend awareness of the sizes of things around us

- Stick the photographs of big and small objects at the bottom of the board, all mixed up, at a height the children can reach. Draw a line down the center of the board. Move one of the pictures of a big object on one side of the line on the board, e.g., the truck. Ask *Is it small?* The children say *No, big*. Choose a picture of a small object. Hold it next to the picture of the large object and ask *Is it like this? Is it big?* The children say *No, small*. Stick the picture on the other side of the line on the board. Call a volunteer to the board to choose a picture and stick it on the correct side of the board, according to its size. Help by asking *Is it big? Is it small?* The rest of the class responds, too. Encourage the child to say *It's a big (car)* or *It's a small (car)*. Repeat until all the pictures have been stuck on the board. Mix up the pictures and repeat the activity with different children.

Ending the lesson

Aim: to review *big/small* and practice the unit song

- Play the song from page T35 (CD 1, Track 51). Mime holding a small ball or a big ball as you sing each verse. The children copy.

Aims

- to review language and values from the unit; to encourage children to reflect on their learning

Recycled language: *big, small*, toys, classroom objects, *I have a ... , Clean up ...*

Optional: colored pencils or crayons, pencils, a selection of big and small objects (e.g., a big book, a small book, a big doll, a small doll, a big bag, a small bag), and two large boxes, one with a picture of an elephant on it, one with a picture of a mouse

Language competences: The children will be able to sort objects according to their size. The children will be able to use language from the unit.

Warm-up

Aim: to review *big/small*, toys, classroom objects, and *I have a ...*

- Mime using a big or small object which the children know, e.g., writing with a small pencil. Ask *What is it?* Encourage the children to guess *A small pencil*. Say *Yes! I have a small pencil*. Repeat with different mimes, e.g., carrying a big bag, driving a small car, throwing a big ball, doing a big puzzle, reading a big book, sitting on a small chair.

Practice

7 Think! SB p39 **Look and draw lines. Say "big" or "small."**

Thinking skills: sorting

- Point to the photographs on SB page 39. Say, e.g., *Point to the small book*. The children point. Repeat with *small bag, big bag, big book, small ball*, and *big ball*.
- Say *Look and draw lines*. Demonstrate by pointing to the first picture and asking *Big or small?* Then drawing a line with your finger from the picture to the small square. Repeat for picture 2. The children draw lines for the remaining pictures. Circulate and help. Ask individual children *What's this? Is it big? Is it small?* Encourage them to make a phrase, e.g., *A small ball*.

8 WB p39 **Say the toys. Color the circles.**

Aim: to create a record of learning

- Point to the pictures on WB page 39. The children say the words together.
- The children color the circles if they can say the words on their own.
- Circulate and help as necessary. Ask individual children to say the words.

Extension activity

Aim: to practice sorting objects according to size

- If possible, move your class into the playground, school gym, or an empty classroom.
- Point to the box with the elephant on it, and say *Big or small?* The children say *Big!* Point to the box with the mouse on it, and repeat the question. The children say *Small!* Place the two boxes at one end of the space. Ask the children to stand at the other end. Between the children and the boxes, put a pile of big and small objects which the children know (e.g., books, bags, dolls, toy cars, balls). Choose a volunteer and say, e.g., *Clean up the big book!* The child chooses the correct object and puts it in the appropriate box. Repeat with different children and different items.
- Once the children are playing with ease, you can choose to play it as a team game. You can make the game competitive if you wish, by choosing two children at a time. They race to find the correct object and put it in the right box.

Ending the lesson

Aim: to review language from the unit

- Play the children's favorite game from the unit or sing the unit song.

Phonics

- See page T83 for Unit 4 Phonics.

7 Think! **Look and draw lines. Say “big” or “small”.**

Phonics → page 83 Review → page 92

5 My numbers

1 CD2 02 Listen and point. Say the numbers.

Aims

- to present and practice numbers

New language: *one, two, three, four, Go,* plural: *book/books*

Recycled language: toys, classroom objects, *red, blue, green, orange*

Materials: CD 2, four toy cars / pictures of cars, the puppet (Polly), coloring pencils or crayons, a toy train engine with four separate carriages, or a picture of a train engine and pictures of four carriages (to stick on the board)

Optional: flashcards (toys and classroom objects), classroom objects or small items (e.g., buttons, coins, building blocks), two sets of four for each pair of children

Language competences: The children will be able to count from 1 to 4. The children will begin to recognize plural words.

Warm-up

Aim: to introduce numbers 1 to 4

- Show the toy cars / pictures of cars. Put them slowly one by one on a table (or stick them on the board), counting *One … two … three … four!* Point and count several times. Say it as a chant. The children join in if they wish.
- Mime driving a car and, in L1, say that you need help driving the cars. Draw two lines to make a simple road from left to right on the board, at a height your children can reach. Choose four volunteers. Give each volunteer a toy car / picture and ask them to stand at one end of the "road." Say *One!* The first child "drives" his/her car by moving it along the board. Do the same for the other children (*Two! Three! Four!*). The rest of the class joins in with the counting.
- Repeat with more groups of four children.

Presentation

1 CD2 02 SB p40 **Listen and point. Say the numbers.**

Aim: to present numbers 1 to 4

- Point to each character one at a time on SB page 40. The children say the names. Say *Listen*. Play the audio. The children just listen.
- Say *Listen and point*. Play the audio and show the children how to point to the characters. Say *Listen and point*. Play the audio again. The children point.
- Say *Say the numbers*. Play the audio again. The children point and join in.

Audio script page T97

Practice

- If possible, move your class into the playground, school gym, or an empty classroom.
- Divide the class into four teams. The teams wait at one end of the space in lines.
- Say *Go!* Count *One, Two, Three, Four, Go!* The four who are at the front run to the wall as fast as they can. The winner gets a point for their team. These four children go to the back of the lines. Repeat until everyone has had a turn. The children who have already run help with the counting.

1 CD2 03 WB p40 **Listen and color. Say the numbers.**

Aim: to practice numbers and introduce plurals

- Point to the first ball. Ask *What's this?* and *What color is it?* The children answer *Red / A red ball.* Repeat for the other balls.
- Make sure the children have their colored pencils/crayons ready. Hold up a red pencil/crayon and say *Listen and color.* Play the first line of the audio and stop so that the children can color in the ball. Play the rest of the recording, stopping after each set of balls.
- Circulate and check that the children have used the correct colors for each set of balls.
- When the children have finished coloring, say *Say the numbers.* Point to the picture of the red ball and say *One ball.* The children repeat. Repeat for the other pictures, with the children saying all the numbers and adding the plural "s" if they can.

Audio script page T97

Extension activity

Aim: to practice numbers and counting sets of items

- Stick the toy and classroom object flashcards on the board. Move the toy flashcards into a group together, counting *One, two, three, four* as you do so. The children join in. Repeat for the classroom objects.
- Children repeat with the eight small items handed out to them.

Ending the lesson

Aim: to review numbers

- Hold up the toy train or stick the picture of the train on the board. Attach the carriages / stick them on the board, counting slowly as you do so, *One, two, three, four.* Point to the carriages and count again. Encourage the children to join in.
- Put on the puppet. Play *No, Polly!* using the toy train/pictures (see Introduction, page xvii). Polly points to the carriages and makes mistakes with the counting (e.g., pointing at two carriages, but saying *One, two, three*), or gets the order wrong (e.g., *One, four …*).

Aims

- to practice counting and plural words; to practice recognizing figures 1 to 4; to say a chant

Recycled language: *one, two, three, four, Show me …* , classroom objects, toys

Materials: CD 2, four pencils, groups of four other known items (e.g., dolls, cars, balls), pencils

Optional: a doll, toy car, puzzle, ball, bag, book, or pencil for each child, but no fewer than two or more than four of each thing in total (e.g., four toy cars, three dolls, two balls, four puzzles, two bags, etc.)

Language competences: The children will be able to use plural forms. The children will be able to join in with a chant.

Warm-up

Aim: to practice numbers 1 to 4 and counting

- Hold up one finger and say *One!* Hold up two fingers and say *Two!* Do the same for *three* and *four*. Repeat with the children copying the words and actions.

Note: Some children will find this more difficult than others. Encourage the children to help one another.

- Say, e.g., *Show me three!* The children hold up the correct number of fingers.

Presentation

2 CD2 04 SB p41 **Listen and match. Chant.**

Aim: to practice counting and recognizing figures 1 to 4 to say a chant

- Point to the first picture on SB page **41** and say *One book*. Point to the figure **1** and the dot and say *One*. Point to the books in the second picture, saying *Book, book, two books!* Again, point to the figure 2 and the dots. Repeat for pictures 3 and 4.
- Say *Listen and match*. Play the first line of the chant (*Book! One Book!*). Show the children how to trace from the picture of the book down to the figure **1** with their fingers. Repeat for the other lines. Children trace the lines with a pencil. Circulate and check the children are matching correctly. Repeat for the second verse.
- Say *Chant*. Play the first section of the chant, pausing after each line for the children to repeat. Play the second section through for the children to join in.

Audio script page T97

Practice

- Hold up a pencil. Say the first line of the chant, but using the word *pencil* instead of *book*. Hold up two pencils for the next line, then three for the next line, and so on. Encourage the children to join in. Repeat with groups of four different items (e.g., dolls, cars, balls).

2 WB p41 **Look and circle. Say the sentences.**

Aim: to practice counting and recognizing shapes

- Point to the first picture in the key on WB page **41** and say *Look and circle the puzzle*. Show the children how to find the puzzle and circle it with their pencils. Hold up your finger and say *One puzzle*. Point to the picture of the car in the key, elicit the word, and say *Look and circle the cars*. Circulate and help. Then ask *How many cars?* The children say *Two cars*. Repeat the process for *dolls* and *balls*.
- Once the children have found all the items, say e.g., *Cars?* The children point and count along with you *One, two cars*. Repeat for the other items in the puzzle.
- The children then work in pairs. Child A says the name of an item in the key, e.g., *Doll*. Child B points and counts the dolls aloud. Circulate and check that the children are counting correctly and adding an "s" to plural nouns.

Extension activity

Aim: to work together and practice counting

- If possible, move your class into the playground, school gym, or an empty classroom.
- Give a toy car, doll, puzzle, ball, book, pencil, or bag to each child in the class. Point to individuals. They say, e.g., *I have a book*.
- Tell the children, in L1, to find people who have the same type of object. Encourage the children to make sentences with *I have …*
- When all the children are sitting down, help each group count the objects they have, one at a time, e.g., the children with the bags hold them up and say *One, two, three, four*.

Ending the lesson

Aim: to practice the chant

- Play the chant again for the children to join in. They stand up and count on their fingers as they chant.

2 CD2 04 Listen and match. Chant.

1

2

3

4

3 CD2 05 06 Listen and act. Listen and color.

1

2

3

4

Aims

- to practice counting forwards and backwards

New language: *rocket*

Recycled language: numbers 1 to 4, colors, instructions (*Clap your hands, Throw, Catch*, etc.)

Materials: CD 2, flashcards (numbers), the puppet (Polly), a toy rocket or picture of a rocket stuck on thin cardboard, colored pencils or crayons in red, green, blue, and yellow

Language competences: The children will be able to follow instructions. The children will be able to count from 1 to 4, forwards and backwards.

Warm-up

Aim: to review numbers 1 to 4 and practice counting backwards

- Review numbers 1 to 4 using the flashcards.
- Put on the puppet. Play *Disappearing flashcards* (see Introduction, page xvii) using the number flashcards.
- Stick the number flashcards on the board again but in reverse order, 4, 3, 2, 1. Point to the flashcard with four spots and elicit the number. Repeat with the rest of the flashcards. Practice counting down from 4 to 1 with the class. Ask in L1 *When do we hear a countdown like this? Yes, at a rocket launch.*

Presentation

3 CD2 05 SB p42 **Listen and act.**

Aim: to practice counting backwards and listening and responding physically

- Show the toy rocket / picture of a rocket and say *Look! A rocket*. The children repeat *Rocket*.
- Start the countdown *Four … , three … ,* in a "NASA" voice. Encourage the children to join in with *Two … , one …* Make the rocket take off into the air, adding "blast off" noises. Repeat several times together, then choose volunteers to make the rocket blast off, some counting and some making the sound effects. Help them if needed.
- Say *Stand up*. Play the audio and show the children the following actions:
  Four = Stand up with your arms out.
  Three = Put your arms up above your head, making a rocket shape.
  Two = Bend your knees.
  One = Jump in the air.
- Play the audio for the children to listen and copy. When the rocket launch sound effect plays, they jump in the air.
- Say *Listen and act*. Play the audio again for the children to join in with the countdown and act out being a rocket on their own.
- Give more instructions, adding language from earlier units, e.g., *Throw your ball. Catch your ball. Sit down. Stand up. Hands up.*

Audio script page T97

Practice

3 CD2 06 SB p42 **Listen and color.**

Aim: to practice numbers and listening

- Say *Listen and color*. Remind the children, in L1, that they have to color the circles below the pictures the correct color. Play the first line of the audio and point to the circle next to picture 1. Then play the rest of the audio, pausing for children to color the circle each time.
- Point to picture 2 and elicit the color and the number. Repeat for pictures 3 and 4.

Audio script page T97

5

3 CD2 07 WB p42 **Listen and circle.**

Aim: to practice numbers, listening, and pencil control

- Point to the pictures on WB page 42 and elicit *One* and *Four* (according to the child's pose).
- Say *Listen and circle. One or four?* Play the audio. The children point to the correct picture. They circle the first picture.

Audio script page T98

Extension activity

Aim: to practice counting and listening carefully

- Say *Listen and count*. Ask *How many?* Clap your hands three times. Say *Three*. Do it again with *two*. Then, clap your hands and ask the children *How many?* Repeat, clapping a different number of times at different rhythms (up to four).

Ending the lesson

Aim: to practice counting backwards

- Put on the puppet. Start to count backwards, *Four, three …* and make Polly prepare to fly. The children join in. When you get to *one*, Polly doesn't fly; make her look as if she is still waiting. Then make her say *Go?*, and you say *Yes, go!* Point to all of them and say *Go!* The children realize that they need to say *Go!* Repeat the countdown. Polly "takes off" on the word "Go!" and flies around the class.
- Make Polly land on a child's head or shoulder. That child does the countdown from *four* and says *Go!* Polly flies and lands on a different child. Repeat several times.
- Make Polly wave and say *Goodbye!* The children wave and say *Goodbye, Polly!*

Aims

- to sing a song with the class; to practice following instructions and numbers 1 to 4

New language: *purple, sing*

Recycled language: *mom, cars, puzzle, colors*

Materials: CD 2, flashcards (colors, numbers, *mom, brother, car, puzzle*), a piece of thin purple cardboard (or thin cardboard colored purple), purple, green, and blue pencils or crayons

Optional: the puppet (Polly), No cards

Language competences: The children will be able to join in with a song. The children will be able to follow instructions.

Warm-up

Aim: to review counting backwards and colors, to present *purple*

- Review *red, green, blue,* and *yellow* with the flashcards. Show each flashcard and say the color. Show the cards in different orders. The children say the colors.
- Show a piece of thin purple cardboard and say *Purple*. The children repeat.
- Mix up the flashcards, adding the purple card. Call four volunteers to the front and ask them each to choose a card. They hold their cards so the class can't see the colors.
- Count down and say *Go!* The children join in. On "go," the children at the front turn, one by one, their flashcards to face the class. Everyone says the color. Repeat with different volunteers.

Presentation

4 CD2 08 09 SB p43 **Listen and sing.**

Aim: to practice numbers and sing a song

- Point to the picture on SB page 43. Say *Point to mom*. The children point. Point to the number next to the woman and say *Mom is one*. Point to her clothes and ask *What color?* The children answer *Purple*. Repeat with the other pictures.
- In L1, ask what the boy next to number 4 is doing. Point to the musical notes. Say/Elicit that the boy is singing. Say *Sing*.
- Play the song, pausing after the first two lines. Ask the children to point to the correct picture and number. Continue in this way until the end of the verse.
- Play the chorus for the children to listen.
- Play the rest of the song. The children point and begin to join in.
- Play the song again, pausing to teach each line. Tell the children in L1 that some words in the song sound similar (*one* and *mom, two* and *blue, green* and *three, four* and *more*). Listen for this when the children sing. The children point to the people and toys as they sing.

Audio script page T98

Practice

4 CD2 10 WB p43 **Listen again and color.**

Aim: to practice listening for specific information (colors)

- Point to the picture of mom and ask *Who's this?* Elicit *Mom*. Repeat for the other two pictures.
- Play the audio, pausing after the first two lines so that the children have time to color in mom. Continue in this way, pausing after each object for the children to color.
- Circulate, checking that the children have used the correct colors. Ask individuals *What's this? What color is it?*

Audio script page T98

Extension activity

Aim: to practice listening skills and review numbers

- Play *Singing Polly* (see Introduction, page xvii). Make Polly sing, e.g., *One, one, one, my green mom. Three, three, three, my cars are blue. Two, two, two, my doll is green. Four, four, four, let's jump some more!*
- For the last verse, make Polly sing correctly and encourage everyone to join in, standing up and dancing.

Ending the lesson

Aim: to practice the song

- Stick the one flashcard on the board. Stick the remaining number flashcards below and ask a volunteer *Where's two?* Stick *two* next to *one*. Repeat for *three* and *four*.
- Stick the flashcards puzzle, mom, boy, and car on the board. Say *Listen and match*. Play the first two lines of the song. Elicit/Show the children that the first picture is mom. Say *One, mom*. Stick the flashcard mom above the one flashcard. Play the next two lines and elicit *Cars*, and so on for verse 1.
- Play the rest of the song for the children to join in.

4 CD2 08 09 **Listen and sing.**

5 CD2 11 Sticker

Where's Polly?

Values

1

2

3

4

Aims

- to present a picture story; to review language from the unit

New language: *I'm here, Now ...*

Recycled language: numbers 1 to 4, *Hello*, character names, *Where's ... ? Is it there? Show me*

Materials: CD 2, four small objects for each child (e.g., four building blocks / plastic toys), flashcards (characters), the puppet (Polly), a large toy car or ball, colored pencils or crayons

Language competences: The children will be able to listen to and follow a picture story. The children will be able to use *Where's* (name)? and *I'm here!*

Warm-up

Aim: to review numbers

- Hand out the small objects – four to each child. Say *Stand up, please*. Say *Show me one!* The children hold up one object. Repeat with *Show me two! Show me three!* and *Show me four!* Demonstrate the first time, until the children are following with ease. Then mix up the numbers. The children hold up the correct number of items each time.
- Ask volunteers to lead the activity by giving the instructions.

Presentation

5 CD2 11 SB pp44–45 **Story: Where's Polly?**

Aim: to listen and follow a picture story

- Point to the characters on SB page 44 and ask *Who's this?* The children say, e.g., *(It's) Polly*. Alternatively, use the character flashcards. Point to picture 1, and ask in L1 what Gina is doing and why (covering her eyes, because the other animals are hiding). Explain/Elicit that they are playing *Hide and seek*. Ask the children if they like playing *Hide and seek*. Ask what Gina is doing in pictures 2 and 3 and how she feels in picture 4 (puzzled/sad). Ask what Mike and Leo are doing (giggling). Turn to page 45 and ask what is happening. Ask *Does Gina feel different? How does she feel?*
- Play the CD. The children point to the pictures as they listen.
- Play the story again, stopping after each picture. In L1, the children explain what's happening and the funny joke at the end of the story. Elicit a translation for *I'm here!* The children practice pointing at themselves and saying *I'm here!*
- Put on the puppet, Polly, and explain that she likes playing *Hide and seek*. Call a volunteer to the front. Make Polly cover her eyes with her wings and count slowly from one to four. The children join in with the counting. The volunteer hides somewhere in the classroom.
- Polly uncovers her eyes and flies around looking for the hidden child (e.g., in cabinets, under desks, etc.). She asks *Where's* (name)? Pretend that Polly can't find the child. Make Polly look tired and sad. Encourage the child to come out and say *I'm here!* Polly cheers up.

Audio script page T98

Practice

5 CD2 12 WB p44 **Listen and color the correct circle.**

Aim: to listen and identify the correct picture

- Point to the first picture on WB page 44. Ask *Who's this?* The children say the name. Repeat for the second picture. Say *Listen and color the circle*. Point to the circles. Play the audio. Elicit the answer (the second picture).
- Play the audio again. Check the children's work as they color.
- Play the recording again. The children listen and repeat Gina's lines.

Audio script page T98

Extension activity

Aim: to practice numbers, *Where's ... ?* and *I'm here!*

- If possible, move your class into the playground or an outside area with places for the children to hide. Make sure the area is safe to play.
- The first time you play the game, do the counting to four yourself, slowly, to give the children time to hide. Look for the children asking *Hmm. Where's* (name)? *Is he/she here?* When you find a child encourage him/her to say *I'm here!*
- The second time ask a confident volunteer to do the counting and seeking.

Note: If it is not possible to play the game in a large space, hide flashcards of the characters around the classroom for the children to find.

Ending the lesson

Aim: to practice numbers and *Where's ... ?*

- Show the children the toy car or ball. Ask them to close their eyes and count aloud to four. Hide the toy somewhere in the room. Ask *Where's the (ball)?* The children stand up and look for the toy. If you have a large class, choose three or four volunteers to look. Encourage the children who are looking to say *Where's the (ball)?* and suggest places to look by saying *Is it there?* The child who finds the toy gets to hide it in the next game.

Aims

- to talk about the meaning of a story; to review language from the unit

Recycled language: *Where's* (name)? *I'm here*, numbers, toys, *I have a (car)*, *It's (blue) / My (car) is (blue)*, *Go*

Materials: CD 2, flashcards (numbers, colors, and toys), Unit 5 stickers, colored pencils or crayons, the puppet (Polly), cars, a ball, a puzzle, or dolls for each group of three or four children, pencils

Optional: character masks

Language competences: The children will be able to appreciate the values shown in the story. The children will be able to use and respond to language from the story.

Warm-up

Aim: to review *Where's ... ?* and *I'm here!*

- Say *Stand up, please*. Tell the children that you are going to close your eyes and you want them to all change places and sit down in someone else's seat. They have to be ready when you say *Four!* Close your eyes and count slowly to four.
- Look around the classroom and act being very confused. Say *Oh, no! Where's* (name)? Encourage the child to stand up and say *I'm here!* Repeat until everyone is standing up. The children return to their usual places.

Practice

5 CD2 11 SB pp44–45 **Story: Where's Polly? Listen to the story. Stick.**

Aim: to review the story

- Ask the children to tell you what they remember about the story in L1. Ask *What are the animals playing? Who is hiding? Who is seeking? Does Gina find everyone? How does she feel?*
- Play the story again, pausing to ask what is happening and what the characters are saying. Ask what happened at the end (all the animals played together).
- Hand out the stickers for Unit 5. Say *Where's two?* The children point to the correct sticker. Repeat for *four*.
- Point to the picture on SB page 45. Say *Where's two?* The children point to the sticker outline. The children peel off the sticker and hold it up. Check that they all have the correct sticker. Then say *Stick*. The children stick the sticker in their books. Repeat for the other sticker.

Audio script page T98

Story values SB pp44–45

Aim: to think about the meaning of the story: playing together

- Play the story again. The children listen and point. Pause after picture 1. Ask what Gina says (*Where's Leo?*). Play the next part of the story. Pause after picture 4 and ask where Polly is (hiding – she has flown into the air for a joke). Play the rest of the story. Ask what Polly says to let Gina know where she is (*I'm here!*). Talk about how important it is to play together, and not to leave people out.
- Call three or four volunteers to the front. Give them a toy car each. Encourage them to sit together and say *Hello*. They count their cars aloud in English and say the colors (e.g., *I have a car. It's red. / Look! A red car.*). Tell the children to race their cars. Encourage them to count down in English *Four, three, two, one! Go!*
- Make groups of three or four and give out the toys. Give the children time to play together freely.

6 WB p45 **Complete the face. Color the picture.**

Aim: to apply values from the story to new situations

- Tell the children in L1 *We're going to look at some children now. Look at the picture and think*. Ask *How do the children feel?* (Happy.) *Why?* (They are playing together.) *What are they doing?* (A jigsaw.)
- Point to the happy face and remind the children in L1 that if they think the children are doing the right thing, they trace the happy smile. Circulate and check as they draw. Then the children can color the picture.

Extension activity

Aim: to reinforce understanding of the story

- Invite four volunteers to the front. Assign them the roles of Gina, Polly, Leo, and Mike. The children playing the characters put on the masks. Play the story. The children act out the story along with the CD.
- Invite another group of four children to come to the front and act.

Ending the lesson

Aim: to practice language from the unit

- Put on the puppet, Polly. Play *No, Polly!* (see Introduction, page xvii) with the number, color and toy flashcards.

Value: Playing together

Quantity

6 CD2 13 **Listen and point. Trace and say the numbers.**

1

2

3

4

1 2 3 4

Aims

- to integrate other areas of the curriculum through English: Numeracy

New language: *train*

Recycled language: numbers 1 to 4, toys, classroom objects

Materials: CD 2, flashcards (numbers), four small objects for each child (e.g., building blocks, pencils, plastic toys), a photocopy of a drawing of a train with four carriages for each child with figures 1 to 4 on the carriages, a glue stick, different colored small circles of thin cardboard (ten per child), colored pencils or crayons, pencils

Optional: ten large toys in number groups – e.g., one robot, two dolls, three balls, four teddy bears, four large pieces of thin cardboard each with a number from 1 to 4 on it, character masks

Language competences: The children will be able to count sets of objects.

Warm-up

Aim: to practice recognizing figures 1 to 4

- Repeat the Warm-up activity from page T44. This time, as you say, e.g., *Show me one!* hold up a flashcard with the figure 1 on it. When the children are playing the game with ease, show only the flashcards, without saying anything. See if the children can recognize the numbers and show you the correct number of objects. Don't insist that they get it right at this stage.

Presentation

6 CD2 13 SB p46 **Listen and point. Trace and say the numbers.**

Aim: to practice counting sets of objects and recognizing figures 1 to 4

- Ask the children to look at SB page 46. Point to the first picture and ask *What's this?* Elicit *Car.* Elicit the colors of the car. Say *How many?* Elicit/Say *One car.* Point to the figure 1 below the picture. Repeat for the other pictures. Encourage the children to add the plural "s" for *Two bags*, etc.
- Play the first section of the recording. The children listen and point to each picture one at at time. Join in yourself. Play the second section with the numbers in a different order. Point along with the children. Play the third section for the children to point on their own.
- Say *Trace the numbers*. Trace the line in the figure 1 with your finger. At the same time, say *One*. The children copy. Do the same for the other numbers. The children trace and say the numbers.

Audio script page T98

Practice

7 WB p46 **Make a number train.**

Aim: to take part in a craft activity and encourage recognition of figures 1 to 4

- Show the pictures on WB page 46. Explain in L1 that the children are going to make a train with circles on the carriages, like the girl in the pictures. Explain what to do, using the pictures on page 46. Show the children that they need to stick the correct number of circles to each carriage, using the figures 1, 2, 3, 4 to help them. If necessary, write the numbers on the board, at a height your children can reach, and ask volunteers to the front to draw the correct number of circles next to each one.
- Hand out a worksheet, ten thin cardboard circles, and a glue stick to each child. Circulate and help the children count and stick. Ask individual children *What number?* and encourage them to count the circles aloud.
- The children compare their trains in pairs and count the circles on each carriage.

Extension activity

Aim: to practice recognizing figures 1 to 4 and working together

- If possible, move your class into an area with four corners and a large space at the center. In the corners of the room, place a number flashcard and the appropriate number of toys.
- Divide the class into four teams. Name them Leo, Polly, Gina, and Mike. The children in each team can wear the appropriate character mask.
- Say, e.g., *Gina! Four! Go!* The children in the Gina team run to the corner with four toys. Repeat for the other numbers and teams. Call the class back to the center. Remove the toys so that the children are playing by recognizing the figures on the cards.

Ending the lesson

Aim: to practice the unit song and recognize figures 1 to 4

- Play the song from page T43 (CD 2, Track 8). Hold up the number flashcards you used in the Warm-up as prompts while the children sing.

Aims

- to review language and values from the unit; to encourage children to reflect on their learning

Recycled language: numbers 1 to 4, toys, *Show me ...*

Materials: pencils, colored pencils or crayons

Optional: large piece of display paper for each group of four children with the outline of a number on it (1, 2, 3, or 4), small pieces of colored paper / tissue paper (red, blue, green, or yellow), glue

Language competences: The children will be able to count objects and match them to figures 1 to 4. The children will be able to use language from the unit.

Warm-up

Aim: to review figures 1 to 4

- Write numbers 1 to 4 (as figures) on the board. Point to each one. The children say the number.
- Say *Stand up, please*. Say *One* and draw the figure 1 in the air with your finger. The children copy you. Do the same for the rest of the numbers. Repeat several times. Then say *Show me one!* The children draw the figure in the air, using the numbers on the board to help. Repeat for the rest of the numbers. Say *Sit down, please*.

Practice

7 Think! SB p47 **Look and match. Say the numbers.**

Thinking skills: describing with numbers

- Point to the first photograph on SB page 47. Say *How many? One? Two?* The children count and put up their hands when they know the answer. Elicit *Three (balls)*.
- Point to the figure 1 and elicit/say the number. Say *Look and match*. Trace a line with your finger from the number to the picture of one ball. The children draw lines for the remaining numbers. Circulate and help. Ask individual children *What number?* and ask them to show you the correct photograph. Encourage them to use plural "s," e.g., *Three. Three balls*.

8 WB p47 **Say the numbers. Color the circles.**

Aim: to create a record of learning

- Point to the numbers on WB page 47. The children say the numbers together.
- The children color the circles if they can say the numbers on their own.
- Circulate and help as necessary. Ask individual children to say the numbers.

Extension activity

Aim: to practice recognizing figures 1 to 4 and make a class display

- Divide the class into four groups (if you have more than 16 children in your class, have more groups, each with three or four children).
- Hand out a piece of paper with the outline of a number to each group (1 to one group, 2 to another group, etc.). The children in each group stick small pieces of colored paper within the outline to make a collage-style picture for each number. If possible, give one group red paper, one yellow, one blue, and one green.
- When the pictures are finished, stick them on the walls, if possible, as part of a display of a train with numbered carriages. Get the children to help you decide on the correct order from 1 to 4. Ask, e.g., *One. What color?* Display the numbers to use in future classes.

Ending the lesson

Aim: to review language from the unit

- Play the children's favorite game from the unit or sing the unit song.

Phonics

- See page T84 for Unit 5 Phonics.

Review

- See page T92 for Unit 4 & Unit 5 Review.

7 Think! Look and match. Say the numbers.

1 2 3 4

Phonics → page 84 Review → page 92

6 My pets

1 CD2 16 Listen and point. Say the pets.

 bird, rabbit, fish, cat

6

Aims

- to present and practice pets

New language: *bird, rabbit, fish, cat, pet*

Recycled language: *Look! It's my ...* , numbers

Materials: CD 2, a photograph of a cat, flashcards (pets), pencils, a piece of thin cardboard or thick paper (to cover the flashcards)

Optional: Yes/No cards

Language competences: The children will be able to name pets.

Warm-up

Aim: to introduce the topic of pets and present *cat*

- Show a picture of a cat and say *Look! It's my cat. I have a cat.* Make a cat noise. Say *Cat.* The children repeat. Pretend to pet the cat and say *It's my cat.* The children copy you, while saying *It's my cat.* Ask the children in L1 if they have any pets at home, what animals they are, and what they are called.

Presentation

1 CD2 16 SB p48 **Listen and point. Say the pets.**

Aim: to present pets

- Point to the characters one at a time and ask *Who's this?* The children say the names.
- Show the pet flashcards. Say each word. The children repeat.
- Point to the fish, rabbit, bird, and cat and say *Look! Pets!* Explain in L1 that Leo, Gina, Mike, and Polly all have pets. Say *Gina?* Show the fish. Elicit *Fish* from the children. Do the same with the other animals.
- Say *Listen.* Play the audio. The children listen.
- Say *Listen and point.* Play the audio. The children listen and point to the pets.
- Play the audio again. The children point and say.
  Audio script page T98

Practice

- Show the pet flashcards. Say each word. The children repeat.
- Show the flashcards in different orders. The children say the correct word.
- Teach a mime for each animal:
  Bird = Flapping your arms like wings.
  Rabbit = Hands on your head like a rabbit's ears, jumping.
  Fish = Waving your hand as if swimming and making noises like a fish blowing bubbles.
  Cat = "Washing" your ears with one hand like a cat with its paw and meowing.
- Say the pet and do the action along with the children. When they are doing the actions confidently, say the pet and the children mime without your help.

1 WB p48 **Look and circle the different pictures. Say the pets.**

Aim: to practice pets

- Point to the pictures in the first row and say *Bird, cat, bird, bird.* The children copy you. Point to the picture of the cat and say *Look! Cat is different.* Confirm in L1. Remind the children how to draw the circle around this picture.
- The children find the different picture in the other rows and circle with a pencil. Circulate and help as necessary. Ask individual children to point at the rows and say the words.

Extension activity

Aim: to practice pets and review numbers 1 to 4

- Give each child their Yes/No cards. Say *Yes* and *No* in different orders. The children pick up the correct card.
- Show the rabbit flashcard and say *It's a cat.* The children say *No!* and hold up the No card. Repeat with the other flashcards, mixing up true and false sentences.
- Write numbers 1 to 4 on the board. Point to the numbers and say them along with the children. Point to the numbers. The children say them without you. Stick a pet flashcard next to each number. Repeat the Yes/No activity, this time making sentences with the numbers, e.g., *Two is cat.*

Ending the lesson

Aim: to review pets

- Show the pet flashcards. The children say the words.
- Hold up one of the flashcards covered with a piece of thin cardboard or thick paper. Slowly reveal the picture, looking at it and asking *What's this?* The children say the pet when they recognize it. Repeat for the rest of the cards.

Aims

- to present *What is it?* and practice *It's my ...* and pets; to say a chant

New language: *What is it?, brown*

Recycled language: *bird, rabbit, fish, cat, It's* (color), colors

Materials: CD 2, flashcards (pets, colors), colored pencils or crayons, thin brown cardboard

Optional: flashcards (pets, toys, colors, classroom objects, numbers)

Language competences: The children will be able to answer the question *What is it?* and describe the color of an animal. The children will be able to join in with a chant.

Warm-up

Aim: to review pets

- Show the pet flashcards one at a time. Say the names. The children repeat.
- Choose one of the flashcards, but keep it secret. Do the mime for the pet on the card from the previous lesson (see T48 Practice). The children say the pet. Repeat with another flashcard. Then call on volunteers to come to the front, choose a flashcard, and mime for the rest of the class to guess.

Presentation

2 CD2 17 SB p49 **Listen and color. Chant.**

Aim: to present *What is it?*, review pets and colors and say a chant

- Show the color flashcards. The children say the colors. Practice by asking individuals to point to items in the classroom, e.g., *Clara, show me something green.*
- Point to each pet one at a time on SB page 49. The children say the word (e.g., *Bird*). Rephrase, adding the article each time, e.g., *Yes. A bird.* Show the children a brown card and say *Brown*. Ask children to repeat the word.
- Say *Listen and color.* Make sure the students have colored pencils or crayons in red, blue, brown, and green. Play the first verse of the chant. Encourage the children to point to the correct animal (the rabbit). Ask *What color?* Elicit *Brown*. Give them time to color the rabbit. Repeat for the rest of the chant.
- Say *Listen and chant.* Play the chant again line by line. The children listen and repeat. Play the chant again for the children to join in. They point to the pets as they chant.

Audio script page T98

Practice

- Choose a confident volunteer. Point to one of the pets on SB page 49 and ask *What is it?* The child replies, e.g., *A bird.* Remind the child to use the article "a" if he/she doesn't use it. Say slowly *Yes, a bird.* Repeat with the other pictures.
- Children do the same activity in pairs. Child A points to one of the animals and asks *What is it?* Child B replies *A rabbit. / It's a rabbit.* Circulate and encourage the children to always use the article "a."

2 CD2 18 WB p49 **Listen and connect the dots. Say the sentence.**

Aim: to practice pets and pencil control

- Ask in L1 if they have done a dot-to-dot picture like this before. Explain that they need to complete the picture by drawing a line from one small picture of an animal to the other. Play the audio. The first time, they listen and trace with their fingers. Play the audio again. The children listen and connect the dots.
- Play the sentence at the end again. The children point to their finished picture and repeat.

Audio script page T98

Extension activity

Aim: to practice asking and responding to *What is it?*

- If possible, move your class out into the playground, school gym, or an empty classroom.
- Have ready enough flashcards so that each child in your class can have one. Make sure that the flashcards make up groups of three or four.
- Give a flashcard to each child. Tell the children to keep their card hidden. Demonstrate the activity – hold a flashcard yourself and move around the classroom, asking individuals about their card *What is it?* Encourage the children to reply, e.g., *It's a pencil.* When you find a child with a card which is from the same group as the card you are holding, tell the class in L1 that it is the same group. Explain that the children need to find all the other people in the class who have cards from the same group.

Ending the lesson

Aim: to practice the chant

- Play the chant again. The children join in and do actions when they say the names of the pets.

2 CD2 17 Listen and color. Chant.

3 CD2 19 20 Listen and act. Listen and color.

1

2

3

4

Aims

- to present and practice responding to *jump, walk, fly, swim*

New language: *jump, walk, fly, swim*

Recycled language: pets, *What is it? It's a (rabbit)*, instructions (*Hands up, Hands down, Throw, Catch, Show me three*, etc.)

Materials: CD 2, flashcards (pets), the puppet (Polly)

Optional: CD of lively music

Language competences: The children will be able to follow new and familiar instructions.

Warm-up

Aim: to review *What is it?* and *It's a ... .*

- Review pets using the flashcards.
- Divide the class into two teams. Stick the pet flashcards on the board at a height your children can reach. Call one child from each team to the front. They stand at either side of the board. Explain in L1 that they need to listen and touch the right card on the board, as quickly as they can. Say, e.g., *It's a cat.* The child who touches the correct flashcard first wins a point for their team. If it's a tie, award a point to both teams. The children sit down and the next two children come to the front. Repeat until one of the teams reaches ten points. As the children become familiar with the game, encourage the class to ask *What is it?* before you say *It's a ...* each time.

Presentation

3 CD2 19 SB p50 **Listen and act.**

Aim: to present pets, *jump, walk, fly, swim*, and practice listening and responding physically

- Books closed. Ask the children to sit in a circle. Sit in the center. Play the first line of the audio, mime being a rabbit, and do the action (jump). Encourage the children to copy you. Say *Jump.* Do the action again, along with the children. Play the next line, mime and do the action. The children copy. Repeat for the rest of the recording.
- Play the audio again without pausing, doing the actions with the children. Repeat several times, until the children are confident. Play the audio for the children to do the actions without your help.

Audio script page T98

Practice

3 CD2 20 SB p50 **Listen and color.**

Aim: to practice new instructions and listening

- Say *Listen and color.* Remind the children by doing the action, that they have to color the circles below the pictures the correct color. Play the first line of the audio, point to the example, and show them the color they need to use for the circle under the picture. Then play the rest of the audio, pausing for children to color the circles each time.
- Point to picture 1 and elicit the color. Repeat for pictures 2 and 4.

Audio script page T98

3 CD2 21 WB p50 **Listen and circle.**

Aim: to practice new instructions, listening, and pencil control

- Point to the pictures on WB page 50 and elicit *A rabbit! Jump!* and *A cat! Walk!*
- Say *Listen and circle.* The children practice the circle shape in the air.
- Say *Listen! A rabbit! Jump! or A cat! Walk?* Play the audio. The children point to the correct picture. They draw the circle around the second picture. Circulate and elicit *A cat! Walk!* from individuals.

Audio script page T98

Extension activity

Aim: to practice responding to *jump, walk, fly, swim*

- If possible, move your class out into the playground, school gym, or an empty classroom.
- Play the traditional party game *Musical statues* with the children. Say one of the action words, e.g., *Fly, birds!* Put on the CD of lively music. The children move around like birds. When you stop the music, the children freeze like statues. Say another action, e.g., *Jump, rabbits!* as you start the music again. The game continues in this way. As the children gain confidence, you could add other known instructions.

Ending the lesson

Aim: to practice *jump, walk, fly, swim* and following instructions

- Put on the puppet. Play *Polly says* (see Introduction, page xvii) with the new verbs and instructions from earlier units (e.g., *Polly says "Stand up!," Polly says "Clap your hands!," Polly says "Hands up!," Polly says "Sit down!," Polly says "Go to sleep!"*). Review numbers 1 to 4 by saying, e.g., *Polly says "Show me three!"* The children hold up three fingers.
- End the lesson by asking the children to say *Goodbye!* to Polly.

Aims

- to sing a song with the class; to review pets and *jump, walk, fly, swim*

New language: *What is this? It's a ...*

Recycled language: *It's my ...* , pets, *jump, walk, fly, swim*, colors

Materials: CD 2, flashcards (pets, toys, classroom objects), red, blue, and green colored pencils or crayons for each child, the puppet (Polly)

Language competences: The children will be able to join in with a song.

Warm-up

Aim: to review *jump, walk, fly, swim*

- Do one of the actions from the previous lesson, e.g., fly like a bird. The children say the pet name and the action (e.g., *Bird! Fly!*). Repeat with the other pets.
- Ask the children to sit in a circle. Name each child with a pet word, around the circle, e.g., *Rabbit, cat, bird, fish*. Then say, e.g., *Rabbits! Jump!* All the children who are rabbits go into the center of the circle and jump around. Then say *Rabbits! Sit down, please.* Repeat for the other pets and actions (*Cats! Walk!*; *Birds! Fly!*; *Fish! Swim!*). Then repeat the game, but naming the groups in different orders. Sometimes repeat pets so that a group of children has to go into the center twice in a row.

Presentation

4 CD2 22 23 SB p51 **Listen and sing.**

Aim: to review pets, *It's my ...* , *jump, walk, fly, swim*, and sing a song

- Point to the girl on SB page 51 and ask *Who's this?* Elicit/Say *Rosemary*. Point to the pets in the picture and elicit the words. Say, e.g., *Point to the bird*. The children point. Repeat for *cat* and *fish*. Point to the swing and explain in L1 that the swing is singing to Rosemary. It wants to know what all the animals in the picture are.
- Play the song. The children listen and point to the appropriate animal in the picture for the verses.
- Play the song again, pausing to teach each line. The children mime being the animals mentioned in the verses while they sing.

Audio script page T98

Practice

4 WB p51 **Look and color.**

Aim: to practice *What is this? It's a ...* and colors

- Review colors (yellow, red, green, or blue) and classroom objects (pencils, chairs, bags, books). Point and ask *What is this?* Encourage the children to reply with a complete phrase, e.g., *A blue chair. / A green book.*
- Point to the puzzle on WB page 51 and elicit the colors. Make sure all the children have red, blue, and green crayons/pencils. Explain in L1 that they need to color all the sections with dots in the color shown. Demonstrate with the first few sections.
- Circulate and help as necessary. Point to the animals revealed as the children color and ask *What is this? What color?*

Extension activity

Aim: to practice the song

- Divide the class into two groups. One group is the swing, the other group is Rosemary. Play the song. The groups join in with the chorus or the verses, as appropriate. They all do the animal mimes. Swap roles and repeat.

Ending the lesson

Aim: to practice *What is this?* pets, toys, classroom objects, and *It's ...* .

- Hand out to eight volunteers one flashcard each of pets and toys. Point to each flashcard and ask the child *What is this?* He/She says *It's a ...* .
- Put on the puppet. Make Polly fly to one of the children with a flashcard and land on their head or shoulder. Polly asks *What is this?* The child replies *It's a (cat)*. Polly then flies to children who don't have flashcards, landing on their bags/chairs/books, etc. and asks *What is this?* Encourage the children to reply *It's my (bag)*.
- End the lesson by asking the children to say *Goodbye!* to Polly.

4 CD2 22 23 **Listen and sing.**

5 CD2 24 Sticker

The cat

Values

Aims

- to present a picture story; to review language from the unit

New language: *Let's go, Yippee, tree*

Recycled language: pets, *fly, walk, swim, jump, Look, Thank you*

Materials: CD 2, flashcards (pets)

Language competences: The children will be able to listen and follow a picture story.

Warm-up

Aim: to practice the song

- Play the song (CD 2, Track 22). Stick the bird, cat, and fish flashcards on the board as prompts. The children join in. Encourage them to mime being the animals (flying, walking, and swimming) as they sing.
- With the karaoke version (CD 2, Track 23), tell the children that together you can sing about the rabbit.

Presentation

5 CD2 24 SB pp52–53 **Story: The cat**

Aim: to listen and follow a picture story

- Point to each of the characters in the first picture on SB page 52 and ask *Who's this?* The children say, e.g., *(It's) Gina*. Point to the cat and ask *What is this?* The children reply *(It's a) cat*. Ask how Gina, Mike, and Leo feel in L1 (worried/ surprised) and why (because the cat is stuck in a tall tree).
- Play the CD. The children point to the pictures as they listen.
- Play the story again, stopping after each picture. The children explain what's happening in L1. Ask how the cat feels at the end of the story (happy). Point to the rabbit and the bird on page 53 and elicit the words.

  Audio script page T98

Practice

5 CD2 25 WB p52 **Listen and color the correct circle.**

Aim: to listen and identify the correct picture

- Point to the first picture on WB page 52 and ask in L1 who is speaking (Leo). Do the same for the second picture (Polly). Say *Listen. Leo or Polly?* Play the audio. Elicit the answer *Leo*.
- Remind the children that they have to color the correct circle. Play the audio again. Check their work as they color.
- Play the recording again. The children repeat Leo's line.

  Audio script page T98

Extension activity

Aim: to practice responding to instructions

- If possible, move your class out into the playground, school gym, or an empty classroom.
- Play a game to review instructions and extend the Ending the lesson activity. Divide the class into four groups: Rabbits, Cats, Birds, Fish. Give instructions to everyone at first, e.g., *Stand up! Hands up! Trees!* (encourage the children to stretch up like trees) *Clap your hands! Jump!* When the children are following with ease, mix in instructions addressed to the groups, e.g., *Cats – walk, Rabbits – jump, Fish – swim, Birds – fly.* Only the children in the named group do the action.
- You can make the game competitive – any child who joins in with the action of the wrong group is out. Then the group with the most people left at the end wins.

Ending the lesson

Aim: to practice listening and responding physically

- Ask in L1 where the cat was in the story (in a tree). Present *tree*. Draw a tree on the board. Tell the children that they are going to pretend to be trees.
- Do the following actions for the children to copy, giving instructions in English: *Stand up!* (stand up straight and tall with hands by your side), *Hands up!* (reach high up above your head, on tiptoes, arms outstretched as if they are branches), *Let's go!* (moving arms gently from side to side, as if they are branches moving in the wind), *Wheeee!* (moving arms more quickly), *Go to sleep, hands!* (stop moving your arms).

Aims

- to talk about the meaning of a story; to review language from the unit

Recycled language: pets, language from the story

Materials: CD 2, simple jigsaw made from a large picture of a pet (cut into five pieces with poster putty on each piece), Unit 6 stickers, colored pencils or crayons, pencils, a toy parachute (with handles for the children to hold), and a soft ball

Optional: character masks, cat flashcard (or a picture of a kitten)

Language competences: The children will be able to appreciate the values shown in the story.

Warm-up

Aim: to review pets and introduce the topic of working as a team

- Choose five volunteers. They stand at the front. Give each one a piece of the jigsaw you have made of a pet. Don't give them instructions, apart from pointing to the board. Leave the volunteers to work together to stick the pieces in the right order.
- Ask the rest of the class to give the volunteers a round of applause. Ask in L1 how they managed to complete the puzzle (by working together / as a team).

Practice

5 CD2 24 SB pp52–53 **Story: The cat**
Listen to the story. Stick.

Aim: to review the story

- Ask the children to tell you what they remember about the story on SB pages 52 and 53 in L1.
- Play the story again, pausing to ask what's happening and what the characters are saying.
- Hand out the stickers for Unit 6. Say *Bird*. The children point to the correct sticker on the sheet. Repeat for *rabbit*.
- Point to the picture on SB page 53. Say *Where's the bird?* The children point to the sticker outline. They peel off the sticker and hold it up. Check that they all have the correct sticker. Then say *Stick*. The children stick the sticker in their books. Repeat for the other sticker.

Audio script page T98

Story values SB pp52–53

Aim: to think about the meaning of the story: working as a team

- Play the first part of the story. Pause after picture 1 and ask in L1 *Who notices the cat in the tree?* (Leo.) Play the next section, and after picture 2 ask *Who comforts the cat?* (Polly, because she can fly up into the tree.) Play the next part of the story. Pause after picture 3 and ask *Who can rescue the cat?* (Gina, because she is tall.) *What is Mike doing?* (He's showing the way down.) Play the next part of the story, and after picture 4 ask *How does the cat get down?* (It slides down Gina's neck, in Mike's arms.) Play the rest of the story. Talk about how when we work as a team we can do things we couldn't do alone (all the animals play a part in helping the cat).

6 WB p53 **Complete the face. Color the picture.**

Aim: to apply values from the story to new situations

- Tell the children in L1 *Let's look at a family now.* Point to the dad in the picture on WB page 53 and ask *Who's this?* The children say *Dad*. Repeat with *brother* and *sister*. Point to the face and remind the children in L1 that if they think the picture shows people doing the right thing, they draw a happy smile. Circulate and check as they draw. Then the children can color the picture.

Extension activity

Aim: to reinforce understanding of the story

- Draw a tree on the board, with branches at a height your children can reach. Stick the cat flashcard or picture on one of the branches.
- Invite four volunteers to the front. Assign them the roles of Gina, Polly, Leo, and Mike. They put on the masks and act out the story along with the CD. Repeat with a different group.

Ending the lesson

Aim: to practice working as a team

- If possible, move your class out into the playground, school gym, or an empty classroom.
- Show the parachute and ask about its colors, if known. Show the children the soft ball and ask *What is this?* The children say, e.g., *It's a red ball.* Tell the children in L1 that they have to make the ball jump in the air and catch it again. But the ball can't fall on the floor. They stand in a circle and hold the handles of the parachute. Throw the ball into the middle of the parachute. Say *Throw the ball! Catch the ball!* Point out in L1 that it is important to work as a team, even in games.

Note: If you don't have a parachute, play *Tag* together (see Introduction, page xvii).

Family fun!

Value: Working as a team

Species

6 CD2 26 **Listen and point. Draw lines and say.**

1

2

3

Aims

- to integrate other areas of the curriculum through English: biology

New language: *hand*

Recycled language: *rabbit, cat, bird, fish, colors, What is this? It's a … , This is my … , walk, jump, fly*

Materials: CD 2, flashcards (pets), the puppet (Polly), materials for the project (a paper plate, cans of paint, paintbrush, one stick-on eye, a piece of letter size paper for each child), a "handprint bird" you have prepared (similar to the one on WB page 54)

Optional: playdough or modeling clay (one piece for each child)

Language competences: The children will be able to identify related animals.

Warm-up

Aim: to review pets and introduce the topic of species

- Put on the puppet. Play *Disappearing flashcards* using the pet flashcards (see Introduction, page xvii).
- Ask the children in L1 what kind of animal Polly is (a bird). Point out that there are different types of birds, and that they look different from one another, but they are all birds.

Presentation

6 CD2 26 SB p54 **Listen and point. Draw lines and say.**

Aim: to identify animals of different species

- Ask the children to look at SB page 54. Say *Listen and point*. Play the first section of the recording. The children listen and point to each picture one at a time. Join in yourself. Play the second section for the children to point without your help.
- Say *Draw lines*. Point to the line between the pictures of the birds. At the same time, say *Bird, bird, bird*. Explain in L1 that these animals are all part of the same group or species. Elicit things that all three birds have (e.g., wings, two legs, beaks).
- The children draw lines between the other groups of pictures. Circulate and help, pointing to some of the pictures and asking individual children *What's this?*

Audio script page T98

Practice

7 WB p54 **Make a handprint bird.**

Aim: to take part in a craft activity and review parts of a bird

- Show the pictures on WB page 54. Explain in L1 that you are all going to make a handprint bird. Show your hand and say/elicit *Hand*. The children repeat. Hold up the bird you have made and say *Look! This is my hand! This is my bird.* Explain how you made the bird in L1, using the pictures on WB page 54.
- Hand out the materials. Circulate and help the children make a print of their hand to form the head, body, and tail of the bird, then paint the beak and legs and stick on the eye. Ask individual children *What is this?* Elicit *Bird.* Point at the body, legs, and beak and ask *What color?*

Extension activity

Aim: to review vocabulary and practice fine motor skills

- Make a playdough model of a bird. Show the class and ask *What is this?* Tell the children they are going to make a model of one of the animals from the unit. Show the flashcards and elicit the words. Stick them on the board.
- Hand out playdough to each child. The children make the animal of their choice (rabbit, bird, fish, or cat). Circulate and help as necessary. Ask *What is this?* Show some of the best models to the class. Confident children can show and say, e.g., *This is my cat.*

Ending the lesson

Aim: to encourage the children to think about birds

- Ask the children to hold up or point to the handprint birds they have made. Encourage them to say *This is my bird.* Ask in L1 what they added to the handprint to make the birds (legs, beaks, eyes). Ask in L1 whether we have each of these things. The children say that we have legs and eyes, but we don't have beaks. Birds have beaks. Ask who has wings – people or birds?
- When the handprint birds are dry, the children hold them up and follow your instructions. Say *Birds, walk! Birds, jump! Birds, fly!*

Aims

- to review language and values from the unit; to encourage children to reflect on their learning

Recycled language: pets, *jump, walk, fly, swim, What's this? It's a ... .*

Materials: flashcards (pets, classroom objects, family, toys), a piece of thin cardboard with a hole cut in the middle (in order to reveal part of a flashcard picture), colored pencils or crayons

Optional: magnifying glasses (one for each pair or small group of children), items/material from the natural world for the children to look at in detail (e.g., feathers, tree bark, leaves, shells, acorns), if possible one per pair or small group

Language competences: The children will be able to make deductions based on visual evidence. The children will be able to use language from the unit.

Warm-up

Aim: to review vocabulary and introduce the idea of making deductions

- Show one of the flashcards from the course so far, covered by a piece of thin cardboard with a hole in it (the hole should be about five centimeters in diameter). Ask *What is this?* The children guess. Don't confirm answers. Move the card around so a different part of the flashcard is visible and ask again. If the children are having problems guessing, ask, e.g., *Is it a chair? Is it a doll?*
- Reveal the flashcard and elicit the answer. Point out that the children were using things they knew about the object (color, size, shape) to help them work out what it was (and what it wasn't).

Practice

7 Think! SB p55 **Look and say the words.**

Thinking skills: making deductions

- Point to the photographs on SB page 55. Say *Look and say the words.* The children work in pairs. They point to each picture and say what they think it is (in English).
- Point at the first photograph and ask *What is this?* The children say *It's a rabbit.* Talk about how they figured this out (the big foot, the tail). Repeat for the cat, bird, and fish.
- The children work in pairs. Child A points at one of the photographs and asks *What is this?* Child B replies *It's a (fish).*

8 WB p55 **Say the words. Color the circles.**

Aim: to create a record of learning

- Point to the pictures on WB page 55. The children say the words together.
- The children color the circles if they can say the words on their own.
- Circulate and help as necessary. Ask individual children to say the words.

Extension activity

Aim: to look at details of objects in the natural world

- Say *Let's look!* Show a magnifying glass and ask the children in L1 what it does (makes things bigger). Make pairs or small groups and give each one a magnifying glass and an object to look at. The children take turns looking at both sides of the object in detail. Circulate and ask the children what they notice (shape, colors, texture).

Note: If you don't have magnifying glasses, the children can make pictures by placing leaves or feathers below thin paper and rubbing a crayon on top. This reveals details of the shape and texture of the leaves in a similar way.

Ending the lesson

Aim: to review language from the unit

- Play the children's favorite game from the unit or sing the unit song.

Phonics

- See page T85 for Unit 6 Phonics.

7 Think! **Look and say the words.**

1

2

3

4

Phonics → page 85 Review → page 93

7 My food

1 CD2 28 **Listen and point. Say the food.**

pasta, salad, rice, cake

Aims

- to present and practice food

New language: *pasta, salad, rice, cake, food*

Recycled language: *I have ... , Where's the (salad)? It's there, big/small (cake)*

Materials: CD 2, a lunchbox or bag with five or six food items inside (e.g., an orange, a banana, some sandwiches, a tomato), flashcards (food), the puppet (Polly), pencils

Language competences: The children will be able to name food.

7

Warm-up

Aim: to introduce the topic

- Mime being hungry and take out your lunchbox. Open it and remove the items one by one, saying *Mmm ... Food* or *I have food* each time. Point to all the food and say *Look! My food!* Encourage the children to repeat food and tell them in L1 that they will be learning how to talk about food in English.

Presentation

1 CD2 28 SB p56 **Listen and point. Say the food.**

Aim: to present food

- Point to the characters and ask *Who's this?* The children say the names.
- Say *Listen*. Play the audio. The children just listen.
- Say *Listen and point*. Play the audio. The children listen and point to the food items with you. Make sure they are pointing from left to right and that they point to the correct picture for cake.
- Play the audio again. The children point and say.

Audio script page T98

Practice

- Show the food flashcards. Say each word. The children repeat. Say the words at different volumes. The children repeat in the same way.
- Draw a simple table on the board (two legs and tabletop) at a height the children can reach, and large enough for the four food flashcards. Stick the flashcards on the "table," point and say the words. The children repeat.
- Call a volunteer to the board and ask, e.g., *Where's the salad?* The child points. Encourage him/her to say, e.g., *Salad*. Confirm by saying *Yes. Salad. It's there*. Repeat with different volunteers.

1 WB p56 **Look and match. Say the food.**

Aim: to practice food and recognize size and shapes

- Point to each food one at a time and say the words. The children copy you. Repeat. Point to one of the big pictures and ask *Is it big? Is it small?* The children say *Big*. Repeat with different pictures.
- Say, e.g., *Point to the big cake*. The children point. Repeat for all the pictures.
- Say *Look and match*. Show the children how to draw a line from one of the big pictures (e.g., the big cake) to the smaller matching picture. They draw lines using pencils. Monitor and make sure they are matching the right pictures and using the correct grip. Ask individual children to point to the pictures and say, e.g., *Small pasta*.

Extension activity

Aim: to practice food

- Ask the children to sit in a circle. Place the food flashcards in the center, face up. Choose a confident child and say, e.g., *Rita, pasta!* The child comes to the center of the circle to collect the correct flashcard and sits back down. Point to the flashcard and ask *What's this?* He/She holds up the card and says, e.g., *(It's) pasta / I have pasta.*
- Repeat with different children for the other flashcards. Replace the flashcards when all four are taken and call on different children. Once the children are confident, call two children to take different flashcards, e.g., *Yolanda, rice! Mario, cake!* The two children come to the center together and see who can choose the correct card quickest. The game can also be played calling three children or even four children to take the cards.
- If you have less space, stick the flashcards on the board and call children to come to the front and choose.

Ending the lesson

Aim: to review food

- Put on the puppet. Play *No, Polly!* with the food flashcards (see Introduction, page xvii). Polly either points at the flashcards and says, e.g., *It's rice* or she holds them and says, e.g., *Mmm. I have salad!*
- Make Polly wave and say *Goodbye!* The children wave and say *Goodbye, Polly!*

Aims

- to present *I like (rice)* and practice food; to say a chant

New language: *I like (rice), eat*

Recycled language: *pasta, salad, rice, cake, I have... , It's ... ,* colors

Materials: CD 2, flashcards (food, colors), Yes/No cards, colored pencils or crayons, pencils

Optional: shopping bags (one for each pair of children), play cash register/calculator, play money with a picture of the food, not numbers (for each pair of children)

Language competences: The children will be able to talk about food they like. The children will be able to join in with a chant.

Warm-up

Aim: to review food

- Show the food flashcards one at a time. Say/Elicit the names. The children repeat.
- Show the flashcards again and ask *What is it?* The children reply *It's (pasta).*
- Give out the Yes/No cards. Say *Show me Yes.* The children hold up the correct card. Repeat for No.
- Hold up the rice flashcard and say *Mmm! Cake!* The children hold up the No card. Repeat several times for the other foods, mixing correct and incorrect sentences. Make some sentences with *I have* … and *It's* ….

Presentation

2 CD2 29 SB p57 **Listen and trace. Chant.**

Aim: to present *I like* … and *eat*, review food, and say a chant

- Show one of the food flashcards, e.g., pasta, lick your lips / rub your stomach, look very happy and say *I like pasta.* Mime eating pasta. Repeat for two more flashcards. Translate *I like* … into L1.
- Point to the food flashcards. The children say the food words.
- Play the first verse of the chant. Show the children how to trace the line from the first boy to the picture of the rice. Repeat the audio. The children trace the line with a pencil. Make sure they are tracing from left to right.
- Repeat for the rest of the chant, pausing after each verse for the children to trace.
- Say *Listen and chant.* Play the chant again line by line. The children listen and repeat. Mime eating each food for the *Eat, eat, eat* lines. Play the chant again for the children to join in and copy your mimes. They trace the lines from the children to the food as they chant.

Audio script page T99

Practice

- Hold up a food flashcard and say *I like* … . The children say the food. Say the whole sentence e.g., *Yes! I like cake.* Repeat with the color flashcards, e.g., *Yes! I like red.*

2 WB p57 **Draw something you like. Say the sentence.**

Aim: to practice *I like* … and food

- Point to the example drawing on WB page 57 and the heart. Elicit/Say *I like salad.* Point to the frame. Show some crayons and say *Draw something you like.* Translate into L1. Make sure the children understand that they have to draw pasta, rice, salad, or cake.
- Circulate and encourage individual children to say a sentence about their picture, e.g., *I like rice.* The children can also practice talking about their pictures in pairs.
- Invite volunteers to show their picture to the class and say a sentence with *I like* … .

Extension activity

Aim: to practice *I like* …

- Draw a shelf on the board. Stick the food flashcards on the "shelf" and elicit the words.
- Tell the class that you need a volunteer to be a sales clerk.
- Place a grocery bag at the front. Take one of the flashcards from the "shelf" on the board, and show it to the class. Say, e.g., *I like pasta* and put it in your shopping bag. Repeat for the other flashcards.
- Stand next to the sales clerk and pass him/her the items from your bag one by one. Encourage the child to say, e.g., *Pasta, thank you* and pretend to ring up the price on the cash register/calculator. Use play money to "pay." Put the food back in your bag and say *Goodbye!* to the sales clerk. Repeat the whole game with a different volunteer.
- The children can play the game in pairs using imaginary food instead of flashcards.

Ending the lesson

Aim: to practice *I like* …

- Mime eating a food, e.g., eating a slice of cake with your fingers. The children copy your mime and say the food. Say, e.g., *Yes, I like cake.*

2 CD2 29 Listen and trace. Chant.

3 CD2 30 31 Listen and act. Listen and color.

1

2

3

4

Aims

- to present and practice responding to *Eat the pasta, It's yummy* and *Wash your face*

New language: *Eat the … , It's yummy, Wash your face*

Recycled language: food, *I like … ,* instructions (*Go to sleep, Wake up, Stand up, Sit down, Walk, Jump, Fly, Swim,* etc.)

Materials: CD 2, the puppet (Polly), colored pencils or crayons, pencils

Language competences: The children will be able to follow new and familiar instructions.

Warm-up

Aim: to review food and *I like … .*

- Play the chant (CD 2, Track 29). The children join in and mime eating the different foods.

Presentation

3 CD2 30 SB p58 **Listen and act.**

Aim: to present new instructions and practice listening and responding physically

- Point to picture 1 on SB page 58 and say *Look! Pasta. Ooooo!* Model looking down at a plate of food and licking your lips. The children copy the action. Do the same for the other pictures (*Eat the pasta, It's yummy, Wash your face*). Translate *It's yummy* into L1.
- Play the first line of the audio. The children join in and do the action. Do the action along with the children. Repeat for the rest of the recording.
- Play the audio again without pausing, doing the actions with the children. Repeat several times. Play the audio for the children to follow the instructions without your help.
- Give more instructions, adding language from earlier units, e.g., *Stand up, please, Jump, Fly, Sit down, please, Go to sleep, Wake up, Stand up, please, Swim, Sit down, please, Eat the pasta, It's yummy.* The children follow. Speed up as they become more confident.

Audio script page T99

Practice

3 CD2 31 SB p58 **Listen and color.**

Aim: to practice new instructions and listening

- Say *Listen and color.* Remind the children that they have to color the circles the correct color. Play the first line of the audio and elicit the color. Show the children how to color the circle for picture 1, if necessary. Then play the rest of the audio, pausing for children to color the circle each time. Point to each picture one at a time and elicit the color and the sentence (e.g., for picture 1 *Red. Eat the pasta.*).

Audio script page T99

3 CD2 32 WB p58 **Listen and circle.**

Aim: to practice new instructions, listening, and pencil control

- Point to the first pair of pictures on WB page 58 and elicit *It's yummy* and *Wash your face.*
- Say *Listen and circle. It's yummy or wash your face?* Play number 1 on the audio. The children point to the correct picture. They draw the circle around the second picture. Elicit *Wash your face* from individuals.
- Point to the second pair of pictures and elicit *Eat the pasta (Yum, yum, yum)* and *Look! Pasta.* Say *Listen and circle.* Play number 2 on the audio.

The children choose the correct picture and circle. Elicit *Eat the pasta! Yum, yum, yum!* from individuals.

Audio script page T99

Extension activity

Aim: to practice following instructions and responding to new language

- If possible, move your class out into the playground, school gym, or an empty classroom.
- Divide the class into two teams (e.g., Reds and Blues). Give an instruction to each team one at a time (a mixture of familiar instructions and *Wash your face*, etc. from this lesson), e.g., *Reds, stand up! Blues, stand up! Reds, eat the pasta! Blues, wash your face! Reds, jump!* The children follow your instructions, with the two groups doing different actions at the same time.
- Once the children are following your instructions with ease, tell the children that they must say the action while doing it. For example, when you say *Reds, jump!* they'll have to say *Jump* while jumping.

Ending the lesson

Aim: to practice following instructions

- Put on the puppet. Play *Polly says …* using known instructions *Eat the pasta, Wash your face*, etc. (see Introduction, page xvii).

Aims

- to sing a song with the class; to practice *I like …* . and food

New language: *munch, crunch, lunch, yum*

Recycled language: food, *I like … , yummy (cake)*

Materials: CD 2, flashcards (food), character masks, a lunchbox (if possible filled with a lunch: sandwiches, fruit, drink, etc.), Yes/No cards, pencils

Optional: the puppet (Polly)

Language competences: The children will be able to join in with a song.

Warm-up

Aim: to review *Eat the pasta, It's yummy, Wash your face*

- Divide the class into four groups. Name them Leo, Mike, Gina, and Polly. Hand out character masks to each group (the children in the Leo group all wear Leo masks, etc.).
- Give instructions to each group, using the character names, e.g., *Leo! Eat the pasta.* The children in that particular group follow the instructions. Mix in some instructions for the whole class, e.g., *Everybody! Stand up and jump!*

Presentation

4 CD2 33 34 SB p59 **Listen and sing.**

Aim: to present *lunch* and sing a song

- Show the children the lunchbox. Take out the contents. Put them on your desk and say *Look! My lunch! Yum!* Pretend to start eating and then say in L1, *No, it's not lunchtime yet. This is my lunch.* Pack the food away and say again *Lunch.* The children repeat the word several times.
- Point to food on the table on SB page 59 and say *Look! Lunch! Yum!* Say *Where's the rice?* The children point to the bowl of rice on the table. Repeat for *salad, cake, tree,* and *rabbit.*
- Play the song. The children listen and point to the food on the table.
- Play the song again, pausing to teach each line. The children point to the foods and/or clap along as they sing.

Audio script page T99

Practice

4 WB p59 **Follow the path.**

Aim: to practice pencil control

- Point to the boy and the food and say *Oh, no! Where's lunch?* Explain in L1 that this is the boy from the song and the children need to help him find his lunch. Say, e.g., *Point to the rice.* The children point to the correct picture at the exit of the maze. Repeat for the other items.
- Show the children how to trace the route through the maze with their fingers. When they have figured out the route, they draw it with a pencil. Circulate and check they are using the correct grip and working from left to right. Encourage individuals to pretend to be the boy and say, e.g., *I like rice. Yum, yum, yum!*

Extension activity

Aim: to practice listening skills and review food

- Play *Singing Polly* (see Introduction, page xvii). Make Polly sing different nouns instead of the food in the song, e.g., *Munch, munch, munch, Crunch, crunch, crunch, I like yummy chairs!* Explain to the children that when they put up the No card, they have to say the word they think is wrong, e.g., *Chair.* They can also replace *yummy lunch* with *Polly's lunch* in the line *I like yummy lunch!*
- For the last chorus and verse, make Polly sing correctly and encourage everyone to join in, standing up, clapping, and dancing.
- Confident volunteers can come to the front and sing along with Polly.

Ending the lesson

Aim: to practice the song

- Play the song for the children to join in. Stick the flashcards rice, salad, and cake on the board as prompts.

4 CD2 33 34 **Listen and sing.**

Family fun!

The cake

5 CD2 35 Sticker

Values

Aims

- to present a picture story; to review language from the unit

New language: *Here's your cake, I have an idea. Let's get some ice cream, great, wonderful*

Recycled language: food, *lunch*, numbers, *dad*, *I like (cake)*, *yummy*, *Yes*, *Oh*, *no*, *What is it? It's ...*

Materials: CD 2, the puppet (Polly), flashcards (food, numbers), a picture of some ice cream, colored pencils or crayons

Optional: a large bowl and four spoons, character masks

Language competences: The children will be able to listen and follow a picture story.

Warm-up

Aim: to review *lunch, yummy* and *I like ...*

- Show the food flashcards. Say *I like ...* . The children say the food. Show a flashcard to a volunteer. The child says, e.g., *I like pasta*. Stick the flashcards on the board.
- Put on the puppet. She flies to a child and "lands" on his/her head or shoulder. She says, e.g., *I like the yummy pasta!* The child gives the pasta flashcard to Polly. Repeat with the other flashcards and different volunteers.

Presentation

5 CD2 35 SB pp60–61 **Story: The cake**

Aim: to listen and follow a picture story

- Show the picture of ice cream and say *Look! Ice cream*. The children repeat the word. Say *I like ice cream*. Invite volunteers to say *I like ice cream*.
- Point to the characters in the first picture on SB page 60 and ask *Who's this?* The children say *Leo* and *Dad*. Say *Yes. What's Leo's dad holding?* Point to the cake he is holding and say *What's this?* The children say *Cake*. Ask the children in L1 what kind of cake it is (a birthday cake).
- Play the CD. The children point to the pictures as they listen.
- Play the story again, stopping after each picture. The children explain what's happening in L1. Ask what is happening in picture 4 and what the cloud means (the children tell you in L1 that Gina has an idea – she is thinking about ice cream). Ask what the animals are doing in picture 5 (eating the ice cream) and where the candles are. Explain the meaning of *I have an idea* and *Let's get some ice cream*.

Audio script page T99

Practice

5 CD2 36 WB p60 **Listen and color the correct circles.**

Aim: to listen and identify the correct picture

- Point to the characters in the first pair of pictures on WB page 60. Ask *Who's this?* Say *Listen and color the circle*. Remind the children that they have to color one of the circles. Play the audio for number 1. Confirm the answer (the first picture).
- Play the audio again. Check the children's work as they color in the shaded circle.
- Repeat for the second pair of pictures.
- Play the whole recording again. The children repeat the two lines.

Audio script page T99

Extension activity

Aim: to practice language from the story

- Divide the class into four groups. Each group repeats and mimes a line from the story. Group 1 says *I like ice cream!* Group 2 *Yes, it's great!* Group 3 *Wonderful!* and Group 4 *Yummy!* Say each line several times, at different volumes. The children repeat in their groups. Encourage them to be enthusiastic.
- Choose a volunteer from each group. They stand at the front and put on character masks (1 Leo, 2 Mike, 3 Gina, 4 Polly). Put a large bowl in front of the children and give them each a spoon. They all mime eating and say the lines they have been practicing. Repeat with different volunteers.

Ending the lesson

Aim: to practice counting

- Draw four birthday cakes on the board, with one to four candles on each cake (e.g., three candles on one cake, two on the next, etc.). Make sure your children can reach the pictures.
- Point and say *Cakes! Yummy! I like cakes*. Count the cakes aloud with the children. Then point to the candles on the first cake and ask *How many?*
- Stick the number flashcards in order at the bottom of the board. Count them aloud with the children. Point to the flashcards in different orders and elicit the numbers.
- Call a volunteer to the board. He/She counts the candles on the first cake, chooses the correct number flashcard, and sticks it next to the cake. Repeat for the rest of the cakes.

Aims

- to talk about the meaning of a story; to review language from the unit

Recycled language: food, language from the story

Materials: CD 2, Unit 7 stickers, a piece of toy food (ice cream, pasta, cake, rice, or salad) or picture of known food items – one per pair of children, colored pencils or crayons

Optional: character masks, toy cake or cake flashcard, a large bowl, four spoons

Language competences: The children will be able to appreciate the values shown in the story. The children will be able to use and respond to language from the story.

Warm-up

Aim: to review language from the story

- Pretend that you have just thought of something and say *I have an idea!* Show the picture of the ice cream and say *Let's get some ice cream!* Encourage the children to reply *Wonderful!*
- Practice the lines *Let's get some ice cream* and *Wonderful*, with the children repeating after you. Make sure the children say *Wonderful* with enthusiasm and that they stress the first syllable. Once they are confident, add an action for each line (eating with a spoon for *Let's get some ice cream* and jumping up and down for *Wonderful*).

Practice

5 CD2 35 SB pp60–61 **Story: The cake**
Listen to the story. Stick.

Aim: to review the story

- Ask the children to tell you what they remember about the story on SB pages 60 and 61 in L1. Ask *What do Leo and his dad have at the beginning? What happens to the cake? What's Gina's idea? Do the animals like ice cream?*
- Play the story again, pausing to ask what is happening/elicit what the characters are saying.
- Hand out the stickers for Unit 7. Say *I like rice.* The children point to the correct sticker. Repeat for *pasta*.
- Point to the picture on SB page 61. Say *Where's the rice?* The children point to the sticker outline. Mime peeling the sticker of the rice off the sheet. The children peel off the sticker and hold it up. Check that they all have the correct sticker. Then say *Stick.* The children stick the sticker in their books. Repeat for the sticker of the salad.

Audio script page T99

Story values SB pp60–61

Aim: to think about the meaning of the story: sharing

- Play the story again. The children listen and point. At the end of the story ask in L1 *Who's eating the ice cream?* Talk about how important it is to share. Ask the children in L1 what they can share in class and at home (toys, books, crayons, etc.).

6 WB p61 **Complete the face. Color the picture.**

Aim: to apply values from the story to new situations

- Tell the children in L1 *We're going to look at some children now. Look at the picture and think.* Point to the cake and ask *What is it?* Ask in L1 *What are the children doing?* (Sharing.)

Elicit/Explain what the children are saying when they share – *Here's some cake. Thank you.* Point to the face and remind the children in L1 that if they think the children are doing the right thing, they draw a happy smile. Circulate and check as they draw. Then the children can color the picture.

Extension activity

Aim: to reinforce understanding of the story

- Invite five volunteers to the front. Assign them the roles of Leo, Leo's dad, Gina, Polly, and Mike. The children playing the main characters put on the character masks. Give "Leo's dad" a toy cake or the cake flashcard. Have a large bowl and four spoons ready for the last scene.
- Play the story. The children act along with the CD. Encourage them to join in with the CD and do the actions.
- Invite another group of five children to come to the front and act.

Ending the lesson

Aim: to practice sharing

- Hand a piece of toy food/picture of known food to a child. Say, e.g., *Here's some salad.* The child takes it and says *Thank you. (I like salad.)* Repeat with different children. Collect the toys/pictures.
- Hand out a piece of toy food/picture to each pair of children. They practice sharing, saying *Here's some …* and *Thank you. I like ….* Once they have practiced with one food, they swap their toy/picture with another pair and repeat. Circulate and help.

5
7

Solids and liquids

6 CD2 37 **Listen and point. Trace and say the food.**

1

2

3

4

Aims

- to integrate other areas of the curriculum through English: physics

New language: *soup, water*

Recycled language: food, *I have an idea ... , Let's get some ... , I like ...*

Materials: CD 2, flashcards (food, toys), materials for the project (green, red, and yellow colored pasta (e.g., fusilli), a piece of blue letter size thin cardboard and PVA glue with a brush for each child), character masks, pencils

Optional: pictures/photographs/real objects to show liquids and solids in the world around us, character masks

Language competences: The children will be able to differentiate between liquids and solids.

Warm-up

Aim: to review foods and *I have an idea. Let's get some ...*

- Review food using the flashcards.
- Divide the class into two teams. Stick the food flashcards on the board at a height your children can reach. Call one child from each team to the front. They stand at either side of the board. Explain in L1 that they need to listen and touch the right card on the board, as quickly as they can. Say, e.g., *I have an idea. Let's get some rice*. The child who touches the correct flashcard first wins a point for their team. Repeat until one of the teams reaches ten points. You could also add the toy flashcards to the board (and say, e.g., *Let's get a puzzle*) when the children are playing with ease.

Presentation

6 CD2 37 SB p62 **Listen and point. Trace and say the foods.**

Aim: to differentiate between solid and liquid food

- Ask the children to look at SB page 62. Point to the first picture and say *Look! Soup! Yummy! I like soup*. Say *Soup* again. The children practice saying the word. Repeat for the other pictures.
- Play the first section of the recording. The children listen and point to each picture one at a time. Join in yourself. Repeat for the second section. Play the third section for the children to point without your help.
- Point to the line around the first picture and trace it with your finger. At the same time, say *Soup*. The children copy. Do the same for the other pictures. The children trace around the pictures and say the words. Ask in L1 which foods go together (soup and water, pasta and cake). Do not try to explain "liquid" and "solid" in L1 – say, e.g., that we can drink soup and water, but we eat pasta and cake because they are hard.

Audio script page T99

Practice

7 WB p62 **Make a pasta fish.**

Aim: to take part in a craft activity and encourage recognition of texture

- Show the pictures on WB page 62. Explain in L1 that you are all going to make a picture of a fish, like the girl in the picture. Point to the fish in the picture and ask *What is this?* Elicit *Fish*. Point to the red, green, and yellow pasta and elicit the colors. Show the real pasta and elicit *Pasta*.
- Hand out the materials. Circulate and help the children make their picture, following the steps shown in the pictures. Ask individual children *What is this? What color is it?*
- Ask volunteers to show their pictures to the class and say *Look at my pasta fish!*

Extension activity

Aim: to extend awareness of liquids and solids around us

- Stick the pictures of liquids and solids at the bottom of the board, at a height the children can reach (or place them on a table). Draw a line down the center of the board or draw a line on the table with a piece of chalk. Move one of the pictures of a liquid on one side of the line on the board. Choose a picture of a solid. Hold it next to the picture of the liquid and ask in L1 *Is it like this? Can we pour it / drink it / swim in it?* The children say *No*. Stick the picture on the other side of the line on the board. Repeat until all the pictures have been stuck on the board.

Ending the lesson

Aim: to review foods, toys, and language from the unit

- If possible, move your class into the playground, school gym, or an empty classroom.
- Stick the food flashcards in the four corners of the room.
- Divide the class into four teams. Name them Leo, Polly, Gina, and Mike. The children in each team can wear the appropriate character mask.
- Say, e.g., *Leo! I like cake!* The children in the Leo team run to the corner with the cake flashcard. Repeat for the three other flashcards, giving instructions to each team. Call the class back to the center. Play until the children are all following with ease.

Aims

- to review language and values from the unit; to encourage children to reflect on their learning

Recycled language: *soup, water,* food

Materials: colored pencils or crayons

Optional: flashcards (colors, toys, numbers, animals, food), cardboard box/basket for each team

Language competences: The children will be able to identify objects by their shape. The children will be able to use language from the unit.

Warm-up

Aim: to review food and *water, soup*

- Mime eating or drinking one of the foods from the unit (e.g., drinking water from a glass). Encourage the children to guess *Water.* Say *Yes! Water. I like water.* Repeat with different mimes, e.g., eating spaghetti (pasta), eating hot soup with a spoon, eating a slice of cake with your fingers, eating salad with a fork, eating ice cream from a cone.

Practice

7 Think! SB p63 **Look and match.**

Thinking skills: focusing on detail

- Point to the pictures in the top row on SB page 63. Say, e.g., *Point to the cake.* The children point.
- Say *Look and match.* Demonstrate by tracing your finger along the example line and saying *Cake … cake!* The children draw lines for the remaining pictures. Circulate and help. Ask individual children *What is this?* Encourage them to make a phrase, e.g., *It's cake. / I like cake.*

8 WB p63 **Say the food. Color the circles.**

Aim: to create a record of learning

- Point to the pictures on WB page 63. The children say the words together.
- The children color the circles if they can say the words on their own.
- Circulate and help as necessary. Ask individual children to say the words.

Extension activity

Aim: to practice categorizing and listening skills

- If possible, move your class out into the playground, school gym, or an empty classroom.

Note: This game is similar to the Extension activity in Unit 1, page T11.

- Divide the class into four teams. The teams stand in lines, with one child at the front. In front of each team, place a toy flashcard, a number flashcard, an animal flashcard, a color flashcard, a food flashcard, and, furthest away, a box or basket.
- Make a sentence about one of the flashcard categories, e.g., *I like red, green, yellow, and blue!* The first child in each team runs to pick up the color flashcard in their line of cards, puts it in the box/basket and runs to the back of their team. Say *Four, three, two, one!* The children now at the front run, pick up their team's number flashcard and put it in their box. They run to the back of their team. Do the same for the rest of the flashcards, using different language from the course so far (e.g., *Clean up the … , I have … , Let's get a …*).
- Practice the game slowly at first, then speed up. You can also make the game competitive – the fastest child wins a point for their team each time.

Ending the lesson

Aim: to review language from the unit

- Play the children's favorite game from the unit or sing the unit song.

Phonics

- See page T86 for Unit 7 Phonics.

Review

- See page T93 for Unit 6 & Unit 7 Review.

7 Think! Look and match.

Phonics → page 86 Review → page 93

Thinking skills: Focusing on detail

8 My clothes

1 CD2 40 Listen and point. Say the clothes.

Aims

- to present and practice clothes; to review colors

New language: *T-shirt, pants, dress, shoes, Look at my (pants)*

Recycled language: colors, characters, pets, *I have … , I like … , lovely*

Materials: CD 2, real items of clothing and pictures of clothing: a T-shirt, pants, dress, and some shoes in known colors (red, blue, green, yellow, orange, purple, and brown), a suitcase or bag large enough to hold the clothes, flashcards (colors and clothes), the puppet (Polly), pencils

Optional: shopping bag and/or shoe box (one for each pair of children), play cash register/calculator, play money (some for each pair of children), items of clothing for each pair of children to "buy" (if possible, a T-shirt, dress, pants, and pair of shoes)

Language competences: The children will be able to name clothes.

Warm-up

Aim: to introduce clothes and review colors

- Review colors with the flashcards. Make a point of reviewing purple, orange and brown with colored cards.
- Hold up your suitcase/bag and say *Look! This is my bag. Hmm. What's in my bag?* For each item ask again *What color?* and rephrase the response to make a sentence, e.g., *Yes. That's right. I have orange pants. / I like my orange pants.*

Presentation

1 CD2 40 SB p64 **Listen and point. Say the clothes.**

Aim: to present clothes

- Point to Leo and Gina and ask *Who's this?* The children say the names. Ask what they are doing in L1 (wearing a costume). Ask the children if they like to wear costumes.
- Say *Listen*. Play the audio. The children listen only the first time.
- Say *Listen and point*. Play the audio. The children listen and point to the clothes.
- Play the audio again. The children point and say.

Audio script page T99

Practice

- Show the pictures of the clothes in the known colors. Say each word. The children repeat. Say the words at different volumes. The children repeat in the same way. Ask the color of each item (*What color?*). The children say, e.g., *Blue*. Rephrase their response, e.g., *Yes. It's a blue dress*. Put on the puppet. Make Polly fly to a child who is wearing an item of clothing in a known color (e.g., a red T-shirt). Polly flies/sits near the item of clothing and says *I like your T-shirt. It's blue!* The child / the class correct Polly *No! Red T-shirt*. Polly says, e.g., *Oh, yes! It's a red T-shirt. It's nice*. Repeat with different children.

1 WB p64 **Look and circle. Say the clothes.**

Aim: to practice clothes

- Point to the pictures in the first row and elicit/say *T-shirt, T-shirt, fish*. Repeat with the children copying you. Point to the picture of the fish and say *Look! Fish is different*. Confirm in L1. Remind the children that they need to circle around this picture.
- The children find the different picture in the other rows and circle with a pencil. Circulate and help as necessary. Ask individual children to point at the rows and say the words.

Extension activity

Aim: to practice clothes and *I like …*

- Draw a "shelf" on the board. Stick the clothes flashcards on the shelf. Elicit the words.
- Ask a volunteer to be a sales clerk. Give him/her a toy cash register/calculator.
- Take one of the flashcards and show it to the class. Say, e.g., *Shoes. I like the shoes*. Keep it in your hand. Repeat for the other flashcards.
- Pass the sales clerk the flashcards one by one. Encourage the child to say, e.g., *Shoes, thank you*, and pretend to use the till/calculator. Use play money to "pay." The sales clerk puts the flashcards in a bag. Say *Goodbye!* Repeat the game with a different volunteer.
- The children can play the game in pairs using real clothing.

Ending the lesson

Aim: to review clothes and colors

- Show the clothes in turn. Ask *What is this? What color?* Rephrase the responses, e.g., *Yes, green pants*. Say, e.g., *Look at my green pants* before you put them back in your suitcase/bag.
- Point to the bag and ask *What's in my bag?* Elicit guesses, e.g., *Green pants*. Check in the bag, but don't show the item until someone has guessed. Then say *Yes! I have green pants* and give the item to the child. You can also add classroom objects.

Aims

- to present *I don't like (the purple dress)* and practice clothes; to say a chant

New language: *I don't like (the purple dress), But … , hat*

Recycled language: *T-shirt, pants, dress, shoes, colors, yes, no, I like …*

Materials: CD 2, flashcards (colors, clothes), the puppet (Polly), colored pencils/crayons in red, green, yellow, blue, orange, and purple, real items of clothing: T-shirts, pants, dresses, and shoes in known colors, CD of lively music, a hat, pencils

Optional: real items of clothing, two pieces of paper, one with a large check mark on it, one with a large X on it

Language competences: The children will be able to talk about clothes they like and dislike. The children will be able to join in with a chant.

Warm-up

Aim: to review clothes

- Show the flashcards of the clothes in turn. Say/Elicit the words. The children repeat.
- Put on the puppet. Play *Disappearing flashcards* (see Introduction, page xvii) with the clothes flashcards.

Presentation

2 CD2 41 SB p65 **Listen and color. Chant.**

Aim: to present *I don't like … ,* review *I like … ,* clothes and colors, and say a chant

- Point to the picture on SB page 65. Ask where the children are in L1.
- Point to each item in the window. The children say *Dress* or *Pants*.
- Say *Listen and color.* Play the first three lines of the audio. The children point to the first dress. Ask *What color?* Elicit *Purple*. Give them time to color. Repeat for the last line. Then do the same for *pants* in verse 2.
- Say *Listen and chant.* Teach the chant line by line. Then play it for the children to join in and point at the clothes.

Audio script page T99

Practice

- Show a real item of clothing. Ask *What's this? What color?* Say, e.g., *Blue shoes* and a sentence with *I like … / I don't like …* (e.g., *I like the blue shoes.*). Repeat several times.
- The children sit in a circle. Hand out items of clothing to children who are not next to each other. Elicit an opinion with *like / don't like* from each child with an item of clothing, e.g., *I don't like the green T-shirt*. Play the music. The children pass the clothes to their left. Repeat until everyone has had at least one turn.

2 CD2 42 WB p65 **Listen and cross out the "don't likes." Say the sentences.**

Aim: to practice *I like / don't like … ,* clothes and present *hat*

- Put on a hat and say *I like my hat. Hat!* The children repeat *Hat*. Chant *Hat, hat, my hat*. The children do the same.
- Point to the man on WB page 65 and say *This is Mr. Blue*. The children say *Mr. Blue*. Explain in L1 that Mr. Blue is going to talk about the pictures he likes / doesn't like. For each framed picture say, e.g., *Point to the blue cat*.
- Say *Cross out the "don't likes."* Draw an X on the board and make a large X in the air. The children copy.
- Play the first four lines of the audio and point to the example X. Play the next two lines and ask the children in L1 where to put the X. Give them time to cross out the correct picture. Repeat for the last two lines. Play the audio again. The children listen and repeat.

Audio script page T99

Extension activity

Aim: to practice *I like / don't like … ,* clothes and colors

- If possible, move your class into the playground, school gym, or an empty classroom.
- Stick a piece of paper with a check mark on it on one wall / in one corner and a piece of paper with an X on it on another wall. Hold up an item of clothing, e.g., a green T-shirt and say *Look! I like the green T-shirt.* Move to the check mark on the wall and repeat the sentence. Repeat the process for a negative sentence.
- The children stand in the center of the room. Show an item of clothing and make a sentence with *I like* or *I don't like*. The children run to the part of the room with the check mark or X, as appropriate. Call the class back to the center. Play again.

Ending the lesson

Aim: to practice *I like / don't like … ,* clothes and colors

- Play the chant again. Pretend to be Mr. Blue pointing to the different pictures in the gallery. Smile / give a "thumbs up" sign when you chant *I like …* and shake your head / give a "thumbs down" sign when you chant *I don't like … .* The children copy your miming.

2 CD2 41 Listen and color. Chant.

3 CD2 43 44 Listen and act. Listen and color.

Aims

- to present and practice responding to *Put on a/the ...*

New language: *Put on the shoes/a T-shirt, Stop*

Recycled language: clothes, colors, *Say "hello," dad*, instructions (*Go to sleep, Wake up, Walk, Jump, Swim, Fly, Eat the pasta, please, Wash your face*, etc.)

Materials: CD 2, flashcards (clothes), five or six different hats, CD of lively music, the puppet (Polly), colored pencils or crayons

Language competences: The children will be able to follow new and familiar instructions.

Warm-up

Aim: to review *hat* and *I like / don't like the ...*

- Show one of the hats you've brought and ask *What's this?* Ask about the color, if it is one of the known ones. Put on the hat, pretend to look in the mirror, smile / do a "thumbs up" and say *Look at my hat! I like the (red) hat.* Put on a different hat and look unhappy / do a "thumbs down" and say *I don't like the (purple) hat.*
- The children sit in a circle. Hand out all the hats. The children with hats put them on. Elicit *I like the hat* or *I don't like the hat* from each child wearing a hat. Play the music. The children pass the hats to their left. When the music stops, the children holding hats put them on. Elicit a *like / don't like* sentence from each child with a hat. Repeat until everyone has had at least one turn.

Presentation

3 CD2 43 SB p66 **Listen and act.**

Aim: to present new instructions and practice listening and responding physically

- Books closed. Ask the children to sit in a circle. Sit in the center. Play the first line of the audio and mime putting on shoes. Encourage the children to copy. Say *Put on the shoes!* Do the action again, along with the children. Play the next line, mime, and do the action. The children copy.
- Play the audio again without pausing, doing the actions with the children. Repeat several times, until the children are confident. Play the audio for the children to do the actions without your help.
- Give more instructions, e.g., *Stand up, Walk, Jump, Fly, Eat the pasta, Wash your face, Wash your hands, Clap your hands, Sit down, Put on the shoes.* The children follow. Speed up when they are confident.

Audio script page T99

Practice

3 CD2 44 SB p66 **Listen and color.**

Aim: to practice new instructions

- Say *Listen and color.* Remind the children that they have to color the circles. Play the first line of the audio and elicit the color. Show the children how to color the circle red next to picture 3, if necessary. Then play the rest of the audio, pausing for children to color each time. Point to each picture and elicit the color and the sentence (e.g., picture 1 *Blue. Put on your shoes*).

Audio script page T99

3 CD2 45 WB p66 **Listen and circle.**

Aim: to practice new instructions, listening, and pencil control

- Point to the first pair of pictures on WB page 66 and elicit *Put on a T-shirt* and *Put on a hat.*
- Say *Listen and circle. Put on a T-shirt or put on a hat?* Play number 1. The children point to the correct picture. They draw a circle around it. Elicit *Put on a hat* from individuals. Repeat for the second pair of pictures.

Audio script page T99

Extension activity

Aim: to practice responding to *Put on a/the ...* and present *Stop!*

- If possible, move your class out into the playground, school gym, or an empty classroom.
- Play the traditional party game *Musical statues*. Put on the CD of lively music. The children dance around. Stop the music and shout *Stop!* The children freeze like statues. Give an instruction from the lesson, e.g., *Put on the shoes!* The children mime putting on shoes. Start the music again. The game continues in this way. As the children gain confidence, add other known instructions, e.g., *Eat the pasta, Eat the cake, Wash your face, Clap your hands.*
- You can make the game competitive by telling the children who move in the "statue" phase that they are "out" of the game.

Ending the lesson

Aim: to practice following instructions

- Put on the puppet. Play *Polly says ...* using known instructions and *Put on ...* (see Introduction, page xvii).

Aims

- to sing a song with the class; to present and practice *clothes* and *Stop*

New language: *clothes, Stop*

Recycled language: clothes, *Put on the … , clothes, hat,* instructions, *I like / don't like …*

Materials: CD 2, Yes/No cards

Optional: photocopies for coloring – simple black and white outline drawings of a girl wearing a dress, shoes, and a hat, and a boy wearing pants, a T-shirt, and a hat, colored pencils or crayons, or a large piece of paper, and a set of colored pens

Language competences: The children will be able to join in with a song.

Warm-up

Aim: to review *Put on the …* and clothes

- Draw a stick figure on the board. Say *Put on the hat, please.* Draw a hat on the figure. Point to the picture and say *Put on the hat. Yes or no?* The children say *Yes.* Say *Put on the dress, please.* Draw some shoes on the picture. Say *Yes or no?* The children say *No.*
- Give out the Yes/No cards. Say *Show me Yes.* The children hold up the correct card. Repeat for No.
- Draw another stick figure on the board. Say *Put on the pants!* Draw a T-shirt on the figure. The children hold up the No card. Repeat several times for the other items of clothing, mixing correct and incorrect sentences.

Presentation

4 CD2 46 47 SB p67 **Listen and sing.**

Aim: to present *clothes* and sing a song

- Say *Stand up! Jump!* The children jump on the spot with you until you say *Stop!* Repeat with other known actions (e.g., *Fly, Walk, Swim, Throw the ball*). Each time, the children do the action continuously until you say *Stop!*
- Stick the clothes flashcards on the board. Elicit the words. Point to all the flashcards and say *Look at the clothes. Clothes.* Touch all your clothes and say *Clothes.* The children do the same. Then, point to the flashcards and say *Clothes.* The children repeat.
- Point to the clothes on the clothesline on SB page 67 and say *Look! Clothes. Point to the T-shirt.* The children point. Repeat for all the items on the clothesline.
- Play the song. The children listen and point to the appropriate item of clothing.
- Play the song again, pausing to teach each line. The children point as they sing.

Audio script page T99

Practice

4 SB p67 **Look and match the children with their clothes.**

Aim: to practice *clothes* and recognizing shapes

- Point at the pictures on the left and explain in L1 that they are the girl and boy from the song. Point to the pictures of clothes. Point to the girl and say *Clothes?* Show the children how to match the girl to her clothes. The children match the boy to his clothes. Monitor and help. Ask individual children *What is this? What color?* only pointing to known colors.

Extension activity

Aim: to practice clothes and colors

- Hand out the photocopies for coloring. Make sure the children have colored pencils/crayons in known colors (red, blue, yellow, green, orange, purple, and brown). They color the pictures as they wish. Circulate and help individuals to make phrases/sentences about their picture, according to ability, e.g., *A purple dress. / I like the red hat.*

Note: If you have not prepared pictures for coloring, draw simple figures on a large piece of paper. Stick the paper on the board and ask the children what colors you should use to complete the picture. Ask, e.g., *Hat? What color?* The children say, e.g., *Red hat.* Color the hat red. When the picture is finished, ask volunteers to make sentences with *I like … / I don't like …* about the different items of clothing.

Ending the lesson

Aim: to practice the song

- Play the song. Mime putting on the various items of clothing, and stand very still when you hear *Stop!* The children copy. Play the song again for the children to join in and mime.

8

4 CD2 46 47 **Listen and sing.**

Family fun!

5 CD2 48 Sticker

The party

Values

Aims

- to present a picture story; to review language from the unit

New language: *Don't worry, We can help, I like your (pants) and your (shoes)*

Recycled language: clothes, *hat, I like my ... , Look, Wow, nice, Put on your ...* , numbers

Materials: CD 2, flashcards (clothes), the puppet (Polly), colored pencils or crayons

Language competences: The children will be able to listen and follow a picture story. The children will be able to talk about other people's clothes with *I like your ...* .

Warm-up

Aim: to practice the song

- Stick the T-shirt, shoes, pants, and dress flashcards on the board. The children say the words. Play the song for the children to join in (CD 2, Track 46). Point to the flashcards as prompts.
- Put on the puppet. Play *Singing Polly* (see Introduction, page xvii). Polly makes mistakes with the clothes items, and sings *Show me* instead of *Put on* and *Go!* instead of *Stop!*

Presentation

5 CD2 48 SB pp68-69 **Story: The party**

Aim: to listen and follow a picture story

- Point to the characters on SB page 68 and ask *Who's this?* The children say, e.g., *(It's) Gina.* Ask in L1 why they are dressed up (they are wearing costumes) and if the children have ever been to a costume party. Elicit the clothes Gina, Leo, and Polly are wearing, by pointing to each item and asking *What is this?* (Gina – a dress and shoes, Leo – pants and a hat, Polly – pants and shoes). Point to picture 4 and ask in L1 how Mike feels (sad) and why (he isn't wearing a costume).
- Play the CD. The children point to the pictures as they listen.
- Play the story again, stopping after each picture. The children explain what's happening in L1. Explain the meaning of *Don't worry!* and *We can help*.
- Point to Mike's clothes in picture 5 and ask in L1 what he is dressed as (a king) and where the different items came from (Gina gave him the crown, Leo the pants and Polly the shoes). Ask what the other characters' costumes are in L1 (Gina is a ballerina, Leo is a pirate, Polly is a superhero).

Audio script page T100

Practice

5 CD2 49 WB p68 **Listen and color the correct circles.**

Aim: to listen and identify the correct picture

- Point to the characters in the first pair of pictures on WB page 68. Ask *Who's this?* Say *Listen and color the circle.* Remind the children that they have to color one of the circles. Play the audio for number 1. Confirm the answer (the second picture).
- Play the audio again. Check the children's work as they color in the circle.
- Repeat for the second pair of pictures.
- Play the whole recording again. The children repeat the two lines.

Audio script page T100

Extension activity

Aim: to review clothes and *Put on your ...*

- Mime putting on an item of clothing (shoes, pants, T-shirt, dress, or hat). The children say the clothes and the action e.g., *Put on your shoes!*. Repeat with the other items.
- Ask the children to sit in a circle. Name each child with a number from 1 to 4, around the circle. Then say, e.g., *Number 1! Put on your hat!* All the children who are number 1 go into the center of the circle and mime putting on a hat. Then say *Number 1! Sit down!* Repeat for the other numbers and items of clothing. Then repeat the game, but naming the groups in different orders. Sometimes repeat numbers so that a group of children has to go into the center twice in a row.

Note: You could also do this game using real clothing, depending on your children's ability (some children will not be able to put on pants or T-shirts themselves).

Ending the lesson

Aim: to practice *I like your ...*

- Put on the puppet. Make Polly fly and land on a child's shoulder. She makes a sentence about something the child is wearing or his/her bag, e.g., *I like your T-shirt. It's nice!* Encourage the child to say *Thank you.* Repeat with three or four other children.
- The children work in pairs. Child A compliments Child B about his/her clothing or possessions, e.g., *I like your bag.* Child B says *Thank you.* Then they swap roles.

Aims

- to talk about the meaning of a story; to review language from the unit

Recycled language: clothes, language from the story

Materials: CD 2, CD of lively music, Unit 8 stickers, the puppet (Polly), a bag (small enough for Polly to carry in her beak) with items which could belong to Polly in it (e.g., crayons, feathers, buttons, plastic food)

Optional: character masks, a cardboard/toy crown, a pair of adult-sized shoes, pants in the right size for the children in your class

Language competences: The children will be able to appreciate the values shown in the story. The children will be able to use and respond to language from the story.

Warm-up

Aim: to review *I like your …*

- The children stand up. Play some music. They walk around. Pause the music and say *Stop!* The children make pairs. They take turns saying something about the other person's clothes with *I like your … .* Play the music again. Repeat the activity.

Practice

5 CD2 48 SB pp68–69 **Story: The party**
Listen to the story. Stick.

Aim: to review the story

- Ask the children to tell you what they remember about the story on SB pages 68 and 69 in L1. Ask *Why are the animals wearing costumes? Why is Mike sad? Who helps him?*
- Play the story again, pausing after each picture to ask what the characters are wearing and what they are doing and saying in pictures 4 and 5.
- Hand out the stickers for Unit 8. Say *Where's the hat?* The children point to the correct sticker. Repeat for *pants*.
- Point to the picture on SB page 69. Say *Where's the hat?* The children point to the sticker outline.

Mime peeling the sticker of the hat off the sheet. The children peel off the sticker and hold it up. Check that they all have the correct sticker. Then say *Stick*. The children stick the sticker in their books. Repeat for the sticker of the pants.

Audio script page T100

Story values SB pp68–69

Aim: to think about the meaning of the story: including your friends

- Play the story again. The children listen and point. Pause after picture 4 and ask in L1 *How does Mike feel?* (Sad. He doesn't have clothes.) Ask how the other characters feel in picture 4. *Are they happy?* (No. They feel sad for Mike.) Elicit/Remind the children what they say (*Don't worry. We can help.*). Play the last part of the story and ask how all the animals feel now. Point out that when we include our friends, everyone feels happy. Explain that lending and sharing toys is a way of including others.

6 WB p69 **Complete the face. Color the picture.**

Aim: to apply values from the story to new situations

- Tell the children in L1 *We're going to look at some children now. Look at the picture and think.* Point to the face on WB page 69 and remind the children in L1 that if they think the picture shows the right thing (including everyone in the game), they draw a happy smile. Circulate and check as they draw. Then the children can color the picture.

Extension activity

Aim: to reinforce understanding of the story

- Invite four volunteers to the front. Assign them the roles of Gina, Leo, Polly, and Mike. They put on the character masks. Give the child playing Gina a cardboard/paper or toy crown, the child playing Leo a pair of pants and the child playing Polly a pair of shoes. Help the children put on the items. (If you don't have the clothes, use flashcards.) Play the story. Encourage the volunteers to join in with the CD and act in the same way as the characters. The children take off the crown, pants and shoes and put them on "Mike" at the end of the story. Everyone then acts out being happy and walking off to the costume party.
- Invite another group of four children to come to the front and act.

Ending the lesson

Aim: to practice *Don't worry* and *We can help*

- Put on the puppet. Make her pick up her bag (with small items in) and fly. She accidentally turns the bag upside down and everything falls on the floor. Make Polly say *Oh, no!* Say *Don't worry, Polly.* Pretend that Polly can't hear you and ask the children to join in. Say *Don't worry, Polly* several times all together. Polly cheers up. Say *We can help!* Encourage the children to repeat. Call volunteers to help pick up Polly's belongings and put them back in her bag. Make Polly say *Thank you!* and *Goodbye!* to end the lesson.

5

Wearing a costume

6 CD2 50 **Listen and point. Trace and say the words.**

1

2

3

Aims

- to integrate other areas of the curriculum through English: social studies

New language: *shirt, black*

Recycled language: *I have a … , hat*, clothes, colors, classroom objects, toys

Materials: CD 2, a selection of classroom objects (pencil, book), toys (doll, ball, car), and items of clothing (shoes, hat, T-shirt, pants, dress) all in known colors (red, green, yellow, blue, orange, purple, or brown), a man's shirt, a bag, materials for the project (a paper plate (pre-cut, as on WB page 70), paints, brushes, stars and circles, a glue stick), a hat you have prepared (similar to the one on WB page 70), pencils

Optional: dress-up clothes for the children to play with/share (costumes for, e.g., police officers, doctors, princesses, firefighters, builders)

Language competences: The children will be able to identify items of clothing.

Warm-up

Aim: to review clothes, classroom objects, toys, colors and *I have …*

- Show the children each of the items from your bag. Say, e.g., *I have a blue hat*. Then put it in the bag. Present *Shirt*. The children repeat the new word.
- Invite a volunteer to the front. With eyes closed, he/she takes an object out of the bag. Encourage the child to make a sentence with *I have …* , according to ability. The child takes the object back to his/her place. Repeat with different volunteers. Collect the objects by saying, e.g., *Where's my blue hat?* The child with the correct object puts it back in the bag. Say *Thank you, (name). Good. I have my blue hat.*

Presentation

6 CD2 50 SB p70 **Listen and point. Trace and say the words.**

Aim: to identify items of clothing in costumes

- Ask the children to look at SB page 70. Point to the first picture and ask in L1 what the boy is dressed as (a firefighter). Say *Point to the hat. What color? Point to the pants. What color?* Repeat for the other pictures. Introduce *Black* and ask the children to repeat the word.
- Play the first section of the recording. The children listen and point to the picture. Join in yourself. Repeat for the second and third sections.
- Point to the line around the first picture and trace it with your finger. At the same time, say *A red hat. Blue pants.* The children copy. Do the same for the other pictures. The children trace around the pictures and say the clothes and colors.

Audio script page T100

Practice

7 WB p70 **Make a hat.**

Aim: to take part in a craft activity, review *hat* and colors

- Show the pictures on WB page 70. Explain in L1 that you are all going to make a hat, like the one in the picture. Show the one you prepared earlier.
- Hand out the materials. Circulate and help the children make their hats. Point to the decorations on individual children's hats and ask *What color?* Say *I like your hat! It's great!* Encourage the children to compliment each other in the same way.

Extension activity

Aim: to focus on the lesson topic through play and practice sharing

- Hand out the dress-up clothes and let the children choose what to wear. Encourage the children to share/include their friends and take turns, if you don't have an outfit for every child. Circulate and ask about items of clothing. Say *What's this? What color?* Help individuals to say, e.g., *I have a blue hat and black pants. / I like my shirt*. The children can then talk about what they are wearing in this way in pairs or small groups.

Ending the lesson

Aim: to review clothes, classroom objects, toys, colors and *I have …*

- Show the bag from the beginning of the lesson (see Warm-up), this time with all the objects inside. Ask the children in L1 if they can remember what is in your bag. The children guess, e.g., *A hat*. Ask *What color?* When the children have guessed the object and the color, take it out of the bag. Say, e.g., *Yes! That's right! I have a purple hat.* If the children have problems remembering any of the objects, give clues by miming (putting the item on, if it is clothing; using it, if it is a classroom object; playing with it, if it is a toy).

Aims

- to review language and values from the unit; to encourage children to reflect on their learning

Recycled language: vocabulary Units 1 to 8, *I like … / I don't like …* , *I have …*

Materials: flashcards (clothes, toys, colors, classroom objects, animals)

Optional: Two cardboard boxes per team of children, a selection of objects for each team: two hats / two shirts in different (known) colors, a package of pasta, a bag of rice, two color flashcards, stuffed animals or animal flashcards, pencils, colored pencils or crayons

Language competences: The children will be able to categorize items. The children will be able to use language from the unit.

Warm-up

Aim: to review vocabulary from Units 1 to 8

- Ask the children to sit in a circle. Hand everyone a flashcard, mixing up cards from earlier units and Unit 8, so that there are at least three cards from each category (e.g., for 14 children: three classroom objects, three toys, four animals, four clothes). Take a flashcard yourself. They all name, one at a time, what is on their flashcards.

Practice

7 Think! SB p71 **Circle the clothes.**

Thinking skills: categorizing

- Show your flashcard and say, e.g., *I have a rabbit*. Turn your flashcard face down and put it in front of you. Turn to your neighbor. He/She shows his/her flashcard and makes a sentence with *I have (a) …* , putting the card face down afterwards. Continue around the circle. After three or four children have had a turn, point to one of the hidden flashcards and ask *What's this?* When everyone has spoken, they turn their flashcards over and stand up. Tell them to make groups – demonstrate yourself (e.g., if you have a rabbit flashcard, find the other children who have animals and stand together). Help as necessary.
- Point to the photographs on SB page 71. Say, e.g., *Point to the shoes*. The children point. Say *Yes, clothes*.
- Say *Circle the clothes*. Explain in L1 that the children need to choose only the clothes. Point to the example circle around the T-shirt. Show the children how to complete it. They work individually to circle the photographs of clothes. Circulate and help. Then elicit the names of the clothes which the children have circled.

8 WB p71 **Say the clothes. Color the circles.**

Aim: to create a record of learning

- Point to the pictures on WB page 71. The children say the words together.
- The children color the circles if they can say the words on their own.
- Circulate and help as necessary. Ask individual children to say the words.

Extension activity

Aim: to practice listening skills, vocabulary, and *I like … / I don't like …*

- If possible, move your class into the playground, school gym, or an empty classroom.
- Divide the class into two teams. The teams stand in lines, with one child at the front. In front of the teams, place a selection of objects, so they are easy to see. Further away, place two boxes, one with a large check mark on it and one with a large X on it.
- Take, e.g., a package of pasta and a bag of rice (or flashcards). Say *I like pasta*. Put the pasta in the box with the check mark. Say *I don't like rice*. Put the rice in the box with the X. Confirm in L1 that the box with the check mark is for things you like, and the box with an X is for things you don't like.
- Practice the game slowly at first. Say, e.g., *I don't like the red hat!* The first child in each team tries to be first to pick up the red hat from the objects and put it in the box with the X on it. He/She then runs to the back. Say, e.g., *I like the blue hat*. The children now at the front both try to pick up the blue hat and put it in the box with the check mark. Repeat for all the objects. As the children gain confidence, keep score (whoever puts the object in the correct box first wins a point for his/her team). The team with the most points wins.

Ending the lesson

Aim: to review language from the unit

- Play the children's favorite game from the unit or sing the unit song.

Phonics

- See page T87 for Unit 8 Phonics.

7 Think! **Circle the clothes.**

Phonics → page 87 Review → page 94

9 My park

1 CD2 52 Listen and point. Say the words.

slide, merry-go-round, seesaw, swing

Aims

- to present and practice play equipment; to present and practice *The … 's (yellow)*

New language: *slide, merry-go-round, seesaw, swing, park, The … 's (yellow)*

Recycled language: character names, *cat, and,* colors, *I like (your) …* , instructions

Materials: CD 2, photographs of parks and outdoor playgrounds, flashcards (park), coloring pencils or crayons, the puppet (Polly)

Optional: materials to make junk models of play equipment (e.g., pieces of thick cardboard, cardboard rolls, pipe cleaners, string, drinking straws, Scotch tape/glue, paints, and brushes) or building blocks, a model you have already made (e.g., of a swing)

Language competences: The children will be able to name play equipment.

Warm-up

Aim: to introduce the unit topic

- Show a photograph of a park and say *Look! A park! I like the park*. Say *Park*. The children repeat. Say the word in a whisper. The children whisper back. Repeat with different tones of voice and volumes.

Presentation

1 CD2 52 SB p72 **Listen and point. Say the words.**

Aim: to present play equipment

- Point to the picture on SB page 72. Say *Look! Leo, Gina, Polly, and Mike are at the park.* Point at the cat and ask *What's this?* Say *Listen.* Play the audio. The children just listen.
- Say *Listen and point*. Play the audio and point to the play equipment. Say *Listen and point.* Play the audio again. The children point.
- Say *Say the words*. Play the audio again. The children point and join in. Help them to stress the first syllable of *merry-go-round* and *seesaw* and manage the consonant pairs at the beginning of *swing* and *slide*.

Audio script page T100

Practice

- Say *Stand up! We're at the park!* Teach mimes as follows:
  Slide = Walking up steps, sitting at the top of the slide and pushing off.
  Merry-go-round = Turning around on the spot.
  Seesaw = Squatting down and up again (bending knees).
  Swing = Miming sitting, holding onto the chains, and moving backwards and forwards.
- Show one of the park flashcards, say the word, and do the mime. The children copy. Repeat for the other flashcards.
- Say a word. The children mime. Mix up the words and speed up, as the children become more confident. Add known instructions (e.g., *Clap your hands, Sit down, Go to sleep, Wake up, Throw the ball*).

1 CD2 53 WB p72 **Listen and color. Say the words.**

Aim: to practice play equipment, review colors and practice listening skills, to present and practice *The … 's (yellow)*

- Make sure each child has crayons/pencils (red, blue, green, and yellow).
- Say *Listen and point*. Then say, e.g., *I like the swing*. The children point to the correct picture. Repeat for the rest of the equipment.
- Say *Listen and color.* Play the first line of the audio. Point to the picture of the merry-go-round and say *The merry-go-round's …* . The children reply *Yellow*. Show the children how to color the picture. Play the rest of the audio. Pause after each item for the children to color.
- Point to the finished pictures and say *The (merry-go-round)'s …* . Repeat the sentence after the children say the colors, e.g., *Yes! The merry-go-round's yellow*. The children repeat the whole sentence.

Audio script page T100

Extension activity

Aim: to practice play equipment

- Show the junk model you have made and ask *What's this?* The children say, e.g., *a swing*. Explain in L1 that they are going to make a model of one of the pieces of play equipment.
- Hand out the materials – children can work individually or in pairs. Circulate and help with cutting and sticking as necessary. Ask individuals *What's this?* to practice the new words and say, e.g., *I like your swing*.

Ending the lesson

Aim: to review play equipment

- Put on the puppet. Make Polly say *I like the park!* Make Polly do one of the play equipment mimes and say *I like the …* . The children say the missing word. Repeat for the other pieces of play equipment. The children can join in with the mimes.

Aims

- to practice *is* (*The … 's fun*); to practice playground equipment; to say a chant

New language: *The (swing)'s fun, In our park*

Recycled language: *The (swing)'s (yellow)*, playground equipment, colors, clothes, *Look! A (slide)! Wow!*

Materials: CD 2, flashcards (park), Yes/No cards, finished models of playground equipment (or pictures of playground equipment in known colors), pencils

Language competences: The children will be able to use *is*.
The children will be able to join in with a chant.

Warm-up

Aim: to practice play equipment and *The (swing)'s (yellow)*

- Review the play equipment words with the flashcards.
- Give out the Yes/No cards. Say *Show me No*. The children hold up the correct card. Repeat for Yes.
- Show a picture of a piece of play equipment / one of the flashcards / one of the models from the previous lesson. Make a true sentence about it, e.g., *The seesaw's blue*. The children hold up the Yes card, and say *Yes, the seesaw's blue*. Repeat for the other pieces of playground equipment. The children hold up the appropriate card each time.

Presentation

2 CD2 54 SB p73 **Listen and match. Chant.**

Aim: to present and practice *The (swing)'s fun*, to say a chant

- Show the swing flashcard and elicit the word. Say *The swing's fun!* Look very happy/excited. Translate *fun* into L1. Say the sentence again for the children to repeat. Do the same for the other flashcards.
- Point to the first picture on SB page 73. Say *Listen and match* and play the first verse of the chant. Trace a line from the girl to the swing with your finger. The children copy. Repeat for the other three verses.
- Play the whole chant, pausing for the children to draw lines from the pictures in the top row to the play equipment. Circulate and help.
- Play the chant again. The children listen and follow the lines they have drawn with their fingers.
- Say *Listen and chant*. Play the chant again line by line. The children listen and repeat. Explain the meaning of *In our park* in L1. Play the chant again for the children to join in. They trace the lines they drew as they chant.

Audio script page T100

Practice

- Stick the park flashcards on the board, in the same order as the chant (swing, slide, seesaw, merry-go-round). Play the chant again, doing a mime for each verse. The children copy. Point to the flashcards as prompts.

2 CD2 55 WB p73 **Listen and connect the dots. Say the sentence.**

Aim: to practice *The (swing)'s fun* and pencil control

- Ask the children to look at WB page 73. Remind them in L1 that they need to complete the picture by drawing a line from one small picture to another (as in Unit 6, page 49). Review the clothes words by saying, e.g., *Point to the pants*.
- Play the audio. The first time, the children listen and trace with their fingers. Play the audio again. They listen and connect the dots.
- Play the sentence at the end again. The children point to their finished picture and repeat.

Audio script page T100

Extension activity

Aim: to practice playground equipment, *is*, *I like …* and listening skills

- If possible, move your class into the playground, school gym, or an empty classroom.
- Stick the park flashcards on four different walls.
- The children stand in the center of the room. Make a sentence with one of the words, e.g., *The merry-go-round's red* or *I like the merry-go-round*. The children run to the wall with the picture of the merry-go-round. Tell them that if they hear a false sentence, they must stay in the center. Mix in false sentences about the color of the items.

Ending the lesson

Aim: to practice the chant

- Play the chant again for the children to join in. They stand up and do the mime for each piece of play equipment. Use flashcards as prompts on the board, if necessary.

2 CD2 54 Listen and match. Chant.

1

2

3

4

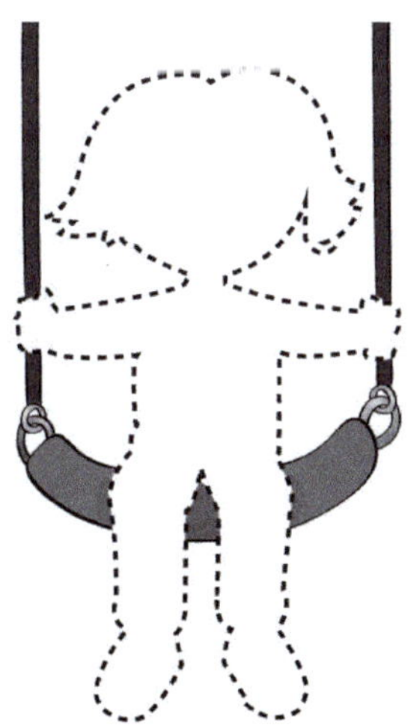

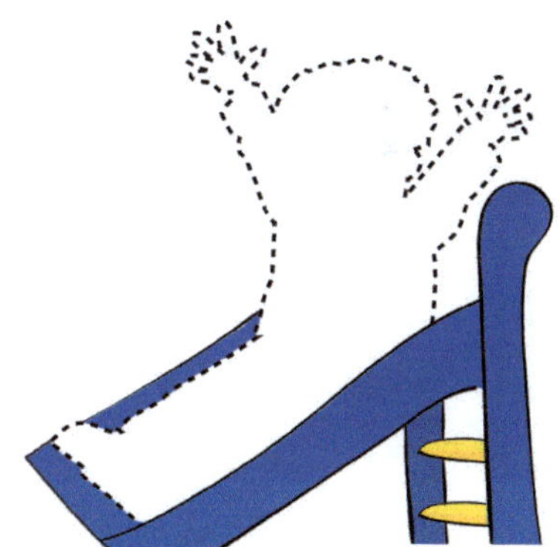

3 CD2 56 57 Listen and act. Listen and color.

Aims

- to practice responding to *Sit down on the …* and *Down/Up you go*

New language: *on the, Down/Up you go*

Recycled language: *Oh, no*, playground equipment, *The (swing)'s fun, In our park*, instructions (*Put on your shoes, Put on your hat, Eat the pasta, Wash your face*, etc.)

Materials: CD 2, pencils, colored pencils/crayons, the puppet (Polly)

Optional: CD of lively music, chairs (one for each child)

Language competences: The children will be able to follow instructions.

Warm-up

Aim: to review play equipment and *The (swing)'s fun, In our park*

- Play the chant (CD 2, Track 54). The children join in and mime playing on the different play equipment.

Presentation

3 CD2 56 SB p74 **Listen and act.**

Aim: to present new instructions and practice listening and responding physically

- Books closed. Ask the children to sit in a circle. Stand in the center. Play the first line of the audio and mime climbing onto one end of a seesaw and sitting down. The children stand up and copy you. Say *Sit down on the seesaw.* Do the action again, along with the children. Play the next line, mime, and do the action. The children copy. Repeat for the rest of the recording (for *Oh, no!* mime taking off from the seesaw into the air, stretching up to the sky).
- Play the audio again without pausing, doing the actions with the children. Repeat several times, until the children are confident. Play the audio for the children to do the actions without your help.
- Give more instructions, e.g., *Sit down, Put on your shoes, Stand up, Put on your hat.* The children follow. Speed up when they are confident.

Audio script page T100

Practice

3 CD2 57 SB p74 **Listen and color.**

Aim: to practice new instructions and listening

- Say *Listen and color.* Remind the children in L1 that they have to color the circles below the pictures the correct color. Play the first line of the audio and elicit the color. Show the children how to color the circle red next to picture 3. Then play the rest of the audio, pausing for children to color the circle each time.
- Point to each picture and elicit the color and the sentence.

Audio script page T100

3 CD2 58 WB p74 **Listen and circle.**

Aim: to practice new instructions, listening, and pencil control

- Point to the first pair of pictures on WB page 74 and elicit *Sit down on the seesaw* and *Oh, no!*
- Say *Listen and circle. Sit down on the seesaw or Oh, no!?* Play number 1. The children point to the correct picture. They draw a circle around it. Elicit *Sit down on the seesaw* from individuals. Repeat for the second pair of pictures.

Audio script page T100

Extension activity

Aim: to practice *Sit down on the … / Stand up* and play a traditional party game

- If possible, move your class into the playground, school gym, or an empty classroom.
- Arrange some chairs in the center of the space in one row (or two rows back to back, depending on numbers). Use enough chairs for all the children.
- Explain in L1 that you are going to play some music and that when it stops the children have to sit down. Play the music. Say *Walk!* The children walk around the outside of the chairs. Stop the music and say *Sit down on the chairs!* The children all sit down. Say *Stand up!* The children stand up and move away from the chairs. Take away one of the chairs. Repeat the procedure. This time when the music stops, one child will not have a chair. This child is "out" and stands to one side / helps with the music. The child who sits down on the last chair is the winner.

Note: Use as much English as you can during the game, e.g., *Stop! Go!* and count the chairs with the children when four, three, two, and only one remain.

Ending the lesson

Aim: to practice following instructions

- Put on the puppet. Play *Polly says …* using known instructions: *Sit down on the seesaw, Up/Down you go, Oh, no!* (see Introduction, page xvii).

Aims

- to sing a song with the class

New language: *Let's go to the park, everyone, Swing on the swing, Slide on the slide, Round the merry-go-round*

Recycled language: instructions, *The (park) is fun*, playground equipment, numbers 1 to 4, toys (optional)

Materials: CD 2, flashcards (park), pencils

Optional: flashcards (toys) or real toys – a doll, a car, a ball

Language competences: The children will be able to join in with a song.

Warm-up

Aim: to encourage children to respond to new instructions and present *Swing on the swing* and *Slide on the slide*

- Say *Stand up, please. Sit down on the seesaw. Up you go. Down you go*, doing the actions at the same time. The children copy. Repeat with the children joining in with the instructions, according to ability.
- When the children are following with ease, add new instructions, e.g., *Sit down on your chair* (the children mime sitting on chairs / actually sit down), *Sit down in the car* (they mime getting into a car), *Sit down on the slide* (they mime climbing the steps of a slide and sitting down), *Sit down on the swing* (they mime getting onto a swing and holding the chains). Join in with the new actions at first, then repeat the instructions for the children to follow on their own.
- Say *Sit down on the swing*, then say *Swing on the swing* and encourage the children to mime swinging back and forth. Do the same for *Slide on the slide* (by gesturing sliding down with your arm).

Presentation

4 CD2 59 60 SB p75 **Listen and sing.**

Aim: to practice following instructions, *The (swing) is fun* and sing a song

- Point to the picture on SB page 75. Ask in L1 *Where are the children?* Elicit *A park* and then the names of the play equipment.
- Say *Listen and point*. Play the chorus and first verse of the song. The children point to the swing. Say *Yes! Swing on the swing. The swing is fun!* Continue in this way for the other two verses.
- Play the song again, pausing to teach each line. Translate *Let's go the park, everyone* into L1 and gesture to help show the meaning of *everyone*. The children mime playing on the swing, slide, and merry-go-round as they sing.

Audio script page T100

Practice

4 WB p75 **Follow the path and count the swings.**

Aim: to practice pencil control and counting

- Point to the boy and the girl from the song and say *Let's go to the park*.
- Show the children how to trace the route through the maze with their fingers. When they have figured out the route, they draw it with a pencil.
- Point to the first swing on the route through the maze. Say *Look! A swing. How many swings?* Point to the rest of the swings along the route. Count them aloud with the class (*One, two, three swings*). Help the children to circle the correct figure (4) in the key.

Extension activity

Aim: to practice *Let's …* , review toys, and sing a song

- Show the toy flashcards one by one (or real toys). The children say the words. Play the karaoke version of the song and teach the following new version:

  Let's play with our toys.
  Our toys are fun!
  Let's play with our toys, everyone!

  Play with your doll.
  Your doll is fun.

  Play with your car.
  Your car is fun.

  Play with your ball.
  Your ball is fun.

- Mime playing with the different toys as you sing each verse. The children copy the mimes. Sing the new version of the song again. The children mime and join in, according to ability.

Ending the lesson

Aim: to practice the song

- Stick the three park flashcards on the board in the same order as the song (swing, slide, merry-go-round).
- Books closed. Play the song for the children to join in. Point to the flashcards as prompts.

4 CD2 59 60 Listen and sing.

5 CD2 61 Sticker

The park

Values

Aims

- to present a picture story; to review language from the unit

New language: *It's my turn, I'm sorry, Let's go home, Come back, Where are they?*

Recycled language: *No, Where's (Mike)? The swing is fun,* numbers, *jump, fly, walk, swim, I'm here*

Materials: CD 2, the puppet (Polly), a simple drawing of a house on a piece of paper with poster putty

Language competences: The children will be able to listen to and follow a picture story.

Warm-up

Aim: to practice the song

- Put on the puppet. Make Polly say *Let's go to the park! Stand up, everyone!*
- Play the song (CD 2, Track 59). Polly acts out playing on the different pieces of play equipment. The children follow her and join in with the words.

Presentation

5 CD2 61 SB pp76-77 **Story: The park**

Aim: to listen and follow a picture story

- Point to the first picture on SB page 76 and ask *Who's on the swing?* The children say *Leo.* Ask what Polly is doing in L1 (she's waiting to use the swing). Repeat for picture 2 (ask about Gina). Then ask how the animals feel in picture 3 (angry) and how Leo feels in picture 4 (sad/lonely). Turn to page 77 and ask what is happening. Ask *How does Leo feel? Who's on the swing now?*
- Play the CD. The children point to the pictures as they listen.
- Play the story again, stopping after each picture. In L1, the children explain what's happening and what Leo does at the end of the story. Elicit/Give translations for *It's my turn, Let's go home,* and *Come back.* The children practice saying the phrases after you.

Audio script page T100

Practice

5 CD2 62 WB p76 **Listen and color the correct circles.**

Aim: to listen and identify the correct picture

- Point to the characters in the first pair of pictures on WB page 76. Ask *Who's this?* Say *Listen and color the circle.* Remind the children that they have to color one of the circles. Play the audio for number 1. Confirm the answer (the second picture).
- Play the audio again. Check the children's work as they color in the circle.
- Repeat for the second pair of pictures.
- Play the whole recording again. The children repeat the two lines.

Audio script page T100

Extension activity

Aim: to review *Where's … ?* and *I'm here!*

- If possible, move your class into the playground or an outside area with places for the children to hide. Make sure the area is safe to play.
- Play *Hide and seek* (as in Unit 5, page T44). At first, do the counting from one to four yourself, slowly, to give the children time to hide. Look for the children, asking *Hmm. Where's* (name)*? Is he/she here?* When you find a child encourage him/her to say *I'm here!* The child you find last is the winner.
- The second time ask a confident volunteer or group of children to do the counting and seeking.

Note: If it is not possible to play the game in a large space, hide flashcards of the characters or the puppet in the classroom.

Ending the lesson

Aim: to practice *Let's go home, Come back,* and review *jump, fly, walk, swim*

- If possible, move your class into the playground, school gym, or an empty classroom.
- Stick the picture of a house on one wall of the room. The children all stand against the opposite wall. Say *One, two, three, four. Let's go home!* Run with the children to the wall with the picture of the house. Walk back to the other wall and say *Come back! Come back!* The children follow you. Repeat until the children are confident following the instructions. Then add different instructions, e.g., *Let's jump home, Let's fly home,* etc.

Aims

- to talk about the meaning of a story; to review language from the unit

Recycled language: *It's my turn, I'm sorry, Let's go home, Come back, Where are they? No, The swing is fun*, toys, play equipment, characters

Materials: CD 2, flashcards (park, toys), Unit 9 stickers, small toy for each pair of children (e.g., car, doll, train), a stopwatch / watch with a second hand, a bell or buzzer, colored pencils or crayons, pencils

Optional: character masks

Language competences: The children will be able to appreciate the values shown in the story. The children will practice taking turns.

Warm-up

Aim: to practice *The ... is ...*

- Stick the merry-go-round on the board and say *Look! A merry-go-round. The merry-go-round is fun.* Say the sentence *The merry-go-round is fun* again. The children repeat. Repeat with other flashcards.

Practice

5 CD2 61 SB pp76–77 **Story: The park**
Listen to the story. Stick.

Aim: to review the story

- Ask the children to tell you what they remember about the story in L1. Ask *Where are the animals? Who is on the swing? Are the other animals happy?*
- Play the story again, pausing to ask what is happening and what the characters are saying. Ask what happened at the end. (Leo felt sad and lonely and gave the other animals a turn on the swing.)
- Hand out the stickers for Unit 9. Say *Where's the slide?* The children point to the correct sticker. Repeat for *merry-go-round*.
- Point to the picture on SB page 77. Say *Where's the slide?* The children point to the sticker outline. The children peel off the sticker and hold it up. Check that they all have the correct sticker. Then say *Stick*. The children stick the sticker in their books. Repeat for the other sticker.

Audio script page T100

Story values SB pp76–77

Aim: to think about the meaning of the story: taking turns

- Play the story again. The children listen and point. Pause after picture 1. Ask what Polly says (*It's my turn*). Elicit a translation. Repeat for picture 2 (Gina). Play the next part of the story and pause after Mike says *Let's go home*. Ask where the animals are going and why (home, because Leo isn't taking turns). Play the rest of the story. Ask how Leo feels and how he asks his friends to come back. Talk about how important it is to take turns, especially at the park / when we play with people we don't know.

6 WB p77 **Complete the face. Color the picture.**

Aim: to apply values from the story to new situations

- Tell the children in L1, and then in English, *We're going to look at some children now. Look at the picture and think.* Ask in L1 where the children are and how many buckets and shovels they have (only one of each).
- Point to the face and remind the children in L1 that if they think the children are doing the right thing, they draw a happy smile. Circulate and check as they draw. Then the children can color the picture.

Extension activity

Aim: to reinforce understanding of the story

- Invite four volunteers to the front. Assign them the roles of Gina, Polly, Leo, and Mike. The children playing the characters put on the masks. Play the story. The children act out the story along with the CD. Encourage the children to join in and act.
- Invite another group of four children to come to the front and act.

Ending the lesson

Aim: to practice taking turns

- Put on the puppet. Make Polly play with a toy, e.g., a car. She makes engine noises and pushes it along. After a minute or so say *Polly, it's my turn!* Make Polly pass you the toy. Say *Thank you, Polly.* Play with the car and say *The car is fun!*
- Say *It's my turn* again. The children repeat.
- Give each pair of children a toy. Tell them in L1 that they must take turns to play with it and that you will let them know when they need to swap. One child plays with the toy. Time one minute. Then ring a bell/buzzer or clap your hands. The other child in each pair says *It's my turn*. The first child passes the toy. Encourage the second child to say *Thank you*. He/She then starts to play. Time a minute again. Repeat so each child has two or three turns.

5
9
Family fun!

Circles and triangles

6 CD2 63 **Listen and point. Count and say the shapes.**

Aims

- to integrate other areas of the curriculum through English: math; to practice recognizing shapes

New language: *triangle, circle*

Recycled language: numbers 1 to 4, *park*, playground equipment, toys, animals, *big, small*

Materials: CD 2, flashcards (park, toys, animals), classroom objects or small items (e.g., crayons, buttons, coins, building blocks): two sets of four for each pair of children, materials for the project for each child (pre-cut paper shapes to make a picture of a cat: one large gray circle, one small black circle (the mouth), two small white circles (the eyes), two very small black circles (the pupils of the eyes), three small pink triangles (ears and nose), four small strips of black paper (whiskers), glue stick), a finished cat picture as a model (similar to the one on WB page 78)

Optional: colorful pipe cleaners or buttons/beads for each child

Language competences: The children will be able to recognize and count shapes.

Warm-up

Aim: to practice numbers 1 to 4 and counting

- Stick the park, toy, and animal flashcards on the board in random order. Say *Look! My toys*. Move the toy flashcards into a group together, counting *One, two, three, four* as you do so. Elicit the words. The children join in. Repeat for the animal flashcards. Invite a volunteer to come and count the park flashcards and move them into a group.
- Hand out eight items to each pair of children – mixed up (e.g., four buttons, four erasers). The children put them into two groups of four, counting aloud. Circulate and ask individuals to count the items.

Presentation

6 CD2 63 SB p78 **Listen and point. Count and say the shapes.**

Aim: to practice recognizing and counting shapes

- Draw a circle on the board. Elicit/Say *Circle* (the children will recognize the word from the instruction "Listen and circle"). Draw a circle in the air with your finger. Say the word again. The children copy you. Draw a triangle and present *Triangle* in the same way (drawing in the air).
- Ask the children to look at SB page 78. Ask *Where's this?* Elicit *A park*. Point to the merry-go-round, tracing the circle shape with your finger, and ask *Circle or triangle?* The children say *Circle*. Point to a triangle on the stroller, and trace the shape in the same way. Ask *Circle or triangle?* The children say *Triangle*.
- Say *Listen and point*. Play the recording. Point to the shapes in the photograph along with the words on the audio. The children copy. Play the audio again for the children to point on their own.
- Say *Count and say the shapes*. Point to the triangles in the photograph from left to right, counting aloud. The children copy. Do the same for the circles.

Audio script page T100

Practice

7 WB p78 **Make a shapes cat.**

Aim: to take part in a craft activity and encourage recognition of shapes

- Show the pictures on WB page 78. Explain in L1 that the children are going to make a picture of a cat, like the girl in the pictures. Explain what to do, using the pictures. Show the children that they need to stick the shapes on the large gray circle to make the cat's face. Show the one you prepared earlier.
- Hand out the materials to each child. Circulate and help with the sticking. Point to shapes and elicit *Circle* or *Triangle* from individuals. Ask *Is it big or small?*

Extension activity

Aim: to practice fine motor skills and review shapes

- Use pipe cleaners to make a circle and a triangle. Show the class, and for each one ask *What's this? What color?* Rephrase answers, e.g., *Yes! It's a red circle.*
- Hand out pipe cleaners to each child. They make a circle and a triangle in the same way. Circulate and ask about the shape and color.

Note: If you do not have pipe cleaners, the children can make the shapes by putting together small items (e.g., buttons or beads).

Ending the lesson

Aim: to practice counting and listening carefully

- Say *Listen and count*. Ask in L1 *How many?* Clap your hands four times. The children listen and put up their hands to say the number. Repeat, clapping a different number of times (up to four).
- When the children are confident, say *Listen and clap your hands*. Say a number. The children clap the correct number of times.

Aims

- to review language and values from the unit; to encourage children to reflect on their learning

Recycled language: *circle, triangle*, numbers 1 to 4, colors, *It's a (red) (triangle), big, small*

Materials: circular and triangular items (or pictures of these), e.g., a hula hoop, a plate, picture of a full moon/the Earth, a cookie, picture of a triangular road sign, a triangular building block, picture of the end of a house showing a triangular gable, picture of a slice of pizza/cake (or toy food), colored pencils or crayons

Optional: ten paper triangles and circles in known colors, five big, five small

Language competences: The children will be able to recognize sequences of shapes. The children will be able to use language from the unit.

Warm-up

Aim: to review shapes

- Draw a triangle and a circle on the board. Point to the triangle and say *Triangle*. Draw a triangle shape in the air as you say the word. The children repeat the word and the action. Do the same for the circle.
- Say *Look and think*. Show the pictures or items you have brought to class in turn. For each one, ask *Circle or triangle?* Help by tracing the shape in the picture / around the edge of the item with your finger. The children say *Circle* or *Triangle* each time.

Practice

7 Think! SB p79 **Look and draw lines. Say the shapes.**

Thinking skills: sequencing

- Point to the first row of shapes on SB page 79. Say the name of each shape and color from left to right. The children watch and listen. Repeat with the children copying you. Then point to the three shapes on the right. Ask in L1 *Which shape comes next?* Trace the example line with your finger. Read out the shapes in the row again, including the answer.
- Repeat the process for rows 2 and 3, helping the children find the answer each time and showing them how to draw a match line.
- The children can then practice saying the names of the shapes in each row in pairs.

Note: Encourage the children to notice patterns around them (in the classroom and outside) and practice different types of patterns in class. There can be patterns when you give instructions (e.g., *Jump, Walk, Clap, Jump, Walk, Clap*), patterns when the children line up (girl, boy, girl, boy), or patterns with objects based on color, size, or shape.

8 WB p79 **Say the words. Color the circles.**

Aim: to create a record of learning

- Point to the playground equipment on WB page 79. The children say the words together.
- The children color the circles if they can say the words on their own.
- Circulate and help as necessary. Ask individual children to say the words.

Extension activity

Aim: to practice recognizing shapes and size

- Show a large paper circle. Ask *What's this?* Rephrase answers, e.g., *Yes, it's a green circle*. Stick it on the board. Show a small circle. Point to the circle on the board and ask *Big or small?* Rephrase answers, e.g., *It's a big circle. A big, green circle*. Say a similar sentence for the small circle, e.g., *It's a small, blue circle*. Stick it on the board. Repeat for a large and a small triangle.
- Stick all the shapes on the board. Make two teams. Call one child from each team to the front. They stand on either side of the board. Explain in L1 that you are going to ask for a shape and both children need to find it first. The first child to take the circle from the board and give it to you wins a point. Then the two children sit down and two more children come to the front. Repeat until all the shapes have been taken. The team with the most points wins.

Ending the lesson

Aim: to review language from the unit

- Play the children's favorite game from the unit or sing the unit song.

Phonics

- See page T88 for Unit 9 Phonics.

Review

- See page T94 for Unit 8 & Unit 9 Review.

7 Think! Look and draw lines. Say the shapes.

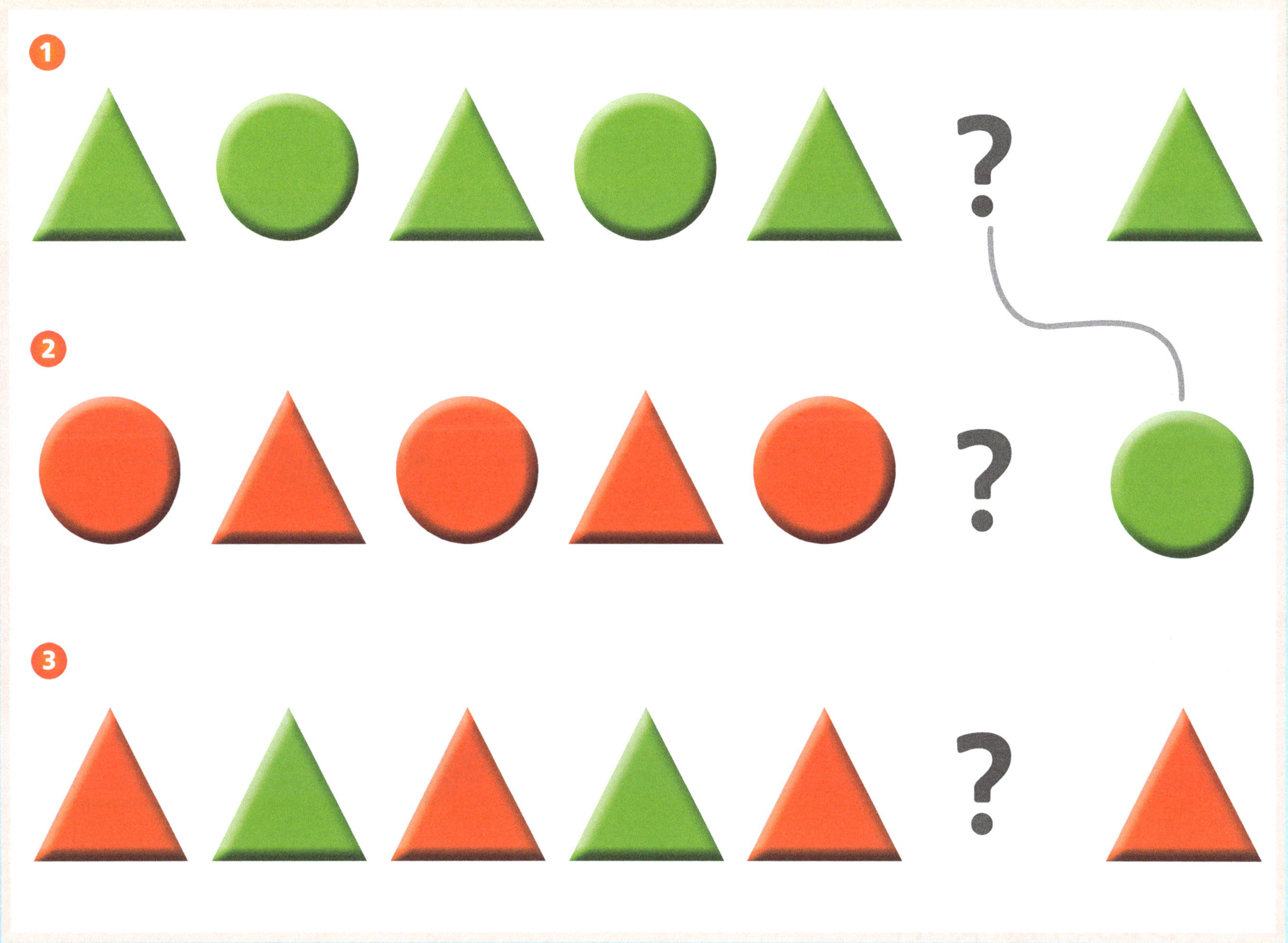

Phonics → page 88 Review → page 94

1 Look and find.

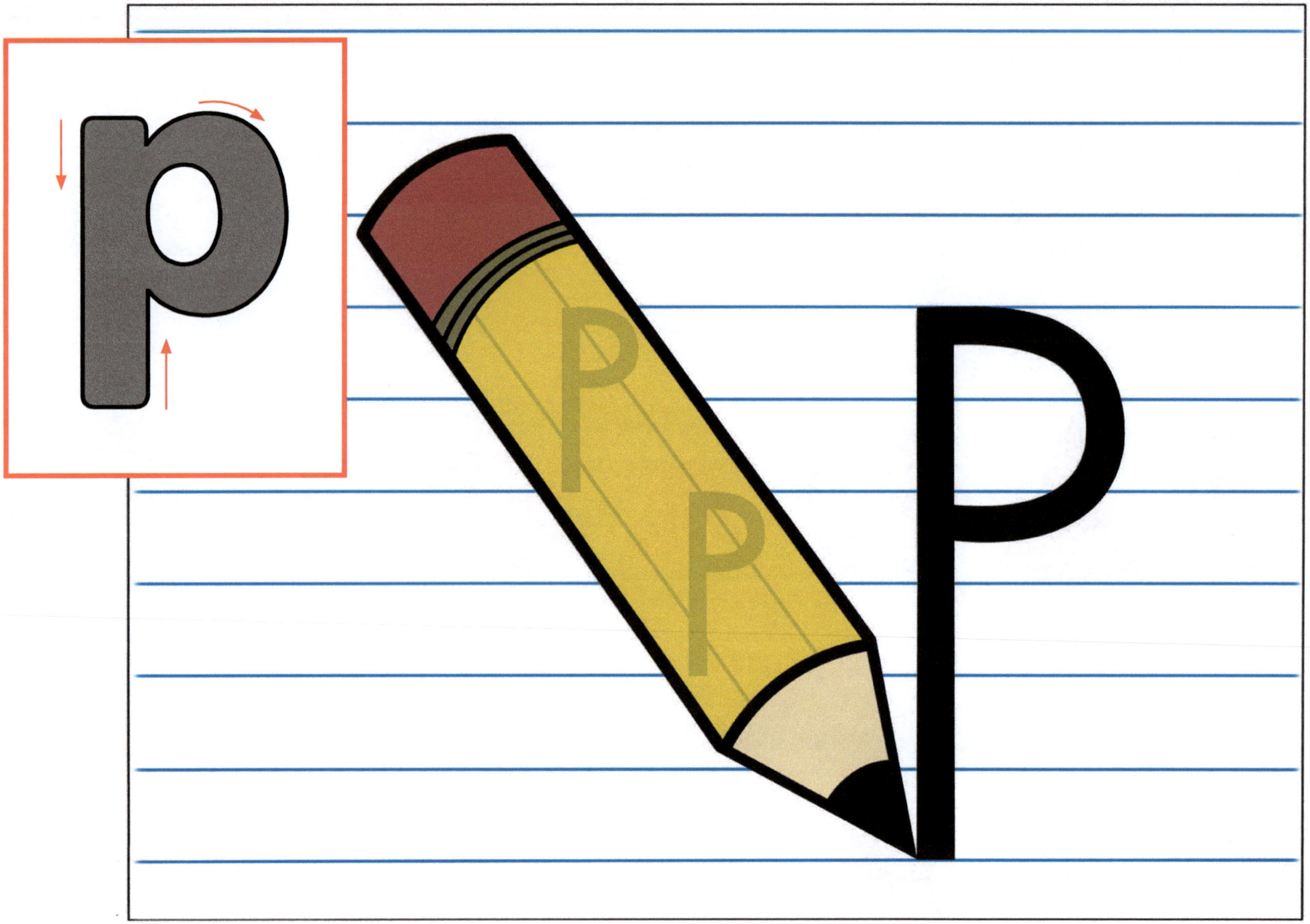

2 CD1 18 Listen and join in.

Aims

- to practice the sound /p/; to practice recognizing and forming the grapheme "p"

New language: *slowly, quickly,* words with different initial consonant sounds

Recycled language: *pencil, Polly,* classroom instructions

Materials: CD 1, pencil flashcard, the puppet (Polly), a pencil for each child, phonics cards pencil and "p" (WB pages 81 and 82), pencils

Language competences: The children will be able to make and recognize the sound /p/. The children will practice forming the grapheme "p."

Warm-up

Aim: to focus on the sound /p/

- Put on the puppet. Ask *Who's this?* Say *Polly.* The children say *Polly.* Say *Yes. It's Polly.* Make Polly wave at the class and say *Hello.* Say *Listen and say. p – p – p – Polly!*

Note: Make the sound, not the name of the letter. The children repeat.

- Say the sound /p/ in isolation. Exaggerate the lip position and movement required to make the sound. The children copy. Explain in L1 that you can feel your breath on your hand exploding out when you make the sound. Demonstrate by making the sound with your hand held to your mouth. The children copy. Give them time to practice. Monitor and check.

Presentation

1 SB p80 **Look and find. Trace the letter.**

Aim: to present and practice forming the grapheme "p"

- Show the pencil flashcard and ask *What's this?* The children say *Pencil.*
- Point to the picture on SB page 80. Say *p – p – p – pencil.* The children copy. Repeat the sound while drawing the shape of the letter in the air, following the strokes as shown on page 80. Say *Draw /p/.* Draw the letter again. The children copy your movements. Practice forming the letter in the air repeatedly. Make the sound /p/ every time.
- Say *Trace the letter.* Show the children how to trace the letter shape on the page with their fingers.
- Say *Find the letters "p" in the picture.*

Chant

2 CD1 18 SB p80 **Listen and join in.**

Aim: to practice the sound /p/ in a chant

- Say *Listen and join in.* Play the chant. Join in with the sounds and words and hold up the pencil card, then the "p" card. Repeat for the children to copy you. Then play the chant for the children to join in without your help.

Audio script page T95

Sound discrimination

- Make sure each child has a pencil. Put a pencil on your desk. Say *Look and listen. Polly /p/?* Look thoughtful and then say *Yes, /p/.* Pick up your pencil. Say *Bag /p/? No!* Signal that you are not going to pick up the pencil. Explain in L1 that you are going to say some words. The children need to listen carefully to the first sound in each word and pick up their pencil if they hear the sound /p/. If they don't hear it, they don't pick it up.
- Say a series of words with initial consonant sounds (not blends), some with the sound /p/, e.g., *Pink, pencil, cat, me, pot, pasta, dog, paint, bat, can, pan, sand.* The children hold up their pencil for the /p/ words. Repeat with the words in a different order.

Extension activity

Aim: to practice the sound /p/

- If possible, move the chairs in the classroom so they are in a long row (or two long rows, one facing the other). Say *Sit down, please.* All the children sit down. Ask in L1 if they know what *The wave* is. Explain that the first person in the row stands up with their hands in the air, then sits down. Then straight away the next person stands up, and so on until the end of the row. Demonstrate yourself, slowly, saying *Stand up, Hands up, Hands down, Sit down.* Practice the wave until the children are confident. Then ask them to make the sound /p/ when they stand up. Repeat until everyone is joining in successfully. Practice starting the wave from different seats (at the other end of the row, in the middle, etc.).

Note: If you can't arrange the chairs in rows, the wave can pass from the child sitting in one corner at the front around the class in a logical direction. Make sure the children know which way the wave is traveling.

Ending the lesson

Aim: to review the sound /p/

- Do a simple clapping chant. Clap three times, and each time you clap make the sound /p/ then say *Pencil.* Say *Stand up! Clap your hands!* Repeat the clapping chant. The children join in. Repeat until everyone is successfully pronouncing /p/.

Aims

- to practice the sound /b/; to practice recognizing and forming the grapheme "b"

New language: words with different initial consonant sounds

Recycled language: *bag*, classroom instructions

Materials: CD 1, bag flashcard, the puppet (Polly), a small bag (for Polly to carry), children's bags, phonics cards bag and "b" (WB pages 81 and 82), pencils

Language competences: The children will be able to make and recognize the sound /b/. The children will practice forming the grapheme "b."

Warm-up

Aim: to focus on the sound /b/

- Put on the puppet. Make Polly wave at the class and say *Hello*. Have Polly pick up a small bag, fly around with it, and then put it on your desk. Ask Polly *What's this?* Polly says *My bag!* Look thoughtful and say *Listen and say. b – b – b– bag!*

Note: Make the sound, not the name of the letter. The children repeat.

- Say the sound /b/ in isolation. Exaggerate the lip position and movement required to make the sound. The children copy. Explain in L1 that you can feel your breath on your hand exploding out when you make the sound. Demonstrate by making the sound with your hand held to your mouth. The children copy. Give them time to practice. Monitor and check.

Presentation

1 SB p81 **Look and find. Trace the letter.**

Aim: to present and practice forming the grapheme "b"

- Show the bag flashcard and ask *What's this?* The children say *Bag*.
- Point to the picture on SB page 81. Say *b – b – b – bag*. The children copy. Repeat the sound while drawing the shape of the letter in the air, following the strokes as shown on page 81. Say *Draw /b/*. Draw the letter again. The children copy your movements. Practice forming the letter in the air repeatedly. Make the sound /b/ every time.
- Say *Trace the letter.* Show the children how to trace the letter shape on the page with their fingers.
- Say *Find the letters "b" in the picture*.

Chant

2 CD1 31 SB p81 **Listen and join in.**

Aim: to practice the sound /b/ in a chant

- Say *Listen and join in*. Play the chant. Join in with the sounds and words and hold up the bag card, then the "b" card. Repeat for the children to copy you. Then play the chant for the children to join in without your help.

Audio script page T96

Sound discrimination

- Ask each child to put their bag on their desk. Put a bag on your desk. Say *Look and listen. Bat /b/?* Look thoughtful and then say *Yes, /b/*. Pick up your bag. Say *Red /b/? No!* Signal that you are not going to pick up the bag. Remind the children in L1 that you are going to say some words. The children need to listen carefully to the first sound in each word and pick up their bag if they hear the sound /b/. If they don't hear it, they don't pick it up.
- Say a series of words with initial consonant sounds (not blends), some with the sound /b/, e.g., *Bad, cat, bag, pat, man, ball, bat, not, pan, back, bake, take*. The children hold up their bag for the /b/ words. Repeat with the words in a different order.

Extension activity

Aim: to practice the sound /b/

- If possible, move your class out into the playground, school gym, or an empty classroom.
- Ask all the children to stand at one end of the space. Explain in L1 that they have to run to the other end, but only when they hear the sound /b/. As they run, they must make the sound /b/. Make a series of sounds, e.g., /t/, /p/, /k/, /l/, /f/, /b/.
- When the children hear /b/ they all run. Encourage them to make the sound /b/ at the same time.
- The children move back to the starting position. Repeat with different sounds.

Ending the lesson

Aim: to review the sound /b/

- Do a simple clapping chant. Clap three times, and each time you clap make the sound /b/, then say *Bag*. Say *Stand up! Clap your hands!* Repeat the clapping chant. The children join in. Repeat until everyone is successfully pronouncing /b/.

Phonics

1 Look and find.

2 CD1 31 Listen and join in.

1 Look and find.

2 CD1 43 Listen and join in.

Aims

- to practice the sound /d/; to practice recognizing and forming the grapheme "d"

New language: words with different initial consonant sounds

Recycled language: *dad*, classroom instructions, *Who's this? It's my (dad)*

Materials: CD 1, the puppet (Polly), dad flashcard, a photograph of your father (or a man of the appropriate age), photocopies of the dad flashcard or a picture of a man who could be a dad, one for each child in the class (if possible, copied onto card), phonics cards dad and "d" (WB pages 83 and 84), pencils

Language competences: The children will be able to make and recognize the sound /d/. The children will practice forming the grapheme "d."

Warm-up

Aim: to focus on the sound /d/

- Put on the puppet. Make Polly wave at the class and say *Hello*. Show Polly the picture of your dad. Make Polly ask *Who's this?* Say *It's my dad!* Look thoughtful and say *Listen and say. d – d – d– dad!*

Note: Make the sound, not the name of the letter. The children repeat.

- Say the sound /d/ in isolation. Exaggerate the lip and tongue position and movement required to make the sound. The children copy. Explain in L1 that you can feel your tongue behind your teeth when you make the sound. Give the children time to practice. Monitor and check.

Presentation

1 SB p82 **Look and find. Trace the letter.**

Aim: to present and practice forming the grapheme "d"

- Show the dad flashcard and ask *Who's this?* The children say *Dad*.
- Point to the picture on SB page 82. Say *d – d – d – dad*. The children repeat. Say the sound while drawing the shape of the letter in the air, following the strokes as shown on page 82. Say *Draw /d/*. Draw the letter again. The children copy your movements. Practice forming the letter in the air repeatedly. Make the sound /d/ every time.
- Say *Trace the letter*. Show the children how to trace the letter shape on the page with their fingers.
- Say *Find the letters "d" in the picture*.

Chant

2 CD1 43 SB p82 **Listen and join in.**

Aim: to practice the sound /d/ in a chant

- Say *Listen and join in*. Play the chant. Join in with the sounds and words and hold up the dad card, then the "d" card. Repeat for the children to copy you. Then play the chant for the children to join in without your help.

Audio script page T97

Sound discrimination

- Hand out a "dad" picture to each child. Have a picture ready yourself. Say *Look and listen. Date /d/?* Look thoughtful and then say *Yes, /d/*. Pick up the picture of the dad. Say *Can /d/? No!* Signal that you are not going to pick up the picture. Remind the children in L1 that you are going to say some words. The children need to listen carefully to the first sound in each word and hold up the "dad" picture if they hear the sound /d/. If they don't hear it, they don't pick it up.
- Say a series of words with initial consonant sounds (not blends), some with the sound /d/, e.g., *Down, pat, ball, nest, dad, Dan, deer, dog, back, tap, door, dinner*. The children hold up the "dad" picture for the /d/ words. Repeat with the words in a different order.

Extension activity

Aim: to practice the sound /d/

- Say *Stand up!* Explain in L1 that the children have to listen carefully and sit down when they hear the sound /d/. Make a series of sounds, e.g., /t/, /p/, /v/, /l/, /f/, /b/, /k/, /d/. When the children hear /d/ they sit down. Encourage them to make the sound /d/ at the same time. The last child to sit down is "out." He/She stands to one side and helps you judge the game. The children stand up again. Repeat, with the sounds in different orders, until only one child is left in. He/She is the winner.

Ending the lesson

Aim: to review the sound /d/

- Do a simple clapping chant. Clap three times, and each time you clap make the sound /d/, then say *Dad*. Say *Stand up! Clap your hands!* Repeat the clapping chant. The children join in. Repeat until everyone is successfully pronouncing /d/.

Aims

- to practice the sound /k/; to practice recognizing and forming the grapheme "c"

New language: words with different initial consonant sounds

Recycled language: *car*, classroom instructions

Materials: CD 1, the puppet (Polly), car flashcard, a toy car or picture of a car for each child, phonics cards car and "c" (WB pages 83 and 84), pencils

Optional: a soft ball or bean bag for each pair of children

Language competences: The children will be able to make and recognize the sound /k/. The children will practice forming the grapheme "c."

Warm-up

Aim: to focus on the sound /k/

- Put on the puppet. Make Polly wave at the class and say *Hello*. Have Polly push a toy car around and make engine noises. Ask Polly *What's this? Your toy?* Polly says *Yes, my car!* Look thoughtful and say *Listen and say. k– k– k– car!* The children copy.
- Say the sound /k/ in isolation. Exaggerate the tongue position and movement required to make the sound. The children copy. Explain in L1 that you can feel your tongue at the back of your mouth when you make the sound. Give the children time to practice. Monitor and check.

Presentation

1 SB p83 **Look and find. Color the letter.**

Aim: to present and practice forming the grapheme "c"

- Show the car flashcard and ask *What's this?* The children say *Car.*
- Point to the picture on SB page 83. Say *k – k – k – car.* The children copy. Repeat the sound, and this time draw the shape of the letter "c" in the air, following the direction shown on page 83. Say *Draw /k/.* Draw the letter again. The children copy your movements. Practice forming the letter in the air repeatedly. Make the sound /k/ every time.
- Say *Color the letter*. Show the children how to color the letter shape on the page.

Chant

2 CD1 57 SB p83 **Listen and join in.**

Aim: to practice the sound /k/ in a chant

- Say *Listen and join in*. Play the chant. Join in with the sounds and words and hold up the car card, then the "c" card. Repeat for the children to copy you. Then play the chant for the children to join in without your help.

Audio script page T97

Sound discrimination

- Hand out a toy car or a picture of a car to each child. Have a toy car ready yourself. Say *Look and listen. Cat /k/?* Look thoughtful and then say *Yes, /k/.* Pick up the toy car. Say *Dog /k/? No!* Signal that you are not going to pick up the car. Remind the children in L1 that you are going to say some words. The children need to listen carefully to the first sound in each word and hold up the toy car/picture if they hear the sound /k/. If they don't hear it, they don't pick it up.

Note: If you don't have a toy or picture, the children can mime driving a car when they hear /k/.

- Say a series of words with initial consonant sounds (not blends), some with the sound /k/, e.g., *Can, cat, call, bad, man, cake, cab, dog, top, not, cap, card*. The children hold up the toy/picture for the /k/ words. Repeat with the words in a different order.

Extension activity

Aim: to practice making the sound /k/

- If possible, move your class out into the playground, school gym, or an empty classroom.
- Demonstrate with a volunteer. You stand facing each other, a short distance apart. Say *Throw the ball!* Throw a soft ball to the volunteer and say *k – k – k – catch!* at the same time. Explain in L1 that whoever throws the ball says *k – k – k – atch!* Then say *Throw the ball!* The volunteer throws the ball back to you. Practice this with the volunteer until he/she is confident.
- Make pairs. The children in each pair stand facing each other and play the game. Monitor and check they are saying *k – k – k – catch!*

Ending the lesson

Aim: to review the sound /k/

- Do a simple clapping chant. Clap three times, and each time you clap make the sound /k/, then say *Car.* Say *Stand up! Clap your hands!* Repeat the clapping chant. The children join in. Repeat until everyone is successfully joining in.

1 Look and find. Color the letter.

2 CD1 57 Listen and join in.

1 Look and find. Color the letter.

2 CD2 14 Listen and join in.

Aims

- to practice the sound /t/; to practice recognizing and forming the grapheme "t"

New language: words with different initial consonant sounds

Recycled language: numbers 1 to 4, classroom instructions

Materials: CD 2, two flashcard, phonics cards two and "t" (WB pages 85 and 86), pencils

Optional: dad flashcard

Language competences: The children will be able to make and recognize the sound /t/. The children will practice forming the grapheme "t."

Warm-up

Aim: to focus on the sound /t/

- March around the classroom, saying *One – Two! One – Two!* as you move your feet. If space permits, encourage the children to join in.
- Ask the children to sit down. Say *t – t – t – two*. Look thoughtful. Say the sound /t/ in isolation. Exaggerate the tongue position and movement required to make the sound. The children copy. Explain in L1 that you can feel your tongue behind your teeth when you make the sound. Give the children time to practice. Monitor and check.

Presentation

1 SB p84 **Look and find. Color the letter.**

Aim: to present and practice forming the grapheme "t"

- Show the flashcard for two or hold up two objects and ask *How many?* The children say *Two*.
- Point to the picture on SB page 84. Count the letters aloud with the children (*One, Two!*) and say *t – t – t – two*. The children copy. Repeat the sound, and this time draw the shape of the letter "t" in the air, following the two strokes shown on page 84. Say *Draw /t/*. Draw the letter again. The children copy your movements. Practice forming the letter in the air repeatedly. Make the sound /t/ every time.
- Say *Color the letter.* Show the children how to color the letter shape on the page.

Chant

2 CD2 14 SB p84 **Listen and join in.**

Aim: to practice the sound /t/ in a chant

- Say *Listen and join in*. Play the chant. Join in with the sounds and words and hold up the two card, and then the "t" card. Repeat for the children to copy you. Then play the chant for the children to join in without your help.

Audio script page T98

Sound discrimination

- Say *Look and listen*. Hold up two fingers and say *Two!* The children copy. Say *Look and listen. Tap /t/?* Look thoughtful, and then say *Yes, /t/.* Hold up two fingers. Say *Cap /t/? No!* Don't hold up any fingers. Remind the children in L1 that you are going to say some words. The children need to listen carefully to the first sound in each word and hold up two fingers if they hear the sound /t/. If they don't hear it, they don't do anything.
- Say a series of words with initial consonant sounds (not blends), some with the sound /t/, e.g., *Take, top, dog, sad, tub, tick, cat, back, tennis, table, land, pink*. The children hold up two fingers for the /t/ words. Repeat with the words in a different order.

Extension activity

Aim: to practice differentiating between the sounds /d/ and /t/

- Practice the sounds /d/ and /t/ one after the other with the children, prompting with the two and dad flashcards. Explain in L1 that we can feel our voice for the sound /d/ but not for /t/. Encourage the children to put their hands on their throats to feel the difference between the two sounds.
- If possible, move your class into the playground, school gym, or an empty classroom.
- Stick the flashcard for two on one wall and the flashcard for dad on the opposite wall. The children stand in the center of the space. Explain in L1 that they need to run to the "two" wall when they hear a word with /t/ at the beginning and to the "dad" wall for /d/ words. Say a series of words, some with initial sound /t/, some with /d/. The children move as appropriate. Mix the words up so that sometimes the children have to stay in the same place, e.g., *Dan, tan, tap, dash, take, dot, tot, time, dime, do*. Repeat with the words in a different order.

Ending the lesson

Aim: to review the sound /t/

- Do a simple clapping chant. Clap twice, and each time you clap make the sound /t/, then say *Two*. Say *Stand up! Clap your hands!* Repeat the clapping chant. The children join in. Repeat until everyone is successfully joining in.

Aims

- to practice the sound /e/; to practice recognizing and forming the grapheme "e"

New language: words with different initial vowel sounds

Recycled language: *egg, This is my … ,* numbers

Materials: CD 2, a toy or hard-boiled egg (see page T30), the puppet (Polly), phonics cards egg and "e" (WB pages 85 and 86), pencils

Language competences: The children will be able to make and recognize the sound /e/. The children will practice forming the grapheme "e."

Warm-up

Aim: to focus on the sound /e/

- Put on the puppet. Make Polly take a toy egg / hard-boiled egg out of your bag. She says *Look! This is my egg*. Make her sit on the egg (as in Unit 3). Say *Egg*. The children repeat. Polly passes the egg to volunteers, saying *This is my egg*. The child says *Egg*. To get it back make Polly say *My egg, please!*
- Say e – e – e – *egg*. Look thoughtful. Say the sound /e/ in isolation. Exaggerate the mouth shape required to make the sound. The children copy. Explain in L1 that you need to open your mouth very wide and smile when you make the sound. Give the children time to practice. Monitor and check.

Presentation

1 SB p85 **Look and find. Color the letter.**

Aim: to present and practice forming the grapheme "e"

- Point to the picture on SB page 85. Say *Look! Eggs! How many?* Count aloud with the children (*One, two, three*).
- Say e – e – e – *egg*. The children copy. Repeat the sound /e/, and this time draw the shape of the letter "e" in the air, with a single movement, following the direction shown on page 85. Say *Draw /e/*. Draw the letter again. The children copy your movements. Practice forming the letter in the air repeatedly. Make the sound /e/ every time.
- Say *Color the letter*. Show the children how to color the letter shape on the page.

Chant

2 CD2 27 SB p85 **Listen and join in.**

Aim: to practice the sound /e/ in a chant

- Say *Listen and join in*. Play the chant. Join in with the sounds and words and hold up the egg card, then the "e" card. Repeat for the children to copy you. Then play the chant for the children to join in without your help.

Audio script page T98

Sound discrimination

- Say *Look and listen*. Mime being a bird sitting down on a nest and say *Egg!* The children copy. Say *Look and listen. End /e/?* Look thoughtful, and then say *Yes, /e/*. Mime being a bird on the nest. Say *In /e/? No!* Don't do any action. Remind the children in L1 that you are going to say some words. The children need to listen carefully to the first sound in each word and mime being a bird with an egg if they hear the sound /e/. If they don't hear it, they don't do anything.
- Say a series of words with initial vowel sounds, some with the sound /e/, e.g., *Extra, exit, and, am, Emma, up, every, Oliver, Ellen, eleven, if, elephant*. The children mime being a bird sitting down on a nest for the /e/ words. Repeat with the words in a different order.

Extension activity

Aim: to practice the sound /e/

- Repeat *The wave* activity with the sound /e/ (see page T80 Extension activity).

Ending the lesson

Aim: to review the sound /e/

- Do a simple clapping chant. Clap three times, and each time you clap make the sound /e/ then say *Egg*. Say *Stand up! Clap your hands!* Repeat the clapping chant. The children join in. Repeat until everyone is successfully joining in.

1 Look and find. Color the letter.

Phonics

2 CD2 27 Listen and join in.

1 **Look and find. Trace the letter.**

2 CD2 38 **Listen and join in.**

Aims

- to practice the sound /s/ at the beginning of words; to practice recognizing and tracing the grapheme "s"

New language: words with different initial consonant sounds

Recycled language: *salad, lunch, munch, crunch, yummy,* classroom instructions

Materials: CD 2, bowl with toy food salad or green tissue paper/cloth inside, phonics cards salad and "s" (WB pages 87 and 88), pencils

Optional: playdough for each child or small objects (buttons, lids, beads)

Language competences: The children will be able to make and recognize the sound /s/. The children will practice forming the grapheme "s."

Warm-up

Aim: to focus on the sound /s/

- Show the children the bowl with "salad" inside and say *Look! My lunch. What is it?* The children say *Salad*. Say *Yes! Munch, munch, crunch! Yummy salad!*
- Say *s – s – s – salad*. Look thoughtful. Say the sound /s/ in isolation. Exaggerate the mouth shape required to make the sound. The children copy. Explain in L1 that your tongue makes a hole shape behind your teeth when you make the sound. Give the children time to practice. Monitor and check.

Presentation

1 SB p86 **Look and find. Trace the letter.**

Aim: to present and practice tracing the grapheme "s"

- Point to the picture on SB page 86. Say *Look! Yummy salad! Point to the salad.* The children point and say *Salad*.
- Say *s – s – s – salad*. The children copy. Repeat the sound /s/, and this time draw the shape of the letter "s" in the air, following the direction shown on page 86. Say *Draw /s/*. Draw the letter again. The children copy your movements. Practice forming the letter in the air repeatedly. Make the sound /s/ every time.
- Say *Trace the letter*. Show the children how to trace the letter on the page. Circulate and check their work.

Chant

2 CD2 38 SB p86 **Listen and join in.**

Aim: to practice the sound /s/ in a chant

- Say *Listen and join in*. Play the chant. Join in with the sounds and words and hold up the salad card, then the "s" card. Repeat for the children to copy you. Then play the chant for the children to join in without your help.
- Say *Find the letter "s" in the picture*.

Audio script page T99

Sound discrimination

- Say *Stand up, please*. The children stand. Say *Sit!* and sit down. The children copy. Say *Look and listen. Sand /s/?* Look thoughtful and then say *Yes, /s/*. Stand up again. Say *Cake /s/? No!* Stay standing. Remind the children in L1 that you are going to say some words. The children need to listen carefully to the first sound in each word and sit down if they hear the sound /s/. If they don't hear it, they stay standing.

Phonics

- Everyone stands up. Say a series of words with initial consonant sounds, some with the sound /s/, e.g., *Sack, bat, can, sum, pick, say, sorry, take, sister, sad, run, sing*. The children sit down for the /s/ words. Repeat with the words in a different order.

Extension activity

Aim: to practice the letter shape "s"

- Make the letter "s" from playdough. Show it to the children and make the sound /s/. Give out the playdough. Circulate and help the children make the "s" shape. Encourage them to say /s/ as they work.

Note: If you don't have playdough, the children can make the shape with small items such as buttons or beads.

Ending the lesson

Aim: to review the sound /s/

- Mime being a snake. Walk around the classroom with your hands in front of you like a snake's head. Make the sound /s/ continuously. The children join in (in their places or walking behind you to make a long snake if possible).

Aims

- to practice the sound /n/; to practice recognizing and tracing the grapheme "n"

New language: *nose*, words with different initial consonant sounds

Recycled language: classroom instructions, *It's my … , Where's the … ? It's here*

Materials: CD 2, phonics cards nose and "n" (WB pages 87 and 88), pencils

Language competences: The children will be able to make and recognize the sound /n/. The children will practice forming the grapheme "n."

Warm-up

Aim: to present *nose* and focus on the sound /n/

- Point to your nose and say *Look! It's my nose! Nose.* The children repeat *Nose*. Say *Point to your nose*. The children point. Give instructions, e.g., *Stand up, Hands up, Clap your hands, Hands down, Jump, Point to your nose, Sit down, Go to sleep, Wake up, Point to your nose*.
- Say *n – n – n – nose*. Look thoughtful. Say the sound /n/ in isolation (be careful not to say "nuh," just make the "n" sound with no vowel). Exaggerate the mouth shape required to make the sound. The children copy. Explain in L1 that your tongue touches the roof of your mouth behind your teeth when you make the sound. Give the children time to practice. Monitor and check.

Presentation

1 SB p87 **Look and find. Trace the letter.**

Aim: to present and practice forming the grapheme "n"

- Point to the picture of the lion on SB page 87. Say *Look! Where's the nose? Point to the nose.* The children point. Say *Yes. It's here*.
- Say *n – n– n – nose*. The children copy. Repeat the sound /n/, and this time draw the shape of the letter "n" in the air, following the direction shown on page 87. Say *Draw /n/*. Draw the letter again. The children copy your movements. Practice forming the letter in the air repeatedly. Make the sound /n/ every time.
- Say *Trace the letter*. Show the children how to trace the letter on the page. Circulate and check their work.
- Say *Find the letters "n" in the picture*.

Chant

2 CD2 51 SB p87 **Listen and join in.**

Aim: to practice the sound /n/ in a chant

- Say *Listen and join in*. Play the chant. Join in with the sounds and words and hold up the nose card, then hold up the "n" card. Repeat for the children to copy you. Then play the chant for the children to join in without your help.
  Audio script page T100

Sound discrimination

- Say *Look! Nose!* Point to your nose. The children copy the action and say *Nose*. Say *Look and listen. Name /n/?* Look thoughtful and then say *Yes, /n/*. Point to your nose. Say *Sit /n/? No!* Don't do any action. Remind the children in L1 that you are going to say some words. The children need to listen carefully to the first sound in each word and touch their nose if they hear the sound /n/. If they don't hear it, they don't do anything.
- Say *Stand up, please*. Say a series of words with initial consonant sounds, some with the sound /n/, e.g., *Nest, top, no, now, sad, need, back, cake, sing, new, nap, Ned*. The children touch their noses for the /n/ words. Repeat with the words in a different order.

Extension activity

Aim: to practice the sound /n/

- Repeat the Extension activity from page T81 with the sound /n/.

Ending the lesson

Aim: to review the sound /n/

- Move around the classroom as if you were driving a car. Make a sound like a siren "nee-naw" continuously. The children join in (in their places or following you if possible).

Phonics

1 Look and find. Trace the letter.

2 CD2 51 Listen and join in.

1 Look and find. Trace the letter.

2 CD2 64 Listen and join in.

Aims

- to practice the sound /ɪ/; to practice recognizing and tracing the grapheme "i"

New language: *igloo*, words with different initial vowel sounds

Recycled language: *It's ...*

Materials: CD 2, a photograph of an igloo, phonics cards igloo and "i" (WB pages 89 and 90), pencils

Optional: a picture of an egg, a picture of an igloo (both large enough to display on the wall)

Language competences: The children will be able to make and recognize the sound /ɪ/. The children will practice forming the grapheme "i."

Warm-up

Aim: to present *igloo* and focus on the sound /ɪ/

- Show the picture of an igloo and say *It's an igloo. Igloo*. The children repeat *Igloo*. Ask in L1 if they know what an igloo is. Explain that igloos are houses made in very cold places. Pretend to be cold and shiver / stamp your feet on the spot. Say *Igloo* and mime being cold at the same time. The children copy.
- Say *i – i – i – igloo*. Look thoughtful. Say the sound /ɪ/ in isolation (say the sound, not the letter name). Exaggerate the mouth shape required to make the sound. The children copy. Give them time to practice. Monitor and check.

Presentation

1 SB p88 **Look and find. Trace the letter.**

Aim: to present and practice forming the grapheme "i"

- Point to the picture of the igloo on SB page 88. Say *Look! Brrr! An igloo. Point to the igloo*. The children point.
- Say *i – i – i – igloo*. The children copy. Repeat the sound /ɪ/, and this time draw the letter "i" in the air, with the downward stroke first and then the dot, following the direction shown on page 88. Say *Draw /ɪ/*. Draw the letter again. The children copy your movements. Practice forming the letter in the air repeatedly. Make the sound /ɪ/ every time.
- Say *Trace the letter*. Show the children how to trace the letter on the page. Circulate and check their work. Encourage them to trace the two parts of the grapheme in the correct order (the dot last).
- Say *Find the letters "i" in the picture*.

Chant

2 CD2 64 SB p88 **Listen and join in.**

Aim: to practice the sound /ɪ/ in a chant

- Say *Listen and join in*. Play the chant. Join in with the sounds and words and hold up the igloo card, then the "i" card. Repeat for the children to copy you. Then play the chant for the children to join in without your help.

Audio script page T100

Sound discrimination

- Stand up and say *Listen! Sit /ɪ/*. Sit down. The children copy the action and say *Sit*. Stand up again. Say *Look and listen. In /ɪ/?* Look thoughtful and then say *Yes, /ɪ/*. Sit down. Say *Egg /ɪ/? No!* Don't do any action. Remind the children in L1 that you are going to say some words. The children need to listen carefully to the first sound in each word and sit down if they hear the sound /ɪ/. If they don't hear it, they don't do anything.
- Everyone stands up. Say a series of words with initial vowel sounds, some with the sound /ɪ/, e.g., *It's, imp, if, end, up, into, Emma, on, in, ink, under*. The children sit down for the /ɪ/ words. Repeat with the words in a different order.

Phonics

Extension activity

Aim: to practice differentiating between the sounds /ɪ/ and /e/

- Practice the sounds /ɪ/ and /e/ one after the other with the children, prompting with the pictures of the egg and the igloo. Encourage the children to think about the way the tongue moves to change from /ɪ/ to /e/.
- If possible, move your class into the playground, school gym, or an empty classroom.
- Stick the picture of the egg on one wall and the picture of the igloo on the opposite wall. The children stand in the center of the space. Explain in L1 that they need to run to the "egg" wall when they hear words with /e/ at the beginning and to the "igloo" wall for /ɪ/ words. Say a series of words, some with initial sound /e/, some with /ɪ/. The children move as appropriate. Mix the words up so that sometimes the children have to stay in the same place, e.g., *Ever, in, Ellen, imp, English, exit, end, if, ill, Ed, ink*. Repeat with the words in a different order.

Ending the lesson

Aim: to review the sound /ɪ/

- Move around the classroom as if you were shivering in an igloo. The children join in (in their places or following you if possible).

Aims

- to review the sounds practiced in Units 1 to 9; to practice recognizing letter shapes

New language: *bingo*

Recycled language: *igloo, pencil, egg, salad, bag, car, nose, dad, two*

Materials: CD 2, the puppet (Polly), flashcards: pencil, salad, bag, car, dad, and two pictures of an igloo, an egg, and a nose, pencils

Language competences: The children will practice recognizing sounds from Units 1 to 9. The children will practice forming graphemes from Units 1 to 9.

Warm-up

Aim: to review sounds from Units 1 to 9

- Stick the flashcards of the key sounds from the phonics lessons on the board, together with the pictures for egg, igloo, and nose. Point to each one in turn and elicit the word and the initial sound for each.
- Put on the puppet. Play *Disappearing flashcards* (see Introduction, page xvii) with the flashcards and pictures on the board. Encourage the children to say the initial sounds, as well as the words.

Review

1 CD2 66 SB p89 **Listen and play bingo.**

Aim: to review sounds from Units 1 to 9 and practice recognizing graphemes

- Help the children find the *Bingo* card on page 89. Say, e.g., *Point to /k/.* The children point to the correct picture (tell them in L1 to use the pictures to help). If they are having problems, say, e.g., *Point to /k/. Car!* Repeat for all the pictures.
- Explain the rules of *Bingo* in L1 if necessary. The children listen and find the sounds on their card as they hear them. The first child to mark all the sounds on the card says *Bingo!*
- Make sure all the children have a pencil. Play the first sound and word on the audio. Ask the children to point to the correct square. Check they are all pointing to the /s/ square. Show them how to mark the square in pencil (with a dot or an X, depending on your children's ability). Play the rest of the audio, pausing for the children to find and mark the squares. They should all shout *Bingo* at the same time.
- Ask the children to erase the marks on the card. Repeat the game, but this time tell the children to choose one row of the card by putting a mark next to it. They only mark sounds from this row when they hear them. Play the audio again. This time there will be a group of winners.

Audio script page T100

Sound discrimination

- Repeat one of the Sound discrimination activities from the Phonics lessons (choose a sound the children find difficult).

Extension activity

Aim: to practice differentiating between sounds

- Play the children's favorite Extension activity game from Units 1 to 9.

Ending the lesson

Aim: to review sounds from Units 1 to 9

- Stick the flashcards and pictures from the Warm-up on the board again, at a height your children can reach. Point and elicit the words and initial sounds.
- Call two volunteers to the front. Explain in L1 that you are going to say a sound, and they both need to try to find it on the board as quickly as possible and give it to you. Say a sound, e.g., */b/*. The children look for the bag card. The first child to give the card to you is the winner. These two children sit down. Put the flashcard back. Repeat with different volunteers.

1 CD2 66 Listen and play bingo.

1 CD1 19 **Listen to the sentences. Color the frames.**

Aims: to review language from the *Hello!* unit and Unit 1

Recycled language: character names, classroom objects, *Hello, Goodbye, I'm* (name), *Yes, No, Look, It's my (pencil), Stand up, Sit down, Say "hello," Clap your hands, Hands up, Hands down, Clean up your (chair)*

Materials: CD 1, character masks, the puppet (Polly), Yes/No cards, colored pencils or crayons in red, blue, green, and yellow, flashcards (characters and classroom objects)

Language competences: The children will be able to use language from the *Hello!* unit and Unit 1.

Warm-up

Aim: to review character names, *Hello! I'm ...* and *Goodbye*

- Put on the Mike character mask (if possible, before the class). Move around like a monkey and say (pretending to be Mike) *Hello! I'm Mike!* Encourage the children to reply all together *Hello, Mike!* Say *Goodbye*. The children reply *Goodbye, Mike!* Take off the mask. Repeat for the other three masks.
- Hand out character masks to pairs of children. They take turns putting on a mask, doing the correct animal action, and saying *Hello! I'm* (character name), then *Goodbye*. Circulate and help as necessary.

Listening

1 CD1 19 SB p90 **Listen to the sentences. Color the frames.**

Aim: to review language from the *Hello!* unit and Unit 1

- Point to the pictures on SB page 90 and say *Listen and color*. Play the first sentence on the audio. Help the children point to the first picture. Explain in L1 that they need to color the frame of the picture the same color as the small circle.
- Repeat for the rest of the audio, pausing after each sentence for the children to color.
- Play the audio again. The children point to the correct picture and repeat the sentence.

Audio script page T95

Practice

- Put on the puppet. Make Polly give instructions from the *Hello!* unit and Unit 1, e.g., *Stand up, Clap your hands, Hands up, Hands down, Say "hello," Sit down, Clean up your pencil.* The children follow.

Game

- Hand out the Yes/No cards. Say *Yes!* The children hold up the correct card. Repeat for No. Do this several times.
- Hold up your book and say *Look! It's my book. Yes or no?* The children hold up the Yes card. Hold up a pencil and say *It's my chair. Yes or no?* The children hold up No. Repeat with different classroom objects, mixing true and false sentences. Then add practice of the character names using the flashcards and correct and incorrect sentences with the names, e.g., *It's Leo.*

Extension activity

Aim: to practice language from the *Hello!* unit and Unit 1

- Choose eight volunteers. Ask them to stand at the front of the class. Mix up the character and classroom object flashcards. Hand each of the children a flashcard. Help each child to show their flashcard to the class and say, e.g., *Look! It's Gina.* He/She then turns the flashcard so the rest of the class can't see it. Tell the class in L1 that they need to look and listen carefully and try to remember where each flashcard is. Ask the children at the front to show their cards and speak again.
- Call on a volunteer from the class. He/She chooses one of the children at the front, points and says, e.g., *Elena. Pencil.* If the guess is correct, the child shows the flashcard and says, e.g., *Yes. Pencil.* Then he/she sticks the flashcard on the board and sits down. The children guess until all the volunteers are sitting down. If they have a problem remembering any of the cards, do a mime to help.
- Point to the flashcards on the board and elicit the words to finish the activity.

Ending the lesson

Aim: to review *Clean up your ...* and classroom objects

- Review classroom objects by saying, e.g., *Point to your chair.* Repeat for *bag, pencil,* and *book*.
- Play the Unit 1 song (CD 1, Track 13). The children join in and clean up their belongings to end the lesson.

Aims: to review language from Unit 2 and Unit 3

Recycled language: colors, family, *It's (yellow), Show me something (red), Paint with me, Paint your (bag), Who's this? Go to sleep, Wake up, Give your dad a hug, Please show me your family*

Materials: CD 1, flashcards (colors and family), the puppet (Polly), colored pencils or crayons in red, blue, green, and yellow, CD of lively music, classroom objects

Optional: CD of relaxing music

Language competences: The children will be able to use language from Unit 2 and Unit 3.

Warm-up

Aim: to review family words and *Who's this?*

- Stick the family flashcards on the board. Point to each one and ask *Who's this?* The children reply with the correct family word. Repeat, pointing to them in different orders. Stick the four flashcards on different walls of the classroom.
- Play the Unit 3 song (CD 1, Track 37). The children sing along and point to the correct flashcard for each verse.

Listening

1 CD1 44 SB p91 **Listen and color the circles. Color the frames.**

Aim: to review language from Unit 2 and Unit 3

- Review colors with the flashcards.
- Point to the pictures on SB page 91 and say *Listen and color the circles.* Play the first item on the audio and point to the first picture. Elicit the color. Confirm by pointing to the green circle.
- Point to the second picture. The children copy. Play the second item. Elicit the color. Give the children time to color the circle. Repeat for the other two pictures. Remind the children that they need to color the frames of the pictures in the same color as the circles. Circulate as they color and ask individuals *What color?*
- Play the audio again. The children point to the pictures and repeat the sentences.

Audio script page T97

Practice

- Make sure the children have crayons in red, blue, green, and yellow. Put on the puppet. Make Polly give instructions from the course so far, e.g., *Stand up, Clap your hands, Show me something blue, Show me something green, Sit down, Go to sleep, Wake up, Stand up, Paint your chair, Paint your bag, Give your dad a hug.* The children follow.

Game

- If possible, move your class into the playground, school gym, or an empty classroom.
- Stick the color flashcards on different walls / in the corners of the room. Make four groups, and put each into one corner / against one wall, near a color flashcard. Ask each group *What color?* They say the color of their flashcard. Stand in the center of the space and give an instruction to each group, e.g., *Green! Clap your hands / Red! Go to sleep / Yellow! Say "hello" / Blue! Hands up.* The groups do the correct action for their color.
- Play the music. Say *Go!* The children walk clockwise to the next flashcard in their groups. Stop the music. Repeat the instruction with different actions for each group. Play slowly at first, then speed up as the children gain confidence.

Extension activity

Aim: to practice language from Unit 2 and Unit 3

- Repeat the *Sleeping lions* game from Unit 3 (see Extension activity page T26).

Ending the lesson

Aim: to review colors and classroom objects

- Show classroom objects and say, e.g., *It's my bag. It's green.* Invite volunteers to show and talk about one of their possessions.

1 CD1 44 Listen and color the circles. Color the frames.

Review

1 CD2 15 **Listen and color the circles. Color the frames.**

Aims: to review language from Unit 4 and Unit 5

Recycled language: toys, numbers 1 to 4, *It's a (blue) (ball), I have a (car), Throw your / the ball, Catch your / the ball, Oh no, big / small, a (big) (red) ball,* plural "s," *orange, purple*

Materials: CD 2, flashcards (colors), one to four of each real toy (e.g., four balls, two cars, three puzzles, four dolls), the puppet (Polly), colored pencils or crayons in red, blue, orange, and yellow, six or seven balls in known colors, some small, some big

Optional: real toys (two balls (one big, one small), three toy cars, a jigsaw puzzle, and four dolls), small classroom objects (a book, a pencil), a tray, and a piece of cloth (to cover the tray)

Language competences: The children will be able to use language from Unit 4 and Unit 5.

Warm-up

Aim: to review toys, numbers 1 to 4, and *I have a ...*

- Show a real toy, e.g., a car and ask *What's this?* The children say *Car*. Encourage them to repeat the word together. Repeat for the other toys.
- Say *Count the toys*. Hold up the balls one by one and count them aloud with the class *One, two, three, four!* Say *Four balls!* The children repeat. Make sure they say the final "s." Do the same for the other groups of toys.
- Hand out the cars, dolls, and balls for the children to look at and play with for a minute (one toy for each child or pair of children). Circulate as they play and help them say, e.g., *I have a ball.*

Listening

1 CD2 15 SB p92 **Listen and color the circles. Color the frames.**

Aim: to review language from Unit 4 and Unit 5

- Review colors with the flashcards.
- Point to the pictures on SB page 92 and say *Listen and color.* Play the first item on the audio and point to the first picture. Elicit the color. Give the children time to color the circle.
- Repeat for the other three pictures. Remind the children that they need to color the frames of the pictures in the same color as the circles. Circulate as they color and ask individuals *What color?*
- Play the audio again. The children point to the pictures and repeat the sentences.

Audio script page T98

Practice

- Review *big* and *small* by saying to volunteers *Point to something big. / Point to something small.*
- Make sure the children have crayons in front of them and four other small items, e.g., building blocks. Put on the puppet. Make Polly give instructions from the course so far, e.g., *Stand up, Show me something blue, Show me three* (the children hold up three blocks), *Show me one, Show me two, Throw your ball, Catch your ball, Paint your book, Point to something big, Point to something small, Sit down.* The children follow.

Game

- Ask the children to stand in a circle. In the centre of the circle, put a selection of balls. Go into the center and pick up each ball saying, e.g., *Look! I have a small, yellow ball.* The children repeat *Small, yellow ball.* Stand in the circle with the children.
- Give volunteers instructions, e.g., *Hector, throw me the big, orange ball.* The child goes into the center of the circle, chooses the correct ball, and passes/throws it to you (according to ability). Say *Yes! I have a big, orange ball* if it is the correct ball. If not, ask the children to help the volunteer find the right ball. Repeat with different volunteers.

Review

Extension activity

Aim: to practice language from Unit 4 and Unit 5

- Repeat the memory game from Unit 4 (see Extension activity page T32). This time, have different numbers of items on the tray, e.g., three toy cars, two balls (one big, one small). The children have to remember the item, how many there were, and (if appropriate) whether the item was big or small.

Ending the lesson

Aim: to review numbers, colors, and toys

- Play the Unit 5 song (CD 2, Track 8). The children join in. Hold up the correct number of fingers every time a number is mentioned in the song. The children copy you.

Aims: to review language from Unit 6 and Unit 7

Recycled language: pets, food, *What is it? What's this? Jump, Walk, Fly, Swim, I like (yummy) (rice), munch, crunch, lunch, Eat the pasta, please, It's yummy, Wash your face*

Materials: CD 2, classroom objects, flashcards (pets, food), the puppet (Polly), colored pencils or crayons in known colors, a handful of dry pasta (if possible in a bowl) for each child

Optional: CD of lively music

Language competences: The children will be able to use language from Unit 6 and Unit 7.

Warm-up

Aim: to review pets, food, and language from Units 6 and 7

- Play *No, Polly* (see Introduction, page xvii) with the pet and food flashcards. Polly makes correct and incorrect sentences using *What's this? It's a … , I have a …* or *I like …* .

Listening

1 CD2 39 SB p93 **Listen and color the circles. Color the frames.**

Aim: to review language from Unit 6 and Unit 7

- Review colors using classroom objects.
- Point to the pictures on SB page 93 and say *Listen and color*. Play the first item on the audio and point to the first picture. Elicit the color. Give the children time to color the circle.
- Repeat for the other three pictures. Remind the children that they need to color the frames of the pictures in the same color as the circles. Circulate as they color and ask individuals *What color?*
- Play the audio again. The children point to the pictures and repeat the sentences.

Audio script page T99

Practice

- Give a handful of pasta to each child (if possible, in a small bowl).
- Make sure the children have crayons in known colors in front of them. Put on the puppet. Make Polly give instructions from the course so far, e.g., *Stand up, Jump, Show me four* (the children hold up four crayons), *Show me something small, Walk, Fly, Sit down, please, Eat the pasta, please* (the children pretend to eat the real pasta), *It's yummy* (they look appreciative/ smile), *Wash your face*. The children follow.

Game

- Review pets and food using the flashcards.
- Divide the class into two teams. Stick the flashcards on the board at a height your children can reach. Call one child from each team to the front. They stand on either side of the board. Explain in L1 that they need to listen and touch the right card on the board, as quickly as they can. Say, e.g., *I like cake*. The child who touches the correct flashcard first wins a point for their team. If it's a tie, award a point to both teams. The children sit down and the next two children come to the front. Repeat until one of the teams reaches ten points.

Extension activity

Aim: to practice language from Unit 6 and Unit 7

- Repeat *Musical statues* from Unit 6 (see Extension activity page T50). Include instructions from Unit 7 (*Eat the pasta, Wash your face*).

Ending the lesson

Aim: to review food and *I like* …

- Play the Unit 7 song (CD 2, Track 33). The children join in. Mime eating the different foods. The children copy you.

1 CD2 39 **Listen and color the circles. Color the frames.**

1 CD2 65 Listen and color the circles. Color the frames.

Aims: to review language from Unit 8 and Unit 9

Recycled language: clothes, play equipment, *Look at my (pants), I don't like (the purple dress), Put on the (hat), Stop, I like this (swing), The (swing)'s fun, Sit on the (seesaw), Down/Up you go*

Materials: CD 2, flashcards (food, toys, clothes, park), Yes/No cards, real items of clothing (T-shirt, pants, dress, shoes), the puppet (Polly), colored pencils or crayons in known colors, grocery bag, and/or shoe box (one for each pair of children), play cash register/calculator, play money (some for each pair of children), items of clothing for each pair of children to "buy" (if possible a T-shirt, dress, pants and pair of shoes)

Optional: CD of lively music, chairs (one for each child)

Language competences: The children will be able to use language from Unit 8 and Unit 9.

Note: If you don't have the equipment for this game, play a version of it using flashcards on the board. Stick the food, toys, and clothes flashcards on the board on "shelves," and call on volunteers to come and choose an item by saying, e.g., *I like the yellow shoes*. They "buy" the flashcard by handing over pretend money to you. Encourage them to use *please* and *Thank you*.

Warm-up

Aim: to review clothes, playground equipment, and language from Units 8 and 9

- Hand out the Yes/No cards. Say *Show me Yes!* The children hold up the correct card. Repeat for No. Do this several times.
- Hold up the park flashcards, the clothes flashcards, or real clothes. Make correct and incorrect sentences, e.g., *Look at my shoes. / I like this merry-go-round. / I don't like this red T-shirt.* The children hold up their Yes/No card as appropriate.

Listening

1 CD2 65 SB p94 **Listen and color the circles. Color the frames.**

Aim: to review language from Unit 8 and Unit 9

- Review colors using real clothes or the clothes flashcards.
- Point to the pictures on SB page 94 and say *Listen and color.* Play the first item on the audio and point to the picture. Elicit the color. Give the children time to color the circle.
- Repeat for the other three pictures. Remind the children that they need to color the frames of the pictures in the same color as the circles. Circulate as they color and ask individuals *What color?*
- Play the audio again. The children point to the pictures and repeat the sentences.

Audio script page T100

Practice

- Make sure the children have crayons in known colors in front of them. Put on the puppet. Make Polly give instructions from the course so far, e.g., *Stand up, Show me something red, Show me something orange, Jump, Sit down on your chair, Eat some cake* (the children mime eating), *Go to sleep, Wake up, Stand up, Sit down on the swing, Swing on the swing, Stand up, Put on the hat* (the children mime putting on a hat), *Put on the shoes*. The children follow.

Game

- Repeat the shopping game from Unit 8 (see Extension activity page T64). Help the children use as much English as possible and use *I like / I don't like* to talk about the items of clothing.

Extension activity

Aim: to practice language from Unit 9

- Repeat the game *Musical chairs* from Unit 9 (see Extension activity page T74).

Ending the lesson

Aim: to review language from Units 8 and 9

- Play the song from Unit 8 or Unit 9 (CD 2, Track 46 or Track 59). The children join in and mime as appropriate.
- Award the certificate from SB page 95 to each student by writing their names on the dotted line if this is your last lesson of the year.

Audio Scripts

CD1, 02

GINA: Hello, I'm Gina.
POLLY: Hello, I'm Polly.
LEO: Hello, I'm Leo.
MIKE: Hello, I'm Mike.
ALL: Hello!
Gina, Polly, Leo, Mike

CD1, 03

Hello, hello, hello!
I'm Jo, I'm Jo, I'm Jo!
Hello, hello, hello!
I'm Jo, I'm Jo, I'm Jo!

Hello, hello, hello!
I'm Mo, I'm Mo, I'm Mo!
Hello, hello, hello!
I'm Mo, I'm Mo, I'm Mo!

CD1, 04

Stand up
Sit down
Stand up

Say "Hello!"
Sit down
Say "Hello!"

Stand up
Sit down
Say "Hello!"

CD1, 05

Say "Hello!"

CD1, 06/07

Clap your hands,
Clap your hands,
Let's go, let's go.
And say "Hello!"

Hello, hello,
Hello, hello,
Hello, hello,
Hello!

Stand up,
Sit down,
Let's go, let's go.
And say "Hello!"

Hello, hello, ...

Clap your hands,
Clap your hands,
Let's go, let's go.
And say "Hello!"

Hello, hello, ...

Stand up,
Sit down,
Let's go, let's go.
And say "Hello!"

Hello, hello, ...

CD1, 08

LEO: Bag!
POLLY: Pencil ... Pencil!
GINA: Book!
MIKE: Chair!
bag, pencil, book, chair

CD1, 09

Look! It's my chair.
Look! It's my chair.
Look! It's my chair.
Look, look, look!

Look! It's my pencil.
Look! It's my pencil.
Look! It's my pencil.
Look, look, look!

Look! It's my bag.
Look! It's my bag.
Look! It's my bag.
Look, look, look!

Look! It's my book.
Look! It's my book.
Look! It's my book.
Look, look, look!

CD1, 10

pencil
bag
book
chair

Ooooh! Look, it's my pencil!

CD1, 11

Hands up
Hands down
Clap your hands
Hands up
Clap your hands

Hands down
Clap your hands
Hands up
Hands down
Clap your hands

CD1, 12

Hands down

CD1, 13/14

Clean up, clean up,
Clean up your book.
Clean up, clean up,
Clean up your book.

Wo-ho ho-ho-ho! Clean clean!
Wo-ho ho-ho-ho! Clean up!

Clean up, clean up,
Clean up your chair.
Clean up, clean up,
Clean up your chair.

Wo-ho ho-ho-ho! Clean clean!
Wo-ho ho-ho-ho! Clean up!

Clean up, clean up,
Clean up your pencil.
Clean up, clean up,
Clean up your pencil.

Wo-ho ho-ho-ho! Clean clean!
Wo-ho ho-ho-ho! Clean up!

Clean up, clean up,
Clean up your bag.
Clean up, clean up,
Clean up your bag.

Wo-ho ho-ho-ho! Clean clean!
Wo-ho ho-ho-ho! Clean up!
Wo-ho ho-ho-ho! Clean clean!
Wo-ho ho-ho-ho! Clean up!

CD1, 15

1. **GINA**: Hello, Polly.
   POLLY: Hello, Gina.
2. **MIKE**: Hello, Leo.
   LEO: Hello, Mike.
3. **TEACHER**: Hello.
   ANIMALS: Hello.
   TEACHER: Sit down, please.
4. **MIKE**: It's my chair.
   LEO: No, it's my chair.
   TEACHER: Mike! Leo! Stop it.
   MIKE, LEO: Oooooph!
5. **LEO**: Sorry.
   MIKE: Ooh. Sorry.

CD1, 16

MIKE: It's my chair.

CD1, 17

look	listen	listen
listen	join in	look
join in	look	join in

CD1, 18

/p/ /p/ /p/ pencil

/p/ /p/ /p/ pencil
/p/ /p/ /p/ pencil
/p/ /p/ /p/ pencil

SLOWLY! /p/ /p/ /p/ pencil

/p/ /p/ /p/ pencil ...

QUICKLY! /p/ /p/ /p/ pencil

/p/ /p/ /p/ pencil ...

CD1, 19

LEO: Hello! I'm Leo.
GIRL: Look! It's my chair!
GINA: Hello! I'm Gina.
BOY: Look! It's my book!

CD1, 20

GINA: Red ...
Blue ...
Green ...
And yellow ...
POLLY: Ooooooo!

red, blue, green, yellow

CD1, 21

Look! It's my pencil.
It's yellow. It's yellow.
Look! It's my pencil.
It's yellow. It's yellow.

Look! It's my book.
It's blue. It's blue.
Look! It's my book.
It's blue. It's blue.

Look! It's my chair.

It's green. It's green.
Look! It's my chair.
It's green. It's green.

Look! It's my bag.
It's red. It's red.
Look! It's my bag.
It's red. It's red.

CD1, 22

Show me something red!
Show me something green!
Show me something red!
Show me something green!

Show me something yellow!
Show me something green!
Show me something yellow!
Show me something red!

Show me something green!
Show me something red!
Show me something yellow!

CD1, 23

red
Show me something red!
green
Show me something green!
yellow
Show me something yellow!

CD1, 24

Show me something yellow!

CD1, 25/26

Oh paint, paint, paint your pencil,
Paint your pencil blue!
Paint, paint, paint your pencil,
Paint your pencil blue!

Oh stand up and paint with me,
Stand up and paint with me!
Stand up and paint with me!

Oh paint, paint, paint your book,
Paint your book green!
Paint, paint, paint your book,
Paint your book green!

Oh stand up and paint with me,
Stand up and paint with me!
Stand up and paint with me!

Oh paint, paint, paint your bag,
Paint your bag red!
Paint, paint, paint your bag,
Paint your bag red!

Oh stand up and paint with me,
Stand up and paint with me!
Stand up and paint with me!

Oh paint, paint, paint your chair,
Paint your chair yellow!
Paint, paint, paint your chair,
Paint your chair yellow!

Oh stand up and paint with me,
Stand up and paint with me!
Stand up and paint with me!

CD1, 27

See CD1, Track 25.

CD1, 28

1. **MIKE, POLLY, LEO:** Hello, Gina.
   GINA: Hello, Polly.
   Hello, Mike.
   Hello, Leo.
   Look!
2. **MIKE, POLLY, LEO:** Oh. Poor Gina.
3. **MIKE:** Yellow, please.
   LEO: Red, please.
   MIKE: Blue, please.
   LEO, MIKE: Green, please.
4. **POLLY:** Look, Gina.
   GINA: Yellow, blue, green, and red.
   Wow!
   Thank you, Polly.
   Thank you, Mike.
   Thank you, Leo.

CD1, 29

GINA: Yellow, blue, green, and red. Wow!

CD1, 30

blue	red	orange
green	orange	green
yellow	yellow	blue
orange	green	red
red	blue	yellow

CD1, 31

/b/ /b/ /b/ bag

/b/ /b/ /b/ bag
/b/ /b/ /b/ bag
/b/ /b/ /b/ bag

SLOWLY! /b/ /b/ /b/ bag

/b/ /b/ /b/ bag ...

QUICKLY! /b/ /b/ /b/ bag

/b/ /b/ /b/ bag ...

CD1, 32

LEO: Look! It's my dad.
MIKE: Ooh.
LEO: Look! It's my mom.
MIKE: Ooh.
LEO: Look! It's my brother.
MIKE: Ooh.
LEO: Look! It's my sister.
MIKE: Ooh.

dad, mom, brother, sister

CD1, 33

Who's this? Who's this?
It's my mom.

Who's this? Who's this?
It's my dad.

Who's this? Who's this?
It's my sister.

Who's this? Who's this?
It's my brother.

CD1, 34

Go to sleep.
Wake up!
Go to sleep.
Wake up!

Give your dad a hug.
Give your dad a hug.

Go to sleep.
Wake up!
Give your dad a hug.

CD1, 35

red
Go to sleep.

blue
Wake up!

green
Give your dad a hug.

CD1, 36

Go to sleep.

CD1, 37/38

Rosemary, Rosemary,
Please show me your family.
Rosemary, Rosemary,
Please show me.

Look, it's my brother.
Look, it's my brother.
Look, it's my brother.
My brother, my brother.

Rosemary, Rosemary, ...

Look, it's my sister.
Look, it's my sister.
Look, it's my sister.
My sister, my sister.

Rosemary, Rosemary, ...

Look, it's my dad.
Look, it's my dad.
Look, it's my dad.
My dad, my dad.

Rosemary, Rosemary, ...

Look, it's my mom.
Look, it's my mom.
Look, it's my mom.
My mom, my mom.

Rosemary, Rosemary, ...

CD1, 39

SNAIL: Who's this?
ROSEMARY: It's my mom.

SNAIL: Who's this?
ROSEMARY: It's my sister.

CD1, 40

1. **MIKE:** Who's this?
   LEO: It's my dad!
   MIKE: Ooh.
2. **MIKE:** Who's this?
   LEO: It's my sister!
   MIKE: Wow!
3. **MIKE:** Who's this?
   LEO: It's my brother.
   MIKE: Ooh. Wow!
4. **MIKE:** Who's this?
   LEO: It's my mom.
5. **MIKE:** And who's this?
   LEO: This? This is my friend!
   MIKE: Ooh.

CD1, 41
MIKE: Who's this?
LEO: It's my sister!
MIKE: Wow!

CD1, 42

the mom	the egg	the baby
the dad	the dad	the egg
the baby	the baby	the dad
the egg	the mom	the mom

CD1, 43
/d/ /d/ /d/ dad

/d/ /d/ /d/ dad
/d/ /d/ /d/ dad
/d/ /d/ /d/ dad

Quietly ... /d/ /d/ /d/ dad

/d/ /d/ /d/ dad ...

LOUDLY! /d/ /d/ /d/ dad

/d/ /d/ /d/ dad ...

CD1, 44
green
BOY: Look! It's green.

blue
MAN: Who's that?
BOY: It's my mom.

red
GIRL: Look! It's red.

yellow
MAN: Who's that?
GIRL: It's my dad.

CD1, 45
POLLY: My ball!
LEO: My car! Vroom, vroom!
MIKE: My puzzle!
GINA: My doll!
DOLL: Hello!
GINA: Ooh!

ball, car, puzzle, doll

CD1, 46
Look! It's a blue ball.
Look! It's a red car.
Look! It's a green doll.
Look! It's a yellow puzzle.

CD1, 47
BOY 1: I have a car. I have a car!
BOY 2: I have a doll. I have a doll!
BOY 3: I have a ball. I have a ball!

BOY 1: I have a car. I have a car!
BOY 2: I have a doll. I have a doll!
BOY 3: I have a ball. I have a ball!

BOY 1: I have a car. I have a car!
BOY 2: I have a doll. I have a doll!
BOY 3: I have a ball. I have a ball!

CD1, 48
Throw your ball.
Catch your ball.
Throw your ball.
Catch your ball.

Throw your ball.
Oh, no!
Clean up the doll! Clean up the puzzle!
Clean up the car!

Throw your ball.
Catch your ball.
Throw your ball.
Catch your ball.

Throw your ball.
Oh, no!
Clean up the doll! Clean up the puzzle!
Clean up the car!

CD1, 49
red
Throw your ball.

blue
Catch your ball.

green
Oh, no!

yellow
Clean up the doll! Clean up the puzzle!
Clean up the car!

CD1, 50
Throw your ball.

CD1, 51/52
I have a small red ball,
A small red ball, a small red ball,
I have a small red ball.
I have a small red ball.

A small ball, a big ball,
A small ball, a big ball,
A small ball, a big ball,
I have a ball.

I have a big red ball,
A big red ball, a big red ball,
I have a big red ball.
I have a big red ball.

A small ball, a big ball, ...

I have a small blue ball,
A small blue ball, a small blue ball,
I have a small blue ball.
I have a small blue ball.

A small ball, a big ball, ...

I have a big blue ball,
A big blue ball, a big blue ball,
I have a big blue ball.
I have a big blue ball.

A small ball, a big ball, ...

CD1, 53
See CD1, Track 51.

CD1, 54
1. **LEO:** Ohhh ... My puzzle. My puzzle! Where is it?
2. **LEO:** Is it there?
   GINA: No!
3. **LEO:** Is it there?
   POLLY: No.
4. **LEO:** Is it there?
   MIKE: No ...
5. **MIKE, GINA, POLLY:** Look! It's there!
   LEO: Oh yes! Thank you.

CD1, 55
LEO: Is it there?
GINA: No!

CD1, 56
a big car
a small car
a big pencil
a small pencil
a big ball
a small ball
a big ball
a small car
a small pencil
a small ball
a big car
a big pencil

CD1, 57
/c/ /c/ /c/ car

/c/ /c/ /c/ car
/c/ /c/ /c/ car
/c/ /c/ /c/ car

Quietly ... /c/ /c/ /c/ car

/c/ /c/ /c/ car ...

LOUDLY! /c/ /c/ /c/ car

/c/ /c/ /c/ car ...

CD2, 02
POLLY: One!
MIKE: Two!
GINA: Three!
LEO: Four!
ALL: Go! Yay!

one, two, three, four

CD2, 03
1 red ball
1, 2 blue balls
1, 2, 3 green balls
1, 2, 3, 4 orange balls!

CD2, 04
One, two, three, four!
One, two, three, four!

Book! One book!
Book! Book! Two books!
Book! Book! Book! Three books!
Book! Book! Book! Book! Four books!

One, two, three, four!
One, two, three, four!

Book! One book! ...

One, two, three, four!
One, two, three, four!

CD2, 05
Four
Three
Two
One!

(x3)

CD2, 06
red
Four

blue
Three
green
Two
yellow
One!

CD2, 07
One!

CD2, 08/09
One, one, one,
My purple mom.
Two, two, two,
My cars are blue.
Three, three, three,
My puzzle's green.
Four, four, four,
Let's sing some more.

One, two, three, four,
Sing some more.
One, two, three, four,
Sing some more.

(Verse and chorus twice more)

CD2, 10
See CD2, Track 08.

CD2, 11
1. **GINA**: One ... two ... three ... four! Hmm ... Where's Leo?
2. **GINA**. Oh - hello, Leo.
   LEO: Ohhh!
   GINA: Hmm ... Where's Mike?
3. **GINA**: Hello, Mike.
   MIKE: Ohhh!
4. **GINA**: Now ... Where's Polly? Hmm ... Oh ... Where's Polly?
5. **POLLY**: Hello, Gina. I'm here!
   GINA: Oh yes!

CD2, 12
GINA: One ... two ... three ... four! Hmm ... Where's Leo?

CD2, 13
one	two	four
two	three	one
three	one	two
four	four	three

CD2, 14
/t/ /t/ /t/ two

/t/ /t/ /t/ two
/t/ /t/ /t/ two
/t/ /t/ /t/ two

HIGH! /t/ /t/ /t/ two

/t/ /t/ /t/ two ...

LOW! /t/ /t/ /t/ two

/t/ /t/ /t/ two ...

CD2, 15
red
I have a puzzle.

orange
I have two books.

yellow
I have 3 dolls.

blue
I have 4 balls! WOO-OO-OO - oops!

CD2, 16
POLLY: Look! It's my bird!
ALL: Wow!

MIKE: Look! It's my rabbit!
ALL: Wow!

GINA: Look! It's my fish!
ALL: Wow!

LEO: Look! It's my cat!
ALL: Wow!
bird
rabbit
fish
cat

CD2, 17
What is it? What is it?
A rabbit. A rabbit. It's brown.
A rabbit. A rabbit. It's brown.

What is it? What is it?
A fish. A fish. It's red.
A fish. A fish. It's red.

What is it? What is it?
A bird. A bird. It's green.
A bird. A bird. It's green.

What is it? What is it?
A cat. A cat. It's blue.
A cat. A cat. It's blue.
Blue?

CD2, 18
fish
cat
rabbit
bird

WOMAN: What is it?
BOY: It's a fish!

CD2, 19
A rabbit! Jump, jump, jump, jump, jump!
A cat! Walk, walk, walk, walk, walk!
A rabbit! Jump, jump, jump, jump, jump!
A cat! Walk, walk, walk, walk, walk!

A bird! Fly, fly, fly, fly, fly!
A fish! Swim, swim, swim, swim, swim!
A bird! Fly, fly, fly, fly, fly!
A fish! Swim, swim, swim, swim, swim!

A cat! Walk, walk, walk, walk, walk!
A bird! Fly, fly, fly, fly, fly!
A fish! Swim, swim, swim, swim, swim!
A rabbit! Jump, jump, jump, jump, jump!

CD2, 20
red
A bird! Fly!

blue
A fish! Swim!

green
A rabbit! Jump!

yellow
A cat! Walk!

CD2, 21
A cat! Walk, walk, walk, walk, walk!

CD2, 22/23
What is this?
What is this?
What is this?

What is this?
What is this?
What is this?

It's my bird,
Fly, fly, fly.
It's my bird,
Fly, fly, fly,
Fly, fly.

What is this? ...

It's my cat,
Walk, walk, walk.
It's my cat,
Walk, walk, walk,
Walk, walk.

What is this? ...

It's my fish,
Swim, swim, swim.
It's my fish,
Swim, swim, swim,
Swim, swim.

CD2, 24
1. **LEO**: Look. The cat! The cat!
2. **POLLY**: Oh, no ...
3. **MIKE**: Let's go! ... Humph.
4. **MIKE**: Yippee!
5. **ALL**: Yay!
   LEO: Oh, thank you. Thank you!

CD2, 25
LEO: Look. The cat! The cat!

CD2, 26
bird, bird, bird
fish, fish, fish
cat, cat, cat
fish, fish, fish
cat, cat, cat
bird, bird, bird

CD2, 27
/e/ /e/ /e/ eggs

/e/ /e/ /e/ eggs
/e/ /e/ /e/ eggs
/e/ /e/ /e/ eggs

HIGH! /e/ /e/ /e/ eggs

/e/ /e/ /e/ eggs ...

LOW! /e/ /e/ /e/ eggs

/e/ /e/ /e/ eggs ...

CD2, 28
POLLY: Mmmm, pasta.
GINA: Mmmm, salad.

LEO: Mmmm, rice.
ALL: Oooooo – and cake!
pasta, salad, rice, cake

CD2, 29

I like rice!
Eat, eat, eat.
I like rice!
Eat, eat, eat.

I like pasta!
Eat, eat, eat.
I like pasta!
Eat, eat, eat.

I like salad!
Eat, eat, eat.
I like salad!
Eat, eat, eat.

I like cake!
Eat, eat, eat.
I like cake!
Eat, eat, eat.

Yeah!

CD2, 30

Look! Pasta. Ooooo.
Eat the pasta. Yum, yum, yum.
Look! Pasta. Ooooo.
Eat the pasta. Yum, yum, yum.

It's yummy! Mmmmmm.
Wash your face!
It's yummy! Mmmmmm.
Wash your face!

Look! Pasta. Ooooo.
Eat the pasta. Yum, yum, yum.
It's yummy! Mmmmmm.
Wash your face!

CD2, 31

red
Eat the pasta.

blue
Wash your face!

green
Look! Pasta.

yellow
It's yummy!

CD2, 32

1. Wash your face!
2. Eat the pasta. Yum, yum, yum.

CD2, 33/34

Munch, munch, munch,
Crunch, crunch, crunch,
I like yummy lunch, lunch!
Munch, munch, munch,
Crunch, crunch, crunch,
I like yummy lunch!

I like yummy rice!
I like yummy rice!
I like yummy rice!
Oh yum, yum, yum, yum, yum, yum, yum!

Munch, munch, munch, ...

I like yummy salad!
I like yummy salad!
I like yummy salad!
Oh yum, yum, yum, yum, yum, yum, yum!

Munch, munch, munch, ...

I like yummy cake!
I like yummy cake!
I like yummy cake!
Oh yum, yum, yum, yum, yum, yum, yum!
Yum!

CD2, 35

1. **DAD:** Here's your cake.
   LEO: Thank you, Dad. I like cake.
2. **ALL:** Oh, no!
3. **LEO:** My cake ...
   ALL: Ohhh ...
4. **GINA:** I have an idea.
   POLLY: What is it?
   GINA: Let's get some ice cream.
   MIKE: Lovely idea!
5. **LEO:** I like ice cream.
   MIKE: Yes, it's great.
   GINA: Wonderful!
   POLLY: Yummy!

CD2, 36

1. **LEO:** Thank you, Dad. I like cake.
2. **GINA:** Let's get some ice cream.

CD2, 37

soup	water	pasta
pasta	pasta	cake
water	cake	soup
cake	soup	water

CD2, 38

/s/ /s/ /s/ salad

/s/ /s/ /s/ salad
/s/ /s/ /s/ salad
/s/ /s/ /s/ salad

SLOWLY! /s/ /s/ /s/ salad

/s/ /s/ /s/ salad ...

QUICKLY! /s/ /s/ /s/ salad

/s/ /s/ /s/ salad ...

CD2, 39

red
BOY: What is it?
GIRL: It's a rabbit.

orange
BOY: I like salad. Mmmmm!

yellow
BOY: What is it?
GIRL: It's a cat.

blue
GIRL: I like rice.

CD2, 40

LEO: Hahaha, look at my T-shirt! Hahaha, and look at my pants.
GINA: Hahaha, look at my dress! And look at my shoes!

T-shirt, pants, dress, shoes

CD2, 41

I don't like the purple dress. No, no, no.
I don't like the purple dress. No, no, no.
I don't like the purple dress. No, no, no.
But I like the orange dress. Yes, yes, yes!

I don't like the blue pants. No, no, no.
I don't like the blue pants. No, no, no.
I don't like the blue pants. No, no, no.
But I like the green pants. Yes, yes, yes!

CD2, 42

Hello, I'm Mr. Blue.
Hello, I'm Mr. Blue.

I like the blue cat,
I don't like the purple hat.

I like the blue dad,
I don't like the green bag.

I like the blue two,
I don't like the red shoe.
I like blue.
Hmm ... yes. I like blue.

CD2, 43

Put on the shoes.
Put on a T-shirt.
Put on a hat.

Put on a T-shirt.
Put on a hat.
Put on the shoes.

Put on a T-shirt.
Put on a hat.
Put on the shoes.
Say "hello" to your dad.

CD2, 44

red
Put on a hat.

blue
Put on the shoes.

green
Put on a T-shirt.

yellow
Say "hello" to your dad.

CD2, 45

1. Put on a hat.
2. Say "hello" to your dad.

CD2, 46/47

Put on your T-shirt.
Put on your T-shirt.
Put on your T-shirt,
And stop!

O-O-O-O, O-O-O-O, clo- clo- clothes!

Put on your shoes.
Put on your shoes.
Put on your shoes,
And stop!
O-O-O-O, O-O-O-O, clo- clo- clothes!

Put on your pants.
Put on your pants.
Put on your pants,
And stop!

O-O-O-O, O-O-O-O, clo- clo- clothes!

Put on your dress.
Put on your dress.
Put on your dress,
And stop!

O-O-O-O, O-O-O-O, clo- clo- clothes!
Stop!

CD2, 48

1. **GINA:** Look! I like my dress and my shoes!
2. **LEO:** Look! I like my hat and my pants!
3. **POLLY:** Look! I like my pants and my shoes!
4. **MIKE:** Look ... I like ...
   GINA, POLLY, LEO: Oh, no! Don't worry. We can help.
5. **LEO:** Wow!
   GINA: I like your pants, your hat, and your shoes!!!

CD2, 49

1. **LEO:** Look! I like my hat and my pants!
2. **POLLY:** Look! I like my pants and my shoes!

CD2, 50

I have a red hat.
And I have blue pants.

I have blue pants.
And I have a white shirt.

I have a black hat. I have black pants.
And I have a blue shirt.

CD2, 51

/n/ /n/ /n/ nose

/n/ /n/ /n/ nose
/n/ /n/ /n/ nose
/n/ /n/ /n/ nose

QUIETLY! /n/ /n/ /n/ nose

/n/ /n/ /n/ nose ...

LOUDLY! /n/ /n/ /n/ nose

/n/ /n/ /n/ nose ...

CD2, 52

MIKE: I like this slide! Woooo-hooo!
GINA: Yay! I like this merry-go-round!
LEO: Mmmm! I like this seesaw!
POLLY: Wooo! And I like this swing!

slide, merry-go-round, seesaw, swing

CD2, 53

The merry-go-round's yellow.
The seesaw's green.
The swing's red.
The slide's blue.

CD2, 54

Swing!

The swing's fun,
The swing's fun,
In our park, in our park!

Slide!

The slide's fun,
The slide's fun,
In our park, in our park!

Seesaw!

The seesaw's fun,
The seesaw's fun,
In our park, in our park!

Merry-go-round!

The merry-go-round's fun,
The merry-go-round's fun,
In our park, in our park!

Yay!

CD2, 55

a seesaw
a merry-go-round
a T-shirt
a slide
pants
a swing

Wow! Look, a slide! The slide's fun!

CD2, 56

Sit down on the seesaw.
Down you go.
Up you go.
Down you go.
Up you go.
Oh, no!

Sit down on the seesaw.
Down you go.
Up you go.
Down you go.
Up you go.
Down you go.
Up you go.
Oh, no!

CD2, 57

red
Up you go.

blue
Oh, no!

green
Down you go.

yellow
Sit down on the seesaw.

CD2, 58

1. Sit down on the seesaw.
2. Down you go.

CD2, 59/60

Let's go to the park,
The park is fun,
Let's go to the park - everyone!

Swing on the swing,
Swing on the swing,
Swing on the swing,
The swing is fun.

Let's go to the park, ...

Slide on the slide,
Slide on the slide,
Slide on the slide,
The slide is fun.

Let's go to the park, ...

Round the merry-go-round,
Round the merry-go-round,
Round the merry-go-round,
The merry-go-round is fun.

Let's go to the park, ...

CD2, 61

1. **POLLY:** It's my turn.
   LEO: No, I'm sorry. It's my turn.
2. **GINA:** It's my turn.
   LEO: No, I'm sorry. It's my turn.
3. **GINA:** Oh! Let's go home!
   MIKE: Yes, let's go home.
4. **LEO:** Where's Gina? Where's Mike? Where's Polly? Where are they? Come back! Come back!
5. **GINA:** This is fun!
   LEO: Yes, the swing is fun.

CD2, 62

1. **GINA:** Oh! Let's go home!
2. **LEO:** Where's Gina? Where's Mike? Where's Polly? Where are they?

CD2, 63

triangle, triangle, triangle
circle, circle, circle, circle
circle, circle, circle, circle
triangle, triangle, triangle

CD2, 64

/i/ /i/ /i/ igloo

/i/ /i/ /i/ igloo
/i/ /i/ /i/ igloo
/i/ /i/ /i/ igloo

HIGH! /i/ /i/ /i/ igloo

/i/ /i/ /i/ igloo ...

LOW! /i/ /i/ /i/ igloo

/i/ /i/ /i/ igloo ...

CD2, 65

red
The merry-go-round's fun! Woooo!

green
I don't like the dress.

yellow
I don't like the shoes.

blue
The swing's fun! Hahaha!

CD2, 66

/s/ /s/ salad
/d/ /d/ dad
/t/ /t/ two
/p/ /p/ pencil
/i/ /i/ igloo
/c/ /c/ car
/e/ /e/ egg

Thanks and acknowledgments

Authors' thanks
The authors would like to thank a number of people who have made significant contributions towards the final form of Super Safari:
Colin Sage, Helen Brock, and Carolyn Wright, our editors, for their expertise in working on the manuscripts, and the support we got from them.
Our designers, Blooberry, for their imaginative layout and all the artists – in particular Bill Bolton – for the inspiring artwork that has brought our ideas to life in such beautiful ways.
Liane Grainger, Managing Editor, and Emily Hird, Publisher, for their many useful suggestions for improvement.
Jason Mann, Editorial Director at Cambridge University Press, for his vision and encouragement.

The publishers are grateful to the following contributors:
Blooberry Design: cover design, book design, publishing management, and page make-up
Bill Bolton: cover illustration
Sarah McConnell: freelance editor
Lisa Hutchins: freelance editor
Alison Prior: picture research
John Marshall Media: audio recording and production
James Richardson: chant writing and production
Robert Lee, Dib Dib Dub Studios: song writing and production

The authors and publishers acknowledge the following sources of copyright material and are grateful for the permissions granted. While every effort has been made, it has not always been possible to identify the sources of all the material used, or to trace all copyright holders. If any omissions are brought to our notice, we will be happy to include the appropriate acknowledgments on reprinting.